Tax and Benefit Reform in Central and Eastern Europe

Tax and Benefit Reform in Central and Eastern Europe

Edited by David M G Newbery

Centre for Economic Policy Research

Published by Centre for Economic Policy Research
25–28 Old Burlington Street, London W1X 1LB

British Library Cataloguing in Publication Data
A Catalogue record for this book is available from the British Library

ISBN: 1 898128 19 7

Contents

List of Tables

List of Figures

Preface

This volume contains papers commissioned under the PHARE contract Taxation and Tax Reform in Central and Eastern Europe, financed by the Commission of the European Communities. The authors were selected for their knowledge of East European tax and benefit reform, and for their empirical expertise in analysing survey data and/or building tax and benefit simulation models. The aim was to bring the best academic minds to bear in a quantified and policy-relevant way on one of the major policy issues facing the governments of the transitional economies of Central and Eastern Europe.

The authors were requested to provide detailed paper outlines which were discussed at an initial workshop held in Brussels with staff from the Commission on 3 May 1994. This workshop, organized by the Centre for Economic Policy Research, was invaluable in refining the scope of the research project and in providing coherence to the resulting set of papers, ensuring that appropriate questions were addressed in a systematic way. The papers were written during the summer, and presented at a CEPR workshop in Brussels on 1 December 1994. In order to ensure that the main message of each paper was sufficiently clear, the papers were presented by the discussants, who were required not only to summarize the main points but comment on the content and structure of the papers. Authors were then allowed to respond, and this reversal of the normal roles was most effective, not only in using the time efficiently, but in sustaining a high level of interest by the participants and the staff from the Commission. The chapters were then revised by the authors, edited by David Newbery and ably copy edited by Linda Machin and Richard Fidczuk.

Tax and budgetary reforms continue apace in the transitional economies, and it was never our intention to evaluate the full programme of reforms, which are in any case incomplete. Rather, we aimed to demonstrate the value of the techniques reported in this volume, and to show how they can be used to address a variety of policy questions that will continue to arise in these economies. As a simple example, on a recent visit to Hungary in March 1995, we discovered that the government was about to radically change the system of child allowances and maternity benefits. The chapter by Jarvis and Pudney in this volume provides methods for assessing the impact of such changes, and it would have been quite easy to use their methodology and data to do so, even though at the time the chapter was written there were no such proposals under discussion.

I therefore believe that the techniques developed and described in this volume will continue to be useful for many years to come. Such hopes are often expressed by editors in defence of the lengthy delays between the presentation of the conference papers and the final appearance of the volume. No such excuse is necessary in the present case, as the efficiency and dedication of the CEPR staff and the cooperation of the authors ensured that less than four months passed from workshop presentation to galley proofs, and less than three months from final corrections and updating to final publication. I would therefore especially like to thank, not only the authors for their professionalism and responsiveness, but Kate Millward for managing the production process, and Richard Portes, who attended both workshops, actively concerned himself with the choice of authors and topics, and negotiated the original contract with the Commission of the European Communities. I should also like to thank Joan Pearce of the Commission for her encouragement, comments at workshops, and involving her colleagues in what has been a most fruitful collaboration between academics and the Commission.

David M G Newbery
27 April 1995

List of Contributors

Michael Burda   *Humboldt University, Berlin, and CEPR*
Christopher Heady   *University of Bath*
Maciej Grabowski   *Gdansk Institute for Market Economics*
Sarah Jarvis   *University of Essex*
Martina Lubyova   *CERGE, Prague*
John Micklewright   *European University Institute*
Gyula Nagy   *Budapest University of Economics*
David M G Newbery   *University of Cambridge and CEPR*
Stephen Pudney   *University of Leicester*
Mark Schaffer   *London School of Economics and Political Science*
Stephen Smith   *University College London and Institute for Fiscal Studies*

1

Tax and Benefit Reform in Central and Eastern Europe

David M G Newbery

The fifth anniversary of the fall of the Berlin Wall is an appropriate moment to take stock of the lessons of fiscal reform in the transitional economies of the Central and East European Countries (CEECs). Fiscal reform is central to the process of transforming a Soviet-type economy to a market economy, for with the emergence of a significant private sector the boundary between the public and private sectors needs to be more sharply drawn. The old system in which the bulk of taxes came directly or indirectly from state-owned enterprises, and were just one part of the system of allocation of resources, has to be replaced by a legally based, incentive-oriented and preferably stable system of raising the revenue needed for continuing public activities. Many of the old revenue-raising activities for providing subsidies to enterprises and financing capital formation are no longer appropriate to a market economy and should disappear with the restructuring of the state sector. Other activities, some of which may have been financed directly by enterprises, such as many social services, education and housing facilities, must now either be transferred to the private sector (in the case of housing and resort hotels, for example) or to the state (Rein and Wörgötter, 1995). In addition, the state inherits new responsibilities with the emergence of open unemployment requiring unemployment insurance payments, while lagging infrastructural investment is unlikely to be entirely privately financed. Although telecommunications is a natural industry to privatize and to attract foreign direct investment and expertise, the transport infrastructure will continue to require state finance, assisted by the growth in revenue from vehicle taxation.

This study concentrates on the experience of the Visegrád countries (Hungary, Poland, and the Czech and Slovak Republics), as these countries were in the forefront of the transitional process, and specifically have made the most progress with tax reform. They also have a strong statistical tradition that enables the process of transition to be studied in sufficient detail to make such a study

1

possible. Hungary led the way with major tax reforms coming into effect from 1 January 1988, while Poland started the process with the 'Big Bang' on 1 January 1990, followed by the then Czechoslovakia on 1 January 1991.

It might appear that the detailed design of an entirely new tax system would be a challenging task, but in practice the choice was fairly tightly circumscribed by the desire of these countries to join the European Union eventually. This meant that enterprise taxes were to be replaced by a standard corporation tax, based on western accounting concepts of profit net of depreciation and interest, a personal income tax, social security taxes financed by employer and employee contributions, withholding through Pay-As-You-Earn (PAYE), value added taxes (VAT) to replace turnover taxes, excise taxes on fuel, alcohol and tobacco, and *ad valorem* customs duties. There are no commonly agreed models for local taxation, property taxation, and even personal capital income taxation, and perhaps for that reason the design of these important elements of the tax system in most transitional countries is still in flux.

If the broad design features of the new tax system were reasonably clear, governments still needed to make difficult decisions about the balance between taxes, the tax rates, the level of revenue as a share of GDP with implications for the amount of redistribution to be achieved through the tax system, the mechanisms to be employed, and the general level of expenditure. Such decisions were always going to be difficult, but were made far more so by the unprecedented collapse in output in the transitional countries. Figures 1.1 and 1.2 show the evolution of real GDP and industrial output in the Visegrád countries, together with Romania and Bulgaria (also aspirants to membership of the EU) from 1989 to 1994 (estimated). The trajectories are shown on logarithmic scales, so that equal proportional changes are shown by equal vertical changes, with equal slopes having equal proportional rates of change. The Czech and Slovak Republics separated in 1992, and their previous evolution is that of the combined CSFR. The figures also show the evolution of the US economy from 1929 to 1934 (exactly 60 years before) through the Great Depression. This comparison reveals that, for some transitional countries, the collapse in output and income has been as dramatic as in the Great Depression, with only Poland apparently rebounding at anything like the rate of growth achieved in the United States after 1933.[1] Compared to the Visegrád countries, most of the countries of the former Soviet Union have experienced substantially larger falls in output (IMF, 1994, chart 2, p. 75).

Even without a fall in output, fiscal reform in the context of a movement to a market economy was bound to create tensions. Soviet-type economies secured most of their revenue through a relatively small number of over-large state-owned enterprises, whose financial flows (if not their economic activity) were transparent to the Ministry of Finance and closely monitored. Essentially all profits were available for reallocation through the state financial system, and wages (effectively after-tax) could be centrally determined. The typical western

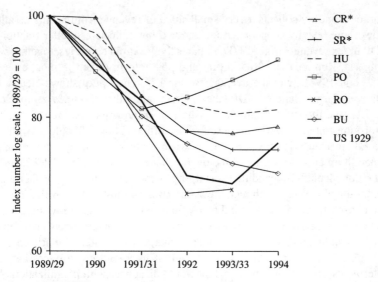

Source: IMF (1994).
Notes: *CSRF before 1992.

Figure 1.1 Real GDP in depression Central Europe 1989–94 and in
United States 1929–34

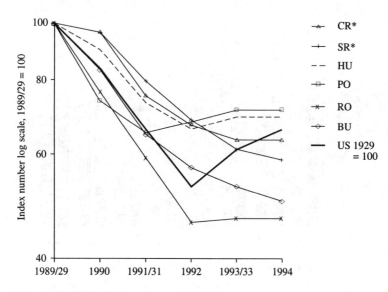

Source: IMF (1994), US Department of Commerce.
Notes: *CSFR before 1992.

Figure 1.2 Real industrial output Central Europe 1989–94 and in United
States 1929–34

market economy collects a very small share of revenue from profits taxation, relies more heavily on personal income tax, but collects a smaller fraction of GDP in tax revenue. Figure 1.3 compares the Visegrád countries, together with Bulgaria, Romania and Russia pre- and post-reform (taken in most cases as 1989 and 1993), with the average for the EU. The figure shows clearly the relatively larger share of GDP taken in taxes and other revenues compared to the EU, and the substantially larger share of enterprise taxes pre-reform. The reforming countries were thus posed with a difficult choice. Should they replace the fall in enterprise taxes by increases in other taxes or by cuts in public expenditure and a lowering of the overall share of taxation in GDP? The case for reducing public expenditure was strong on theoretical and practical grounds. Under the old system, although the state extracted most of the profits from the enterprises, it also directly or indirectly financed much of their investment. In a market economy, responsibility for enterprise investment falls upon the company and the capital markets, and is no longer a charge to the state. Similarly, many of the subsidies were part of a complex web of interventions in prices between enterprises and external markets that would disappear with liberalization. The

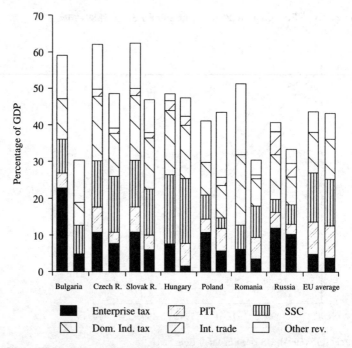

Source: EBRD *Transition Report,* October 1994, Table 6.5.
Notes: Left column is pre-reform. EU domestic industrial and trade taxes combined.

Figure 1.3   General government revenue pre- and post-reform

more difficult question concerned the burden of taxation on individuals, where arguments for increasing taxes or cutting expenditure seemed more finely balanced.

Four factors influence the optimal tax rate (Stern, 1976). The first is the degree of inequality in skills (which is hard to observe, but is related to the degree of pre-tax earnings inequality when workers are paid their marginal product). The higher the degree of inequality, the higher the tax rate is likely to be, other things being equal. The degree of skills inequality appears to be lower in socialist economies, possibly because education is more uniformly allocated than in market economies. One might argue that there are no strong reasons for expecting large differences in the underlying skill distribution between countries at European levels of education, and differences in wage inequality may reflect the operation of implicit tax systems in the more egalitarian CEECs, rather than differences in the distribution of marginal products. Atkinson and Micklewright (1992) provide extensive statistical comparisons of wage dispersions in CEECs compared to the United Kingdom. They find (p. 94) that in the 1970s the Soviet Union and Poland had a higher ratio of the top to bottom decile of earnings than the United Kingdom (at about 3.0), though Hungary and Czechoslovakia were systematically lower, at about 2.5.[2] In the 1980s, Poland's ratio fluctuated widely, but eventually fell to that of Hungary and Czechoslovakia (Hungary actually increased somewhat), while the United Kingdom's inequality rose steadily over the 1980s along with the Soviet Union to 3.3.

The second factor is the level of required government expenditure to be financed by taxes on workers and consumers – the higher the fraction of GDP required, the higher the tax rate. Hungary and Poland have high foreign debts that need servicing, while the Czech and Slovak Republics are better placed in this regard. The main problem facing transitional economies is that enterprise revenue has fallen or is likely to fall sharply, while infrastructural investment demands (especially in transport) have increased, both increasing the uncovered component of required revenue. The other difference with market economies is in the level of foreign interest payments, where Hungary's ratio of foreign debt to GDP puts it among the most heavily indebted developing countries. Given Hungary's intention to retain its international credit standing, debt repayment places a heavy initial claim on the budget. Poland also has a high foreign debt but has been more successful in obtaining debt relief, while the Czech and Slovak Republics had little official foreign debt by 1994.

The third factor is the elasticity of substitution between taxed and non-taxed activities (work and leisure in the benchmark case of a comprehensive tax system in which all goods and services can be taxed). The higher this elasticity, the lower the optimal tax rate, provided taxes are adequate to cover the fixed expenditure requirement. Soviet-type economies have remarkably extensive control over incomes (via state enterprises) and over access to consumption and work, greatly reducing the opportunities for substituting untaxed for taxed activities. The transition threatens this in various ways (Kornai, 1992). The move to a market economy with numerous smaller firms leads to a loss of information about tax liabilities, while the reform of the tax system disrupts existing procedures. Reduced tax efficiency reduces the fraction of income falling within the tax net, raising the marginal cost of tax collection and reducing the optimal tax rate.

Finally, the more egalitarian the government, the higher the tax rate. Most CEECs appear exceptionally egalitarian by western standards, comparable only to very rich and homogenous countries like Sweden. The transition in Eastern Europe is eroding political commitment to the previous degree of equality and, with it, the desired marginal tax rate.

These theoretical considerations pull in different directions. The first two arguments suggest that an increase in taxes might be justified. Marginal products of labour (and hence the correct measure of wages) may become more dispersed with a move to a more internationally exposed market economy, arguing for more redistribution. Pudney (1994) finds a significant growth in earnings inequality in Hungary after 1988, to levels comparable with Western Europe, as does Barr (1994). The component of required public expenditure on infrastructure, debt service and unemployment support not covered by falling enterprise taxes may have to rise as the CEECs reach the limit of prudent international borrowing and attempt to restructure their economies, again requiring tax increases. The last two arguments suggest that optimal tax rates might well fall as a result of transformation, as the ability of the tax system to collect revenue efficiently falters, and public support for equality erodes.

The theoretical arguments appear balanced, and therefore unhelpful. We need to quantify the arguments and see what factors have a large influence on the outcome. Newbery (1994) has done this for a simplified model of CEECs, roughly calibrated to Hungary, and finds that the decrease of tax coverage and/or collection efficiency has a dramatic effect on the optimal tax *rates*. Depending on the exact parameter values, the effect of reducing the tax coverage from 100% to 75% of expenditure would roughly halve the amount of redistributive transfers and the rate of VAT.[3] As reduced tax coverage would lead to a fall in the share of taxes in GDP anyway, a decrease in the optimal rates implies an even greater fall in the desirable share of taxes in GDP, so that a failure to maintain pre-existing tax shares as the tax base erodes is not a reason for increasing the tax rate on the diminished base. This effect appears substantially more important than the increase in inequality, whose effect could be offset by relatively minor decreases in aversion to inequality. Finally, falls in enterprise tax revenue, or increases in required public expenditure, would seem to be primarily (up to three-quarters for most plausible sets of parameter values) at the expense of redistributive transfers, and again provide little justification for sharp increases in personal taxation.

Of course, it would be premature to draw such sharp policy conclusions from what is a highly simplified model of these economies, ignoring important political

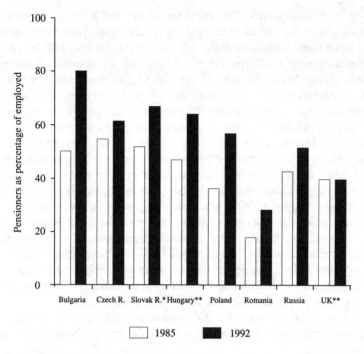

Source: IMF *World Economic Outlook,* October 1994, Table 18.
Notes: * for 1990 not 1985.
** old age or National Insurance only.

Figure 1.4   Dependency ratios 1985 and 1992

realities, and with the standard, if often unrealistic, assumptions of full employment and rational well-informed consumers. Nevertheless, these findings are consistent with the claims that the share of the state is too large in these economies and should, in the medium term, be reduced even at the expense of greater inequality to provide greater incentives for productive growth. Whether that will be politically acceptable, given the very high share of dependents (mostly voters) to active workers, will be one of the sterner tests of a successful transition to a market economy. Figure 1.4 shows the very high dependency ratios (the ratio of pensioners to workers) for CEECs (except Romania) compared to the United Kingdom, and the dramatic increase in these rates since 1985. Given that pensioners vote and are the prime recipients of transfers, the political dynamics of fiscal reform are likely to be extremely difficult.

Once the broad outline of the tax system has been settled, to be compatible with future EU membership, and the level of taxation as a share of GDP decided, perhaps as a long-run target, there remain a variety of detailed questions of fiscal design. These include the balance between direct and indirect taxation, the degree of progressivity of the direct tax system, and the degree of coverage and differentiation of the value added tax and excise taxes. The balance between direct and indirect taxes has a degree of arbitrariness, for there is little apparent difference between a uniform VAT on all goods and a proportional income tax on all incomes. This suggests that progressivity in the overall tax system is best achieved through the direct tax component, while the revenue to be raised from indirect taxes can be set to reduce the number of income tax payers who are required to file an individual tax return, as well as reducing the overall degree of tax evasion. Income taxes are typically evaded by under-reporting or not registering, and become more important as an increasing fraction of income comes from self-employment or is not withheld by the employer. Such income can be taxed when spent through indirect taxes, but some goods and services may be hard to subject to VAT. The relative merits of the two systems of taxation can be put thus: indirect taxes tax all consumers on some goods and services, while income taxes tax the entire potential consumption of some fraction of income earners or income. Direct and indirect taxes are therefore complementary, and together reduce problems of evasion and incomplete coverage. Not surprisingly, we find a considerable similarity in the balance between direct and indirect taxes across countries, as shown in Figure 1.3, which suggests that between one-half and two-thirds of personal income and expenditure taxes together are collected from income taxes, with the balance from indirect taxes, mainly domestic.

The next important question to settle is whether VAT should be levied on all goods and services at a uniform rate (the most broad-based simple system) or whether different goods and services should be taxed at different rates, and whether some goods should be either zero rated or exempt (the distinction being that zero-rated goods can claim back taxes on inputs, but exempt goods cannot). Does differentiating tax rates on goods and services provide an additional leverage over income redistribution that cannot be more effectively achieved through the income tax and transfer system, or is it preferable to treat indirect taxes as the proportional component of the overall tax-raising side of the budget, with most redistribution being achieved through targeted transfers and some progressivity in the income tax system? This question is taken up for the Czech and Slovak Republics by Heady and Smith in Chapter 2, and by Jarvis and Pudney for Hungary in Chapter 3. In other work, Newbery and Révész (1995) find that the indirect tax system in Hungary, which has VAT rates of 0, 15 and 25%, together with various excise tax rates and subsidies for some goods, does have some redistributive effect, but this is almost entirely confined to the taxation of motor transport fuel and to subsidies, mainly to medicine. Relative price changes over the period of tax reforms (1987 to 1993) have had a distributionally neutral effect (Newbery, 1995).

Of course, it does not follow that a move from the present system of taxes to a uniform VAT would have no distributional effect – Heady and Smith show that such changes can lead to a large number of households gaining or losing, even if the pattern of gains and losses is random across the income distribution. This suggests that, while it may be desirable for tax simplicity and administrative convenience to move to a uniform VAT, it may be appropriate to move slowly so that the changes are lost in the noise of normal relative price movements. For countries at an earlier stage of transition, it might be worth considering making the move to uniform taxes as quickly as possible, given that the first step will necessarily have a dramatic impact. In this context, the Czechoslovak device of compensating families with a lump sum transfer (which was subsequently discontinued) that ensured that a majority would not suffer from the initial price shock has considerable political logic.

Other political considerations are also relevant. Most European countries subsidize agriculture by maintaining prices above world market levels, and this is probably true for most agricultural goods in Eastern Europe. Exempting agricultural goods (specifically, food) can then be justified if the agricultural protection is interpreted as a consumer tax and producer subsidy. The commitment value of an explicit set of food taxes and agricultural subsidies is probably lower than the present implicit tax regime, so that farmers would undoubtedly resist strongly a move to an apparently more rational tax system.

1.1   Government Revenues and Expenditure

Compared to richer EU countries, and certainly compared to countries of comparable purchasing power, the CEECs have a higher share of government expenditure in GDP than predicted for market economies. Figure 1.5 shows that, while Bulgaria, the Czech and Slovak Republics, Romania and Russia have succeeded in cutting expenditures, Hungary and Poland have not, perhaps because of the considerable increase in social outlays in both cases. Figure 1.5 also reveals the sharp decrease in subsidies (except for Russia) and expenditure on capital formation, in both cases moving towards the EU average. Social outlays have increased as a share of GDP and interest payments have risen, though high inflation in some countries may exaggerate the real cost of such interest rates, as the real value of the national debt is inflated away.

Figures 1.6–1.8 show the evolution of real government revenue and expenditure in the Visegrád countries between 1989 and 1993 (1987 and 1993 in the case of Hungary, where the tax reforms came earlier). Expenditure is given by the total height of the column, except when the budget is in surplus, in which case the surplus is shown below the line and should be subtracted. Revenues and expenditures are expressed as a percentage of 1989 GDP, while the right-hand column re-expresses the 1993 levels as a percentage of 1993 GDP to show the evolution of tax shares. As real GDP fell in all four countries over this period, even maintaining a constant revenue and expenditure share in GDP would have necessitated cuts in revenue and expenditure.

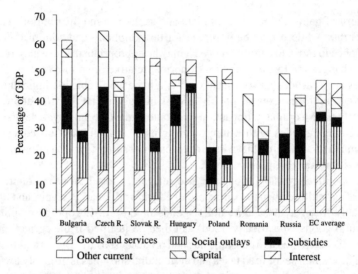

Source: EBRD *Transition Report,* October 1994, Table 6.6.
Notes: For EU, social outlays = transfers to individuals. EU subsidies are to enterprises. Left column is pre-reform.

Figure 1.5   General government expenditure pre- and post-reform

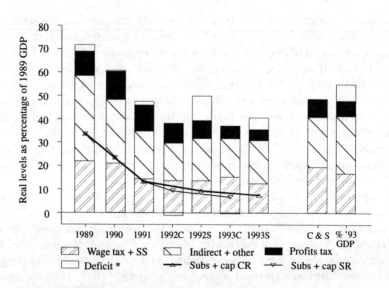

Source: IMF *World Economic Outlook*, October 1994.
Notes: CSFR 1989–91, after shown as C or S. * Surplus shown negative.

Figure 1.6   Real government revenue and expenditure Czech and Slovak Republics 1989–93

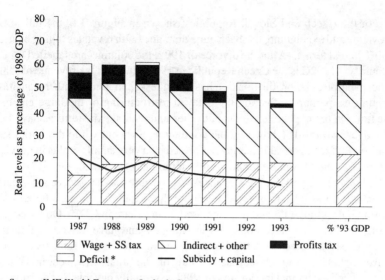

Source: IMF *World Economic Outlook*, October 1994.
Note: * Surplus shown negative.

Figure 1.7   Real government revenue and expenditure Hungary 1987–93

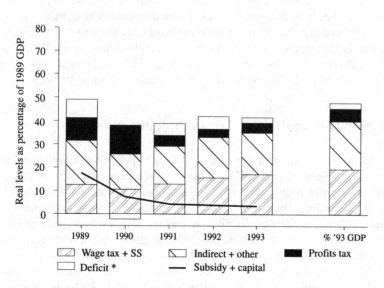

Source: IMF *World Economic Outlook*, October 1994.
Note: * Surplus shown negative.

Figure 1.8   Real government revenue and expenditure Poland 1989–93

In the Czech and Slovak Republics, shown in Figure 1.6, the fall in both revenue and expenditure has been quite dramatic, with revenues falling by nearly 50% in real terms. (After the divorce of 1992, the columns are labelled for each country – 1992C is the Czech Republic in 1992.) Indirect tax revenue has fallen most sharply, and profits taxation has fallen less than in most other transitional countries, perhaps reflecting the delayed restructuring of the large enterprise sector. On the expenditure side, subsidies and capital expenditures have fallen by over two-thirds (shown by the continuous line) but while the initial small deficit in Czechoslovakia has been replaced by a very small surplus in the Czech Republic, the Slovak Republic is still running large deficits.

Neither Hungary (Figure 1.7) nor Poland (Figure 1.8) has succeeded in cutting expenditure as a share of GDP, implying that expenditures have fallen in line with GDP (though Poland has increased its tax share in GDP). On the revenue side, profits taxes have collapsed in Hungary and have halved in Poland as would be expected with the lowering of the profits tax rate, recessionary circumstances, and an increased share of the small-firm sector. Hungary introduced a personal income tax in 1988, essentially payable by enterprises, as wages were grossed up to leave the same after-tax wage, and enterprises withheld through PAYE. Consequently wage (or personal income) taxes and social security taxes increased between 1987 and 1989 in real terms as profits taxes fell, and total taxes increased in real terms until GDP started to fall in 1990. Indirect taxes have decreased modestly in real terms and as a share of GDP.

In Poland, the share of direct personal taxes has moved up to a similar level to that in Hungary and the Czech Republic. Neither Hungary nor Poland have succeeded in addressing persistent government deficits. Hungary has reduced subsidies and capital investment by less than half as much as Poland.

1.2   The Analysis of Tax and Benefit Reform

Comparisons of the structure of taxation and expenditure between countries, particularly between the CEECs and the EU, and over time through the transition are useful in identifying potential problems, tensions and probable directions for further reform. But macro-statistics can conceal important structural details, and are typically silent on distributional issues. The research results presented in this volume go behind these macro-statistical aggregates to probe the efficiency and distributional impacts of the reforms at the household and enterprise level.

All but one of the chapters in this volume present the results of detailed analyses of survey data, ranging in size from several hundred enterprises in the case of Schaffer's chapter, to over 100 000 individuals in the case of Micklewright and Nagy's chapter. The analysis of such detailed micro-data-sets is demanding and time consuming, and is best done by independent academics supported by research grants. Government ministries and statistical offices rarely have the time or resources to explore these issues dispassionately and, even when they undertake policy analyses, are unlikely to publish their findings for the benefit of other, similarly placed countries. We are grateful to the European Commission under the PHARE programme for financing the research reported in this volume, which was discussed at two meetings with the Commission's staff. This volume is not a conference volume, as each piece was specifically commissioned with the intention of providing detailed analyses of fiscal issues in the Visegrád countries, in each case looking for experts in the area chosen.

The resulting book divides naturally into three parts. The first part contains two chapters that look at the impact of tax and benefit reforms on households. Heady and Smith in Chapter 2 simulate the effects of various tax changes in the Czech and Slovak Republics, drawing on detailed modelling of the reforms using household micro-data and a tax simulation model. Their chapter demonstrates the value of constructing such tax simulation models and, although the investment initially required is large, such models can often be reasonably quickly adapted for similar countries. Thus the Slovak model was quite quickly adapted from the Czech model, which itself was originally derived from a model for the United Kingdom. The value of these models in exploring policy alternatives cannot be underestimated. They should alert policy-makers to the likely political opposition to particular tax changes, as they can identify the numbers of different kinds of households that will be adversely affected. Such simulation models allow one to consider the joint impact of a number of potentially interacting tax reforms affecting income taxes, and hence after-tax income and expenditure, together with changes to indirect tax rates and transfers. This opens the prospect of looking for reforms that are revenue-neutral, but simplify the tax structure, improve incentives, and/or improve distribution. The efficiency impacts of tax reforms are judged by looking at the effect on the marginal tax rates of different groups of households, though it is also important to realize that the tax coverage will have a significant effect on distortions and hence efficiency.

Heady and Smith find that making VAT uniform would have adverse distributional effects which could be eliminated by adjusting other taxes and benefits, but only at the cost of increasing the overall marginal tax rate. Similarly, improved targeting of social benefits can reduce poverty and government expenditure, but again at the cost of increasing marginal tax rates. The simulations not only identify the almost inevitable trade-off between equity and efficiency, but allow one to quantify the cost in terms of increased marginal tax rates of improvements in equity.

Chapter 3 by Jarvis and Pudney looks at the scope for redistributional government policies in Hungary, the impact of recent changes in the tax–benefit system, and the potential for improving the income distribution by different targeting techniques. The analysis is based on the 1991 household budget survey of some 12 000 households, and gives a detailed account of the changes to indirect taxation, subsidy reduction, family benefits and unemployment compensation since the reforms began in 1988. Although the personal income tax (PIT) is a relatively small part of the total tax burden in Hungary, as Figure 1.3 shows, it is the most obviously progressive component, as social security contributions, profits tax and indirect taxes are all proportional.[4] Jarvis and Pudney show that the changes in the PIT from 1988 to 1994 substantially raised the tax burden on households and somewhat reduced its progressivity as PIT payments by the lower quintiles of the population increased faster than those in the upper quintiles. In reading their tables, it should be remembered that PIT payments by the lower deciles are a very small fraction of the total tax burden such households face, particularly if they contain active workers, for whom social security payments by employer and employee alone amount to about 55% of the gross wage, compared to a PIT payment of about 5% or less. Nevertheless, their analysis shows that during the period in which incomes were falling and becoming more dispersed, the progressivity of the direct tax system was being somewhat reduced. This is consistent with the modern view of public finance that sees most redistribution occurring not through the revenue side of the budget but through the expenditure side via transfers, benefits and such public expenditures as health and education. It is worth noting that the total Hungarian tax system was still more progressive (and heavier) than the UK system after the changes noted by the authors.

The last part of Chapter 3 demonstrates an innovative technique for identifying desirable directions for tax and benefit reform. The authors point out that the succession of fiscal reforms in Hungary 'has been undertaken without a clear strategy, and particularly without a foundation of research to establish that the areas chosen for policy reform are indeed the areas that really matter in terms of the ultimate objective.' The authors illustrate their approach by asking how one could best reduce a particular measure of poverty by making lump sum transfers to households classified by some characteristics (such as number of children and other demographic attributes, location, employment status, industry of employment). The authors are careful to point out that their findings cannot be immediately translated into policies, and are best seen as a diagnostic technique for identifying better and worse correlates of poverty. These may in turn cast some doubts on the poverty-reducing efficacy of industrial and regional policies, and public rental subsidies. The other major finding of this innovative approach is that poverty would be reduced by making transfers from employed families with children to pensioners and unemployed, starting from the 1991 system of benefits. It is, however, worth noting that the design of tax and benefit policies is likely to be guided by a more comprehensive view of distributional justice than those captured by poverty lines, and will have to take account of disincentive effects and risk reduction (or social insurance), as well as political realities and contractual obligations (to pensioners).

While the techniques are demanding of data and computing resources, Hungary, as well as some other CEECs, are particularly well-endowed with high-quality household budget survey data which can be usefully exploited to inform the policy process in ways such as those demonstrated in this chapter. One of the advantages of using such large data-sets is that they enable the investigator to determine the statistical reliability of any policy conclusions derived from the data. Again, Jarvis and Pudney make important contributions in this area.

Part two of the book deals with the taxation of enterprises, in many ways the pivot of the tax reform and the sector presenting some of the greatest challenges. Chapter 4, by Grabowski and Smith, deals with the taxation of entrepreneurial income both in theory and as illustrated by the experience of Poland. The emphasis is on the smaller, newly emerging private companies, whose rapid rise at the expense of the large simple-to-tax state enterprises lies at the heart of the fiscal problem of replacing lost tax bases. The chapter demonstrates the importance of this sector, and discusses the very real theoretical problems in defining an appropriate tax base for entrepreneurial income, with its ambiguous allocation to labour or capital. It argues convincingly that the tax system should be designed to minimize the administrative resources required, which in turn requires minimum ambiguity and administrative discretion. Presumptive taxes on such unambiguous quantity bases as floor space are attractive, as is maintaining a high level of VAT exemption.

Chapter 5, by Schaffer, discusses the question of subsidies to enterprises, either as explicit budgetary transfers or as tax arrears that may eventually be forgiven and written off. Schaffer finds that the flow of tax arrears appears to be similar in size to the flow of budgetary subsidies, but relatively more important for manufacturing firms, which are now hardly subsidized at all. The evidence from Polish survey data suggests that the tax arrears are concentrated on financially distressed state-owned firms, but to the extent that these firms are still covering current costs out of current income, there may be little urgency in forcing bankruptcy, particularly as the labour market is sufficiently slack to enable appropriate reallocations of labour during the early stages of the transition without further enterprise closures.

The last part of the book deals with the critical area of labour market policy, where the institutions have had to be created from virtually nothing in a very short period. Chapter 6, by Micklewright and Nagy, looks at unemployment insurance in Hungary and the incentives provided for re-employment. The focus of the study is a natural experiment in which the system of unemployment insurance changed sharply in January 1993. It is not often that social scientists have access to an experiment of this kind, where one can study the impact of a regime change on economic behaviour, although as always it is hard to hold everything else constant. The evidence suggests that reducing the generosity of unemployment insurance has a rather small impact in encouraging the unemployed to leave the register more rapidly, and this is even less the case with women than with men. Of course, the pool of unemployed labour in the transitional economies is likely to be rather different from that in developed market economies, and the turbulence surrounding the transition, with unstable expectations about future employment prospects, may be quite different from the state to which the countries will gradually evolve. Given that the major cause in transitional unemployment has been from the demand side, the relative inefficacy of supply-side measures in Hungary may not be so surprising, but it may provide some comfort to those who argue that the disincentive effects of taxes and benefits should not be exaggerated in the turbulence of transition, and that fiscal rectitude and safety-net provision are likely to be the more important determinants of transitional policy. Nevertheless, given the difficulty of making fiscal reforms in quieter times, it remains desirable to attempt to get the basic structure correct as soon as possible, and such a structure will have to take more account of incentives.

The final chapter, by Burda and Lubyova, looks at the impact of active labour market policies in the Czech and Slovak Republics and again offers a fascinating experimental comparison – in this case in the subsequent performance of the two parts of the formally united Czechoslovakia. The data for the analysis come from district labour offices, of which there are 76 in the Czech Republic and 38 in the Slovak Republic. Monthly observations on most variables from January 1992 to July 1994 in the case of the Czech Republic, and until December 1993 in the Slovak case, provide a useful data-set to analyse the impacts of labour market policies. The reassuring finding is that these policies appear to be effective and, although they are associated with a rather modest fraction of job creation, their use can be seen as a catalyst ensuring rapid exit from the unemployment pool. One of the most striking findings is the difference in unemployment experience in the two parts of the former united country, and the divergence between the Czech experience and the other Visegrád countries. It will be interesting to see whether this difference persists, whether it reflects the favoured location of the Czech republic next to its rich neighbour Germany and whether economic expansion in Western Europe, possibly associated with a more open attitude to trade with Eastern Europe, can replicate the Czech experience elsewhere.

1.3   Lessons

Detailed studies of tax and benefit reform based on micro-data-sets are invaluable in providing public finance specialists with evidence from other countries against which to test their theories and prejudices. Studies for transitional economies are particularly useful as many countries further east begin to follow the same sequence of tax and market reforms. One of the salutary lessons of careful case studies is that matters are invariably more complex when studied in detail, and lessons learned from one country should be tested out, preferably using simulation techniques like those illustrated in Chapter 2, before their adoption elsewhere. Nevertheless, it is useful to stand back and ask what lessons emerge from the studies.

The first lesson is that profits tax revenue is almost bound to fall, both in absolute terms and as a share of GDP, but this does not necessarily mean that the share of total tax revenue in GDP will fall – Hungary provides a good counterexample – though whether maintaining the original high tax share is desirable must be doubtful. The second observation is that cutting subsidies to the traded, manufactured sector appears reasonably simple, though consumer subsidies may be more difficult to cut (for example in Hungary). Falling tax revenues combined with falling output do not necessarily imply increased public deficits (which were avoided in the Czech Republic), just as an apparently successful rebound as in Poland does not guarantee that deficits will disappear. Raising direct and indirect taxes on individuals is clearly possible, and the adverse distributional impact of moving to uniform indirect taxes may be offset by adjustments in the tax system, possibly at some cost of increased marginal tax rates (the Czech Republic).

Overall, the benefits of simplifying the tax system and minimizing the administrative burden have a relatively low cost in distributional terms, compared with the revenue gains. Creating a system to handle unemployment insurance appears to have been done more successfully than the admittedly far harder problem of reforming the system of pension payments, which affects a far larger fraction of the population. It is evident that issues of local taxation, property taxation, and capital income taxation have frequently been neglected, but there are few clear models to follow, and most involve politically unattractive choices.

Although the Visegrád countries, being committed to accession to the EU, have chosen to replace turnover taxes by VAT, it may be that other countries would be wise to delay this change, concentrating meanwhile on moving to a more uniform system of purchase taxes, *ad valorem* and excise taxes on the conventional excise goods (fuel, alcohol and tobacco). Although less efficient in principle than a VAT, as they fail to exempt production, the opportunity cost of using scarce administrative resources to introduce a VAT might be too high in some economies. Against this, Gil Díaz (1987) has argued that the Mexican tax reforms which introduced VAT increased company compliance for profits tax, presumably as companies believed that they could now be identified.

Finally, as Jarvis and Pudney point out, too little strategic thinking is being directed at the expenditure side of the budget, and specifically at improving the targeting of transfers to achieve the desired redistribution at minimum total cost. Perhaps because the theory and practice of taxation is reasonably well codified and readily comparable across countries, most tax systems (at least at the central government level) seem moderately sensible, at least in broad outline. It is far harder to judge whether the system of expenditures and transfers is cost effective, and that requires detailed, painstaking, statistical analysis of the kind they illustrate. Fortunately, CEECs are well equipped with survey data, and it is to be hoped that the European Commission will continue to fund research of this directly policy-relevant kind. In this context, the ACE programme to facilitate contacts between EU member countries and researchers in CEECs has been particularly effective, and this project in particular has benefited from the active cooperation of our colleagues in the Visegrád countries.

Notes

1. Comparing levels of output pre- and post-reform is peculiarly difficult, both because of the change in definitions as the countries adopt the SNA system of national accounting, and also because of the difficulty of measuring the true size of the private sector. Figures reported in EBRD (1994), p. 165, fn. 2) suggest that Poland may have reached its previous peak output by 1994, suggesting that Figure 1.1 and 1.2 may overstate the collapse, though the discussion on pp. 186–7 suggests that official output-based GDP may overstate 1993 growth.
2. That is, the ratio of the 90th percentile point to the 10th percentile point.
3. Note that the direct tax equivalent to an indirect tax rate of t on the producer price is $t/(1+t)$, so halving the indirect tax rate with unchanged coverage would reduce tax revenues by less than half.
4. Indirect taxes as a fraction of total expenditure are somewhat progressive as vehicles and motor fuel are heavily taxed and are a larger share of the expenditure of richer than poorer households. Subsidies, which were rapidly reduced, were also progressive. For a more comprehensive analysis of the individual tax burden of Hungary, see Newbery and Révész (1995).

References

Atkinson, A. B. and Micklewright, J. (1992), *Economic Transformation in Eastern Europe and the Distribution of Income*, Cambridge University Press, Cambridge.

Barr, N. (ed.) (1994), *Labour Markets and Social Policy in Central and Eastern Europe: The Transition and Beyond*, Oxford University Press, Oxford.

EBRD (1994), *Transition Report*, European Bank for Reconstruction and Development, London.

Gil Díaz, F. (1987), 'Some lessons from Mexico's tax reform' in D. M. Newbery and N. H. Stern (eds), *The Theory of Taxation for Developing Countries*, Clarendon Press, Oxford, pp. 333–60.

IMF (1994), *World Economic Outlook*, October, International Monetary Fund, Washington, DC.

Kornai, J. (1992), 'The post-socialist transition and the state: reflections in the light of Hungarian fiscal problems', *American Economic Review,* Papers and Proceedings, 82(2), May, 1–21.

Newbery, D. M. (1994), 'Optimal tax rates and tax design during systemic reform', IPR67, January, Institute for Policy Reform, Washington, DC.

Newbery, D. M. (1995), 'The distributional impact of price changes in Hungary and the UK', *Economic Journal*, July.

Newbery, D. M. and Révész, T. (1995), 'The burden of the Hungarian personal tax system', mimeo, Department of Applied Economics, Cambridge. Paper presented at the ACE workshop in Budapest in March, 1995.

Pudney, S. (1994), 'Earnings inequality in Hungary: a comparative analysis of household and enterprise survey data', *Economics of Planning*, 27, 25–76.

Rein, M. and Wörgötter, A. (1995), *Social Protection and the Enterprise in Transitional Economies*, CEPR, London.

Stern, N. H. (1976), 'On the specification of models of optimal income taxation', *Journal of Public Economics*, 6(1,2), July–Aug, 123–62.

2

Tax and Benefit Reform in the Czech and Slovak Republics*

Christopher Heady and Stephen Smith

2.1 Introduction

This chapter discusses the progress which has been made in reforming the personal tax system and the system of social security benefits in the Czech and Slovak Republics, drawing on detailed modelling of the reforms using household micro-data and a tax simulation model.

The Czech and Slovak Republics were created by the dissolution of Czechoslovakia on 1 January 1993. There had been some interim reform of the tax system in the period between Czechoslovakia's 'velvet revolution' and the break-up of the country, but the most significant tax reforms that have been implemented were introduced at the same time as the country divided, based on common legislation that had been passed during 1992. This legislation replaced the existing turnover tax with a VAT, and made major changes to the taxation of corporate and personal incomes, bringing the systems closely into line with Western European practice. The current tax systems of the two Republics remain fundamentally similar, although some differences have subsequently emerged in the rates and rate structures of individual taxes.

Progress in reforming social benefits has been slower. Both Republics are currently in the process of introducing far-reaching reforms to the benefit system, moving away from universal benefits towards a greater emphasis on 'targeting'.

* This chapter is based on research, undertaken jointly with Colin Lawson, which has been supported by the Economic and Social Research Council under grant nos R000 23 2896 and R000 22 1157. This research was also undertaken with support from the European Commission's PHARE-ACE Programme. The authors are grateful to Vera Kamenickova, Karol Peknik, Pavel Stepanek and Drahomira Vaskova for providing data and information, and to Fiona Coulter and Graham Stark, who have constructed the simulation model used in the chapter. The views expressed, and all remaining errors, are the responsibility of the authors alone.

The aim of this chapter is: first, to describe the reforms of personal taxes and benefits that have been made since 1989, including the differences which have begun to emerge between the Czech and Slovak Republics; second, to assess the extent to which the reforms have met the needs of economic transition; and third, to examine the incentive and distributional effects of some of the policy options which are currently under consideration in the two Republics, including simplification of the VAT structure, and measures for targeting of benefits.

2.2   Reform of Tax and Social Security from 1989 to 1993

2.2.1   The Tax System Under the Planned Economy

The tax system in Czechoslovakia prior to the 1989 revolution exhibited many of the features common among the CEECs. The main elements of the tax system – in place since the 1950s – were taxes on enterprise surpluses, payroll and turnover. While taxes on individual incomes (e.g. the wages tax) existed, they were considerably less important than in most Western European economies. The initial function of these taxes had been simply to provide convenient mechanisms for the transfer of enterprise surpluses to the state budget, and to sustain the administratively determined price structure. Incentives in the tax system were not intended to play any role in the economic system. As elsewhere in the centrally planned economies, the 1970s and 1980s had seen some reforms, using tax incentives to support more decentralization in the economic system, but these innovations were less extensive in Czechoslovakia than in Poland and Hungary.

Between them, the three main sources of tax revenue in Czechoslovakia accounted for about four-fifths of total tax receipts. As Table 2.1 shows, profits taxes contributed 24% of total tax receipts in 1989, taxes on payroll 27%, and turnover tax 24%. The wages tax and other taxes on individual incomes contributed 15% of total tax receipts. Total tax revenues were approximately 47% of GDP in 1989.

Taxes on profits and enterprise surpluses were levied on a number of different bases according to the type of enterprise. There were three principal systems of taxation of enterprises, applying, broadly, to state-owned enterprises, enterprises with decentralized ownership (cooperatives, enterprises owned by local governments, etc.), and agricultural enterprises, respectively. In addition to the basic differences between these three profits tax systems, there was substantial differentiation in treatment within each of these systems, applying much lower rates of profits tax to certain types of activity or certain ownership forms.

The differential treatment of different types of enterprises within this schedular structure of profits taxes had the potential to distort the structure of activity, but given the extensive range of other ways in which the state controlled economic

Table 2.1 Consolidated revenues of the federal, republic and local governments, Czechoslovakia, 1989

	Revenue (Kcs billion)	Percentage of total tax revenues
Profits taxes	83	24
Payroll taxes	95	27
Turnover tax (net)	86	24
Wages tax and other taxes on individual incomes	53	15
Other taxes (on agricultural land, trade taxes, etc.)	37	10
Total tax revenues	354 (47% of GDP)	100

Source: Federal Ministry of Finance, 24 January 1992.

Note: These figures may alternatively be presented on a basis which counts the subsidies paid in the form of negative turnover tax rates as public expenditure. If turnover tax receipts and total tax receipts are calculated gross, before deduction of the subsidies through negative turnover taxes, this gives turnover tax receipts in 1989 of Kcs 135 bn and aggregate revenues of Kcs 403 bn. As a percentage of total tax receipts calculated on the gross basis, turnover taxes contributed 33%. Total tax revenues on this basis were 53% of GDP.

activity within the planned economy, it is likely that these effects would have been small (Gray, 1990).

The most distinctive feature of profits taxation under the previous economic system was that there was considerable administrative discretion and scope for negotiation in the tax payments of individual enterprises, both prospectively and after profits had been earned (Vostatek and Vaskova, (1990). This process of negotiation and administrative discretion could encompass a wide range of state objectives, including price and wage restraint, investment and financing, as well as bargaining over more specific state objectives, including the provision of particular local facilities, social provisions, etc. Accordingly, tax administration formed an integral part of the system of central control and influence over economic activity, and the boundaries of tax administration and other functions of central planning and financial control were in practice unclear and overlapping.

The year-to-year negotiation process had the effect that, in the long run, tax payments were partly based on *ex post* information about the profitability of particular investments or enterprises. Tax changes after profits had been earned had the effect that the tax system was not 'parametric' (Kopits, 1990); in other words, tax payments did not bear a predetermined relationship to the tax base. Gray (1990) discusses the reasons for this form of taxation, arguing that it arose ultimately from asymmetry of information between the centre and enterprise managers about the potential profitability of enterprises. She observes, too, the undesirable effects of *ex post* changes in taxation on long-term incentives for efficiency in management.

The *payroll taxes* in Czechoslovakia were the part of the tax system which most closely resembled taxes in market economies. They constituted a simple, flat-rate levy on aggregate payroll, with only limited adjustments and relatively little discretion in administration. As in many market economies, the payroll tax was levied without regard to the individual circumstances of the employees concerned. Unlike in most market economies, this simple form of taxation could be levied at high rates without causing distributional problems. Since the wage structure was determined through an administrative process rather than by market forces, and since there was negligible unemployment, the dispersion of pre-tax household incomes was low, and distributional issues did not need as close attention in the taxation of incomes as is usual in market economies.

The *turnover tax* was extremely complicated. In 1989, the table of turnover tax rates specified separate tax rates for 1 506 different items. 1 078 of these rates were positive, and 428 were negative (Kamenickova, 1990). The subsidies paid in the form of negative turnover tax rates sharply reduced the net yield of the turnover tax; the gross yield of the turnover tax on those goods subject to positive rates in 1989 amounted to some Kcs 135 bn, but this was reduced to a net yield of Kcs 86 bn by subsidies in the form of negative turnover tax rates which totalled nearly Kcs 50 bn (Table 2.1).[1]

A large number of the goods subject to negative turnover taxes were basic foodstuffs, but a wide range of tax rates, including negative tax rates, were encountered in all industrial sectors (Table 2.2). The rate structure supported the system of administered prices; given a set of chosen prices for inputs and for sales to final consumers, the turnover tax rates were designed to absorb the gap between production costs and output prices. Although in theory fixed, turnover tax rates, like profits tax payments, were the subject of negotiation over time, and the extensive subsidy to food and other items through large negative tax rates partly reflected an unwillingness, for political reasons, to adjust retail prices in line with changes in costs.

The *wages tax* was the principal tax on individual income. There were, in addition, a number of other small taxes on particular categories of individual incomes – taxes on literary and artistic activities, on agricultural income, and a population income tax on income from self-employment. The separate, smaller, taxes on different income sources had the effect that the overall taxation of individual incomes had a schedular structure – incomes from different sources were taxed at sharply differing rates, partly with the aim of discouraging the growth of certain types of activity.

In total, the *wages tax* and *other taxes on individual incomes* contributed some 15% of total tax revenues. Wage tax rates were low, and the tax structure complex – tax levels varied according to sex, marital status and age, as well as the number of dependents, and the structure of marginal tax rates varied widely and unevenly. Although apparently designed to ensure that the wages tax burden sensitively reflected differences in taxpayer characteristics, the net redistributive effect of the complexity was small; Coulter *et al.* (1993) show that the

Table 2.2 Range of turnover tax rates within industrial branches

Branch code	Branch	Lowest percentage rate	Highest percentage rate
O	Agriculture, forestry	-240	66
I	Fuels, coal, oil	-189	76
II	Heat, electricity	-181	0
III	Iron and steel	-33	25
IV	Non-ferrous metals	-27	33
V	Chemicals, rubber, asbestos	-216	71
VI	Engineering and metalworking	-291	83
VII	Building materials	-171	20
VIII	Wood-working	-75	46
IX	Paper and pulp	-80	52
X	Glass, china, ceramics	-69	69
XI	Textiles	-137	70
XII	Clothing	-44	79
XIII	Leather, footwear	-222	52
XIV	Printing, culture	-111	76
XV	Foodstuffs	-224	88
XVI	Other industrial products	-100	62
XVII	Building and construction	0	0
	All branches	-291	88

Source: Federal Ministry of Finance: Appendix: Present system of deliveries, taxes and charges in the CSFR, paper prepared for the first joint workshop on tax structure and public finance, Institute of Economics, Prague, 17 September 1990.

distributional incidence of the tax could have been closely mimicked by a simple linear income tax with a constant marginal rate and allowances for dependents.

2.2.2 The Interim Tax Reform

The pre-1989 tax system of Czechoslovakia and other formerly planned economies differed sharply from tax systems in most market economies. It was clear that, during the course of economic transition, major changes would be required to the Czechoslovak tax system, in at least three key areas.

First, and most important, was the need to establish a system of robust, parametric, profits taxation, in which negotiation and bargaining would play a sharply reduced role. Eliminating the scope for discretionary reductions in taxation for less profitable enterprises is a key step towards eliminating the 'soft budget constraint' (Kornai, 1986) which characterized the previous system; in addition, eliminating the risk of *ex post* taxation of successful enterprises is an important component in establishing an incentive-driven market economy.

A second priority was greater uniformity in the tax treatment of different sectors, commodities and forms of ownership, so as to ensure that the market mechanism guided resources into their most productive applications. This implied a reduction in the range of turnover tax rates, and moves to achieve consistency in the schedular systems of income and profits taxation – in other words, systematic taxation of different sources of income and profits according to broadly similar principles.

Third, the anticipated changes in the pattern of individual incomes that would accompany the introduction of a market economy created a need for corresponding adjustments in the taxation of individual incomes, paying closer attention to individual and household circumstances than in the past, since distributional objectives could no longer be secured through the structure of administered wages and supported by adequate employment opportunities.

In the first two years of reform, the Czechoslovak authorities made a number of immediate changes in the tax system, designed to adjust those aspects of the tax system most incompatible with the requirements of a market economy, and to ensure that the system remained capable of delivering sufficient tax revenues to cover public spending. In this latter respect of course, Czechoslovakia was in a very different position compared to its neighbours: the Czechoslovak government budget was in broad balance, and the new government attached a high priority to preventing a fiscal deficit from emerging during the early years of transition.

The first interim step in tax reform was the abolition (in July 1990) of the negative turnover rates (retail price subsidies) on foodstuffs. This increased food prices by some 25%, and was compensated with a state benefit for all citizens of Kcs 140 per month,[2] intended to correspond to the per capita cost of the increase in food prices (Vostatek and Vaskova, 1990). Later, the negative turnover tax rates on non-food products were removed (without compensation), and the number of turnover tax rates was rationalized to a basic structure of four rates – zero, 12, 22 and 32% – with some higher rates applying to goods which are commonly the subject of excises in addition to VAT in the west, including alcoholic drinks and tobacco (Mervart and Vavrejnova, 1992).[3] This reform aimed to ensure that the price increases which arose from the elimination of negative tax rates would be approximately balanced by the reduction in the positive rates of turnover tax.[4]

Other elements of transitional legislation in 1990 extended liability to pay turnover and profits taxes to the newly legalized private business sector, and a new law imposed a personal income tax on private non-wage income.

These reforms, however, were seen as merely temporary steps, to ensure minimal conformity with the requirements of a market system and to maintain budgetary revenues, pending a more thoroughgoing revision of the tax system, based on legislation to be enacted during 1992, and implemented at the start of 1993.

2.2.3   The 1993 Tax Reform

The taxes included in the 1993 reforms (projected 1993 revenues are summarized in Table 2.3) follow the broad outline of Western European practice:[5]

- a Value Added Tax levied at a standard rate of 23% in the Czech Republic and 25% in the Slovak Republic, with a reduced rate of 5% in the Czech Republic and 6% in the Slovak Republic, applying to basic foods, medicines, fuel, books, newspapers and some services including repairs.
- specific excise duties on alcoholic drinks, tobacco products and mineral oils.
- personal income tax, currently levied at comparatively low rates. The tax base includes employment and self-employment income, rental incomes, interest and dividends. A taxpayer allowance of Kc 20 400[6] per annum may be deducted in computing taxable income, and there are also allowances for a spouse and children. Social insurance contributions are deductible. A progressive structure of marginal rates applies to most categories of incomes, beginning at 15% on taxable incomes up to Kc 60 000 per annum (£1 333), and rising to a maximum of 47%; dividends and some other categories of income are taxed at 25%.
- payroll-based social insurance levies, paid partly by employees and partly by employers, for pensions, sickness benefits and unemployment insurance, at combined (employee plus employer) rates of 27.2, 4.8, and 4.0% of gross wages, respectively. In addition, there is a payroll-based health insurance levy, at a rate of 13.5% of gross wages, which is not considered to be part of taxation, and the revenues from which are treated as outside the public budget.

Table 2.3   Projected consolidated revenues of central and local government, Czech Republic, 1993

	Revenue (Kc billion)	Percentage of total projected revenues[1]
Corporate income tax	70.1	17
Individual income tax	25.7	6
VAT	80.6	20
Excise taxes	39.5	10
Other taxes (property tax, road tax, trade taxes, etc.)	41.4	10
Social security contributions (payroll taxes)	107.5	27
Non-tax revenues	36.7	9
Total projected tax revenues and social security contributions	401.5	100

Source: Czech Ministry of Finance, December 1993.

[1]Does not sum to 100% due to rounding.

- corporate profits taxation, based on legislation closely conforming to practice in some Western European countries, with a rate of 45% on taxable profits.

2.3   The Czech and Slovak Tax Reforms and the Needs of Transition

Czechoslovakia, like most of the other formerly planned economies, has evidently looked to Western practice for the basis of its tax proposals. In this section we consider whether modelling the tax system closely on Western practice responds adequately to the particular tax needs of the economy during transition.

Nevertheless, despite this choice of a tax system which, in its general structure, closely resembles tax systems in Western Europe, the implementation of this system may need to take account of the particular features of transition economies which differ from Western European market economies. As we describe below, some of the key constraints on tax policy choice in transition economies differ considerably from those in Western economies; in particular, tax reform must cope with severe administrative limitations. Designing an optimal tax system in the light of these constraints is unlikely to result in systems identical to those of Western European economies.

2.3.1   Administrative Constraints on Reform

Administrative constraints are of central importance in assessing the appropriate pace and direction of tax reform in formerly centrally planned economies. These are of three different basic types, relating to transition costs, scale and administrative culture.

Nearly all tax reforms are likely to involve transitional costs of implementation which are considerably higher than the steady-state costs of annual operation of the system once established. These costs arise partly as a result of the unfamiliarity of taxpayers and tax officials with the new system; both formal training costs and informal training costs in terms of learning-by-doing may be incurred. Also there could be various capital costs, for example in appropriate computer equipment, which would be bunched at the start of a new system. There are likely to be some unavoidable revenue costs in transition as a result of the incompatibility of the previous system and its replacement; to avoid double taxation of certain transactions it is often necessary for transitional provisions to treat taxpayers relatively generously in the first year. Finally, and probably most important, are the revenue losses that will arise through initial inexperience and unfamiliarity of those operating and enforcing it; revenues in the first years of operation are likely to fall substantially short of the levels that could be collected from a well- established VAT system.

A second consideration is the vastly increased scale of tax administration that is necessary in a market economy compared to a planned economy. One aspect of this is simply the number of taxpayers. Planned economies have typically had a highly concentrated industrial structure; in a market economy, much less concentration will be appropriate, and this will inevitably increase the number of taxpayers. Small firms, in particular, involve large fixed costs of tax administration, whilst paying relatively little tax. A second difference which increases the resources required for tax administration is that tax administration can no longer be conducted as a by-product of other operations, such as auditing and financial and management control.

Under the old system, the vast majority of tax payments were made directly by companies, as 'profits' tax, turnover tax, wage tax or payroll tax; liability for tax could be determined as a by-product of other operations. As a consequence, tax administration was cheap, and required few officials for administration. In the new system, tax administration needs to obtain information from reluctant taxpayers. Decades of authoritarian rule have led to acceptance of the legitimacy of tax avoidance, and effective procedures are needed to prevent individual and corporate tax evasion. These new functions imply that more staff will be needed, in an economic context where the sort of skills required are in short supply and are expensive.

There is a third source of important administrative constraints on tax reform as a result of the traditions and attitudes of the existing tax administration. As described above, taxation in the old system was not 'parametric' in the sense that market economy tax systems need to be if firms are to face clear and appropriate budget constraints and incentives. For tax administration and enforcement to function in a way that is compatible with the requirements of a market economy it is necessary that the tradition of negotiation and bargaining in taxation should be broken.

These various administrative considerations imply that phased introduction of a new tax system would face fewer administrative problems than a 'big bang', replacing all aspects of the existing tax structure in one sweeping reform. Constraints on the availability of staff, and the transitional costs and revenue losses may be less serious if phased reform is undertaken. Administrative considerations also imply that different tax policy choices may be appropriate compared to what would be optimal in the West, however, in two areas.

First, to the extent that complexity and sophistication in the tax system has a cost in terms of administration, greater initial simplification will be appropriate; cheap but rough-and-ready taxes may have strong attractions.

Second, the need to make a decisive break with the attitudes of the past regarding tax administration may imply a deliberate preference for tax systems that require the minimum of judgement and discretion in administration. This is needed, not merely because discretion is costly to operate, but also because it is potentially subversive of the shift to a parametric tax system and a market economy. To break past traditions of 'negotiability' in taxation, it may be desirable to design the tax system in a way which avoids the need for tax administrators to make complex judgements, which can then become the subject of bargaining and negotiated trade-offs embracing other aspects of public policy.

These considerations might lead to a number of conclusions for tax policy. The objective of reducing the scale of administrative resources could imply, for example, greater use of exemptions, and higher taxpayer registration thresholds than might be chosen in the West. In the Czech VAT legislation, for example, a relatively high registration threshold of Kc 1.5 million turnover in three consecutive years was chosen, limiting the number of small business taxpayers to whom the system was initially applied.[7] The smaller businesses which are not registered would account for low net VAT payments relative to the administrative and compliance costs of including them in the VAT system.

Similarly, it may be desirable to make as much use as possible of tax systems which permit tax to be withheld at the company level rather than assessed at the personal level. The Czechoslovak system has placed considerably greater weight on the payroll taxes to finance the social security system than on the individual income tax. Maximizing the use of withholding arrangements has clear advantages in terms of reducing the number of taxpayers with which the authorities have to deal (although at the cost of making the taxes less able to reflect the circumstances of individuals and households). It may also make it easier to ensure taxpayer compliance, although Hussain and Stern (1993) warn that this should not be so readily assumed as in the Western European context, since enterprise managers in the planned economy had become highly skilled in concealing information from the authorities.

In addition to those measures which have been taken by the authorities in Czechoslovakia to minimize the administrative burden of introducing and operating a new tax system, we suggest that there would have been scope, and probably would still remain some potential benefit, from further administrative simplification.

The objective of administrative simplification might imply decisions about the coverage of tax systems which in Western European terms would be regarded as a source of distortion and inefficiency. In the case of the Czechoslovak tax reform, the administrative problems of VAT could have been eased by choosing a single-rate system rather than the two-rate system in which a reduced rate is applied to food and other 'necessities'. The distributional objectives which lie behind the choice of a two-rate system in Czechoslovakia might alternatively be met by the exemption (not zero-rating) of the entire food sector. This would sharply reduce the number of VAT taxpayers, at only limited cost in terms of revenue foregone, and would allow the VAT administration to concentrate its resources on taxpayers in other sectors, where the bulk of VAT revenue will in any case be raised (Heady et al., 1993).

Also, as Hussain and Stern (1993) propose, the administrative burden on the revenue authorities in administering and enforcing income tax payments by small businesses could be eased by drawing a link between the VAT system and the income tax system, so as to restrict entitlement to reclaim input VAT to only those small businesses providing verifiable accounts to the income tax authorities. Those which did not provide such accounts would then effectively bear some taxation, through their inability to reclaim the tax on production inputs.

2.3.2   Federalism and Tax Reform

The 1992 tax legislation was formulated at a time when Czechoslovakia was moving towards a highly-decentralized federalism in which all but a limited set of government functions (defence, foreign representation, unemployment insurance and certain infrastructure expenditures) were to be exercised at the Republic level.

Prior constitutional decisions had determined both the basic form of the new tax system, and the assignment of competences in taxation between the federal government and the republics. All of the major taxes were to be the subject of central legislation; these would include all taxes on goods and services (VAT and excises), and also income taxes on individuals and corporations. The taxes which were left to therepublics to determine were to be comparatively minor – property taxes, the road tax, taxes on inheritance and gifts, on property transactions and environmental taxes. It was decided that all tax administration should be the responsibility of the republics. The allocation of revenues between the federal government and the two republics was to be determined by negotiation.

The amount of discretion over taxation which was envisaged for the republics was clearly inconsistent with their rapidly growing strength in the Czechoslovak political system. If the country had not split, it would have been desirable, and probably a political necessity, for the republics to have been given more control over significant parameters of the federal tax system. This would have raised a series of complex, and interacting, issues concerning the form of permissible discretion, the allocation of revenues and the allocation of enforcement responsibility.

Many of these difficulties which would have been encountered were solved – or sidestepped – by the subsequent decision to split the country. In particular, separation has clarified the questions about assignment – of revenues, tax policy and administration. Others have remained problem areas in fiscal relations between the independent Czech and Slovak states.

Political separation has been followed by rapid disintegration of the existing economic linkages between the republics. This has created particular problems for the tax system, for example, over the residence for fiscal purposes of existing enterprises (which during the separation may be more flexible than is usual), and over the correct attribution of the previous history (depreciation allowances, losses, etc.) of individual taxpayers to one state or the other.

Due to the mistrust which appears to have accompanied separation, the opportunity has not been taken to establish institutions and procedures to prevent the emergence of excessive transactions costs in trade or other movements between the two states. As in the European Union, procedures for operating indirect taxes on goods traded between the republics could have a significant effect on the costs of such trade and on the efficiency of VAT administration. Similarly, there would be potential benefits from devising institutional arrangements which could coordinate the basic structure and legislation for taxation (especially corporate taxation), to limit the accounting burdens on firms operating in both halves of the country, and to avoid the emergence of an unpredictable 'tax jungle' of unplanned gaps and distortions between two mismatched tax systems. Indications from the first two years after separation do not encourage the view that this opportunity will be taken. The initial attempt to establish coordinating institutions to govern economic relations between the two halves of former Czechoslovakia, including a monetary union and customs union, disintegrated quickly. Economic relationships between the two states have been soured by disputes over assets and payments, and the degree of economic integration of the two states has been sharply reduced. The Czech Republic, in particular, has moved quickly to introduce border controls on the frontier between the two states, and to place trade relationships with the Slovak Republic on a similar footing to its trade with other partners. Whilst some of these developments may be seen as the consequence of transitional difficulties, there seems to be little recognition of the economic costs that will be incurred in such dis-integration, and currently little attempt to develop fiscal institutions to minimize transactions costs and the potential damage from fiscal competition.

2.3.3   The 1993 Income Tax Reforms

Overall, the tax changes that culminated in the comprehensive reform of January 1993 moved Czechoslovakia (and its successor states) towards a standard European tax system. This system improved the incentive structures by simplifying rates and improving transparency. Our past work has focused in particular on the new income tax and on the pattern of marginal tax rates which it involves.

We have observed that the personal income tax has a structure of allowances that leads to very high marginal tax rate 'spikes' at certain points of the income scale. A problem arises when a married man loses his eligibility to his married man's tax allowance as soon as his wife's earnings exceed Kc 20 400. The experience of the United Kingdom, which used to have similar spikes in the national insurance structure, suggests that this provision could lead to many women deciding to keep their earnings below the level of the spike: a clear adverse incentive.

Our quantitative analysis of changes in the income tax focused on three issues. The first was an analysis of the old wage tax system and a comparison between it and the new income tax (Coulter *et al.,* 1993). This showed that, despite its enormous complexity, the ultimate distributive impact of the wage tax was very similar to a linear income tax with a large child tax allowance for the first child. It also showed that the new income tax, plus the payroll taxes paid by employees, is more progressive than the old wage tax but provides smaller child tax allowances. The increased progressivity is a rational response to an expected increase in the degree of pre-tax income inequality, and the reduction in child tax allowances represents a reduction in a level of state support for children that had been very generous by Western standards.

The reduction in the level of child tax allowances would have been even greater if the income tax law had not been amended in parliament, raising it from Kc 6 000 per child to Kc 9 000 per child. Our second quantitative analysis of the income tax system (Coulter *et al.,* 1992) therefore looked at the distributional effects of this amendment, assuming that the revenue was recovered by a slight increase in the rate of income tax. The model for the whole federation showed that the distributional effects were quite complex, with gainers and losers in all income bands except for those on very low incomes, who are outside the income tax system. It also showed that, on average, people in Slovakia gained from the change while people in the Czech Lands lost.

In view of the plans to separate the two parts of the country, the latter result meant that it was interesting to look at the two republics independently, using the models designed for them and imposing revenue neutrality on each separately. These results confirmed the complexity of the distributional effects. For example, over a third of married couples with children lost from the change because of the increased tax rate required to finance the increased allowances. This point illustrates the importance of modelling the revenue source in any analysis of increased social support.

The final part of the quantitative analysis of the personal income tax was as part of a general examination of the incidence and revenue elasticity of the personal direct and indirect tax system (Coulter *et al.,* 1994). This showed that the income tax is the most progressive part of the tax system and that payroll taxes are also significantly progressive, as the poor receive a smaller proportion of their income as wages. It also showed that the revenue elasticity of income tax is the highest: a 1% increase in nominal income (either from inflation or real income growth) produces a 2.19% increase in income tax revenue. The strictly proportional nature of the payroll tax implies that its revenue elasticity is unity.

In the next two sections of this chapter we look at two further groups of issues concerning the impact on households of the tax and benefit system set up through the 1993 reforms: the structure of the indirect tax system, and the pattern of eligibility and targeting of social security benefits.

2.4   The Simplification of VAT

As discussed above, both the Czech and Slovak Republics have adopted a two-rate structure of VAT (in addition to the zero rate that applies to exports). The rates are 23 and 5% in the Czech Republic; and 25 and 6% in the Slovak Republic. The purpose of this section is to examine the likely effects of simplifying VAT to have only one rate on domestic sales. As the issues involved are essentially the same in the two countries, we report quantitative results for only one of them, the Czech Republic, for which we have built a tax benefit model (CZ) described in Coulter *et al*. (1994). The main data source for this model is the Household Budget Survey, based on 5 000 households from the whole of Czechoslovakia (3 300 from the Czech Republic), collected by the Czech statistical office.

There are two strong reasons for considering the simplification of VAT. First, the application of two different rates involves a distortion of consumer choice between goods in the two tax groups. Second, a move to single-rate VAT would reduce administrative costs, allow cross-checking between VAT and corporation tax assessments, and avoid the rent-seeking activities of producers who wish to have their products included in the lower tax group.

Against these, there are two arguments in favour of having more than one rate of VAT: the setting on non-uniform taxes might encourage labour supply and so reduce the distortionary effect of income taxation, and income distribution can be made less unequal by applying a lower rate of VAT to goods that form a large part of the expenditure of poor people.

It is difficult to test whether the argument in terms of encouraging labour supply can justify the two-rate VAT structure in either the Czech or Slovak Republics: the necessary estimates of complete demand systems are not available for either country. However, work on other countries suggests that such an argument is unlikely to be strong. For example, Ebrahimi and Heady (1988) estimated that the imposition of uniform VAT in the United Kingdom would involve an efficiency loss of less than 0.04% of GNP, compared to optimally non-uniform taxes. It has also been made clear to us that such an argument did not lie behind the decision to adopt a two-rate VAT in either country. The reason for its adoption was its presumed distributional benefits. The remainder of this section will therefore concentrate on evaluating such distributional benefits.

It is first worth considering the extent to which the two-rate VAT in the Czech Republic does favour poorer people. The lower rate applies to basic food, medicines, books, repairs and tourism. Some, but certainly not all, of these items can be expected to form a particularly large share of the budget of poorer households.

A more precise idea of the distributional effects can be obtained by considering the consequences of raising the lower rate of VAT to equal the higher rate. If the cost of such an increase is a higher proportion of the income of poorer households, then the two-rate structure does favour the poor. Table 2.4 shows the results of calculating these consequences using our model, CZ.

Table 2.4   The distributional impact of an increase in the lower rate of VAT to equal the higher rate

(1) Monthly net income range (crowns)	(2) Percentage of households in range[1]	(3) Average monthly cost (crowns)	(4) (3) as percentage of average income
Under 3 000	5.1	167	7.2
3 000 - 4 000	9.6	196	6.6
4 000 - 5 000	6.5	233	6.1
5 000 - 6 000	6.4	291	6.3
6 000 - 7 000	10.0	330	6.1
7 000 - 8 000	10.8	349	5.6
8 000 - 9 000	12.0	387	5.5
9 000 - 10 000	12.2	422	5.4
10 000 - 11 000	9.1	464	5.4
11 000 - 12 000	6.8	507	5.3
12 000 - 15 000	8.3	544	، 5.0
Over 15 000	3.3	623	4.1
All households	100.0	372	5.5

Source: Results from CZ.

[1]Does not sum to 100% due to rounding.

Column (4) of Table 2.4 shows clearly that poorer people would suffer more, in proportion to their income, from an increase in the lower rate. Therefore, it appears that the two-rate structure does favour the poor. It is also clear from column (3), however, that richer people would face the greatest absolute increases in tax payments as a result of simplification. Thus a policy of increasing the lower rate of VAT and using the proceeds to finance a uniform direct payment to all households could produce a substantial redistribution from richer households to poorer households. This is an illustration of part of what lies behind the demonstration by Atkinson and Stiglitz (1976) that uniform sales taxes are optimal in the absence of labour supply effects, provided that the government makes optimal use of direct payments to households.

Of course, the figures in Table 2.4 are averages over households within each income range. Different households will have different consumption patterns, and so will face differing costs as a result of an increase in the lower rate of VAT. A major cause of these different consumption patterns is differences in the demographic composition of households. For example, our CZ model shows that increasing the lower rate of VAT has a particularly large effect on single parents and pensioners. Deaton and Stern (1986) point out that this harmful effect of simplifying sales taxes can be offset by making the direct payments to households depend on their demographic composition.

This discussion shows that, in theory, the simplification of VAT does not have to harm the poor, and could even improve their position. This relies, however, on the government using the theoretically optimal direct payments to households. In fact, the governments of both the Czech and Slovak Republics are unlikely to make use of such direct payments. The 'compensation payments' introduced after the removal of price subsidies are a close approximation to what is required but, as discussed in the next section, these are being phased out. It is more realistic to suppose that the governments of these two countries would use extra revenue from VAT simplification to alter the rates of other taxes and social security benefits. The precise distributional impact of VAT simplification would depend on which rates were changed, and by how much. We now turn to considering some possibilities.

Table 2.5   The distributional impact of an increase in the lower rate of VAT to equal the higher rate and abolition of personal income tax

(a)   By income range

(1) Monthly net income range (crowns)	(2) Average monthly cost (crowns)	(3) (2) as percentage of average income
Under 3 000	154	6.7
3 000 - 4 000	153	5.1
4 000 - 5 000	96	2.5
5 000 - 6 000	148	3.2
6 000 - 7 000	201	3.7
7 000 - 8 000	134	2.2
8 000 - 9 000	59	0.8
9 000 - 10 000	16	0.2
10 000 - 11 000	-80	-0.9
11 000 - 12 000	-134	-1.4
12 000 - 15 000	-318	-2.9
Over 15 000	-1258	-8.3
All households	0	0.0

(b)   By household type

	(2) Average monthly cost (crowns)	(3) (2) as percentage of average income
Single unemployed	125	5.2
Single employed	-158	-4.2
Single parent	7	0.1
Unemployed couple	213	4.9
Single earner couple without children	-6	-0.1
Single earner couple with children	80	1.2
Two earner couple without children	-334	-4.4
Two earner couple with children	-107	-1.3
Single pensioner	198	6.7
Couple pensioner	328	5.2
All households	0	0.0

Source: Results from CZ.

One politically attractive use of the extra revenue from applying the higher rate of VAT to all goods and services would be the abolition of personal income tax: the extra VAT revenue is almost exactly equal to the income tax revenue. The effects of this combined change on income distribution by income range and household type are shown in Table 2.5.[8] As the figures in Table 2.5 represent costs, it is clear that the poor lose and the rich gain from such a change. It can also be seen that the demographic groups that lose are the unemployed and pensioners. Also, looking at single earner and two earner couples, those with children do less well than those without.

Table 2.6   The distributional impact of an increase in the lower rate of VAT to equal the higher rate, combined with increases in the personal tax allowance and selected benefits

(a)   By income range

(1) Monthly net income range (crowns)	(2) Average monthly cost (crowns)	(3) (2) as percentage of average income
Under 3 000	-37	-1.6
3 000 - 4 000	-8	-0.3
4 000 - 5 000	4	0.1
5 000 - 6 000	-9	-0.2
6 000 - 7 000	-20	-0.4
7 000 - 8 000	-16	-0.3
8 000 - 9 000	-11	-0.2
9 000 - 10 000	-27	-0.3
10 000 - 11 000	-6	-0.1
11 000 - 12 000	-1	-0.0
12 000 - 15 000	72	0.7
Over 15 000	186	1.2
All households	0	0.0

(b)   By household type

	(2) Average monthly cost (crowns)	(3) (2) as percentage of average income
Single unemployed	1	0.1
Single employed	63	1.7
Single parent	-39	-0.7
Unemployed couple	-284	-6.6
Single earner couple without children	68	1.0
Single earner couple with children	-20	-0.3
Two earner couple without children	105	1.4
Two earner couple with children	-21	-0.2
Single pensioner	-23	-0.8
Couple pensioner	-47	-0.8
All households	0	0.0

Source: Results from CZ.

It is likely that such strong redistributive effects would not be acceptable, and we have therefore devised a package of changes that will also use all of the extra VAT revenue but have smaller redistributive effects. This involves leaving the income tax rates at their present values, but increasing the individual tax allowance by two-thirds. In addition, pensioners are given a uniform absolute addition to their pensions, child benefits are increased and unemployment benefit is made more generous. The distributional effects of this package are summarized in Table 2.6. This shows a much smaller degree of redistribution. There is some transfer from the richest groups to the poorest, and some from those without children to those with children and to the unemployed.

No doubt, a more careful fine-tuning could have produced even less redistribution, but the results in Table 2.6 are sufficient to show that the two-rate structure of VAT is unnecessary for distributional reasons, at least between the broad groups identified in the table. Any advantage that these groups obtain from the lower rate of VAT could equally well be provided through alteration in taxes and social benefits. There remains the issue of distribution within these groups, where people with unusual consumption patterns may do significantly better or worse than the average. This is an issue we are still working on, but we have no clear results to date.

Finally, it is worth noting the effects of these possible reforms on the marginal rate of tax faced by households, because tax design must take account of efficiency as well as distributional issues. CZ can calculate the overall marginal tax rate that is faced by each household. These rates include the effects of all taxes and benefits,[9] and show the net rate faced by a person working for one additional hour. Table 2.7 reports average values of these marginal tax rates for each of our income ranges, under the various policy alternatives. As one would expect, the simple raising of the lower rate of VAT increases the overall marginal tax rate for all households. This could constitute a major reason for not wishing to spend the proceeds of this tax increase on direct uniform payments to households (which is the most egalitarian option). These high rates can only be reduced by using at least some of the revenue to reduce income-related taxation.

The abolition of income taxation is a clear example of this, and produces marginal tax rates below those of the current system. We have seen above, however, that this policy would harm the poor considerably. The final column relates to the least redistributive policy combination, but still shows an increase in marginal tax rates compared to the current system.

The choice between the current two-rate VAT system and the simplified systems considered here is therefore not clear cut. The advantages of a single-rate VAT appear to be gained at the cost of either increased inequality or increased marginal tax rates. Deaton and Stern (1986) show that there need not be such costs if direct payments to households are chosen optimally. Our problem may be that we have not looked hard enough for a policy combination that will allow VAT simplification without harmful side-effects, or it may be that this is not

Table 2.7 The impact of VAT simplification on marginal tax rates

Monthly net income range (crowns)	Average marginal tax rates (%)			
		VAT simplification		
	Current system	(1)	(2)	(3)
Under 3 000	30	34	32	32
3 000 - 4 000	30	35	32	34
4 000 - 5 000	32	36	32	36
5 000 - 6 000	31	35	32	34
6 000 - 7 000	32	36	32	34
7 000 - 8 000	35	39	33	36
8 000 - 9 000	36	40	32	38
9 000 - 10 000	35	39	32	39
10 000 - 11 000	38	41	32	40
11 000 - 12 000	37	40	32	40
12 000 - 15 000	39	42	32	41
Over 15 000	40	42	30	41

Source: Results from CZ.

Note: VAT simplification options are as follows:
(1) Raise lower rate of VAT to equal higher rate.
(2) As (1) but abolish personal income tax.
(3) As (1) but increase personal tax allowance and selected benefits.

possible without the introduction of additional reforms of the tax and social benefit system.

2.5   Targeting Benefits[10]

From January 1995 the Czech Republic is due to reform its system of social security benefits. The current system consists of a mixture of the social welfare system inherited from the pre-1989 communist government, plus a number of benefits introduced after the Velvet Revolution, in order to deal with the social problems caused by the transition to a market economy. Until now, there has been no major redesign of the benefit system. As a result, it is now urgently in need of reform if it is to be consistent with the operation of the emerging market economy.

The current Czech benefit system consists of three components: a social insurance scheme, providing pensions and contributory benefits for sickness and unemployment; social assistance, which provides benefits for those families with incomes below the subsistence minimum; and the remaining benefits, largely universal in nature, paid to families with children, and pensioners.

The most important of these benefits under the current system are the child allowance, the parents' allowance and the compensation benefit. The combined annual cost paid to families with children through these benefits is estimated for 1994 as Kc 22 600 million, about 2.3% of GDP.

Part of the aim of the reforms is to reduce the cost of benefit payments by restricting eligibility through income testing, thus concentrating payments on low income families. The reforms are intended to be more far-reaching, by replacing a rather *ad hoc* set of benefits with a comprehensive system of state social support. Both the level and entitlement to benefits will depend explicitly on the officially defined subsistence minimum.

The child allowance is currently paid to all families with children, with the amounts depending on the age of the child. In 1994 the rates were Kc 340 per month for a child aged 0 to 5 years; Kc 380 for a child aged 6 to 10; Kc 450 for a child aged 11 to 15; and Kc 490 for a dependent child aged 16 to 26. These amounts are approximately equal to one-third of the value of the subsistence minimum for a child of the relevant age group.

The parents' allowance is paid at a rate of Kc 1 500 per month (the amount for the personal needs of an adult in the subsistence minimum) to a non-working parent who cares for a child aged under three years, or under seven years if the child is disabled.

The compensation benefit was originally introduced in 1990 to compensate for price rises, and was paid to all citizens. It was subsequently restricted to families with children and non-working pensioners, and from 1993 has been restricted to families with income of less than twice the subsistence minimum. It is paid at a flat rate of 220 crowns per month per child and per pensioner.

There are five main reforms due to be introduced in January 1995:

1. The compensation benefit is to be abolished.
2. Pensioners will be compensated for this through an increase in the basic pension.
3. Instead of the compensation benefit, families with children will receive a new benefit, the social additional allowance. Unlike the compensation benefit, however, the amount of the payment is to be explicitly means tested, so that it will depend upon the relationship between family income and the subsistence minimum.
4. A new housing contribution will be introduced. The amount of the benefit payment will not depend at all upon actual housing costs, but will depend upon the amount allowed for housing costs in the calculation of the subsistence minimum. The amount of benefit paid will also be means tested, with the test depending on the relationship between household income and the subsistence minimum.
5. For the first time, both the child allowance and the parents' allowance will be income limited. Families with income greater than a given constant times the subsistence minimum will no longer be eligible for the benefit. In addition, the age limit up to which a child can be considered to be dependent will be reduced from 26 to 21.

The subsistence minimum therefore affects the benefit system in two ways, determining both the level of benefits, and entitlement to the benefits. In the case of the child allowance and the parent allowance, entitlement is determined in a straightforward way – all families with income above a given multiple of the subsistence minimum lose all entitlement to the benefit. According to draft legislation this multiple will be set at 2.5.

The social additional allowance and the housing allowance are more complicated. Families at or below the subsistence minimum receive the maximum benefit. As income rises above this level, the benefit is gradually withdrawn, and reaches zero at K times the subsistence minimum. According to the draft legislation, K is likely to be set at 1.5.

The dependence of these new benefits on household income makes them substantially more difficult to administer than the universal benefits they replace. In addition, experience in other countries suggests that there could be problems of some eligible households not taking up the benefits, as discussed in Dorsett and Heady (1991). As we have no information on the likely take-up rates, the simulations reported below are based on the assumption of 100% take-up.

We used the CZ model to simulate the reforms described above: the income-limiting of the child allowance and the parents' allowance, the introduction of the social additional allowance and the housing contribution, and the abolition of the compensation benefit. We also assume that pensions are raised to compensate for the loss of the compensation benefit. Unfortunately we cannot model the effect of restricting the definition of a dependent child to an upper limit of 21 years, since the data that we have do not allow this, but we are able to model the other main features of the reforms.

Table 2.8 shows our estimated revenue impact of the reforms. Note that this table does not show a prediction for the 1995 benefit system, but shows our simulation of the current 1994 benefit system compared with what would have happened if the reforms had been applied in 1994. This is clearly the comparison that we wish to make, since otherwise interpretation of the results would be confused by the fact that we would have to make assumptions about inflation and consequent uprating of benefit levels.

The table shows in the first column our estimates of tax and benefit payments in 1994 under the current system, while the second column shows the changes caused by the reforms. All increases are shown as positive numbers, so that a positive sign in the second column means that spending on a benefit has increased. For example, the reforms result in an increase in pension spending of 6 500 million Czech crowns per year. The negative value in the second column for all benefits, however, means that total benefit spending falls by 1 300 million crowns.

Similarly, the negative signs against value added and excise taxes in the second column means that revenue from these taxes has fallen. The reason for this is that the fall in benefit payments reduces household incomes, which results in a fall in spending, and hence in indirect tax payments. The final row in the table shows net

Table 2.8   The old benefit system and the new – estimated revenue impact.
Units: millions of Czech crowns per year

	The current system	Differences from current system
Income tax	29 803	0
Social insurance	101 656	0
Health fund	44 667	0
Pensions	84 451	6 551
Child allowance	12 875	-822
Parents' allowance	5 674	-158
Social addition allowance	0	2 284
Housing contribution	0	1 143
Sickness benefit	5 280	0
Unemployment benefit	2 555	-33
Compensation benefit	10 294	-10 294
All benefits	**121 132**	**-1 329**
Value Added Tax	51 291	-184
Excise tax	22 264	-76
All indirect taxes	**73 555**	**-261**
Net Revenue	**128 550**	**1 067**

Source: Authors' tax benefit model, CZ.

revenues to the government, that is, the sum of tax payments minus benefit spending. We can see that overall revenue increases by 1 100 million Czech crowns per year.

We can see from the table that revenue is raised mainly through the abolition of the compensation benefit. We assume that pensioners are fully compensated for the loss of the benefit, so that 6 500 million crowns of this revenue is spent on increasing pensions. This is rather more than we estimate is spent currently on the compensation benefit to pensioners (about 5 400 million crowns). This is because, under the current system, some pensioners are excluded from the benefit because of the income limit, while we assume that all pensioners receive an increase in the pension.

Much of the remaining revenue is spent on the introduction of the social additional allowance and housing contribution. The estimated 2 300 million crowns per year spent on the social additional allowance is substantially smaller than the amount currently spent on the compensation benefit to families with children, which we estimate as 4 900 million in 1994.

The effects of income limiting the child allowance and the parents' allowance are quite small – spending on the child allowance falls by about 820 million crowns per year, while spending on the parents' allowance falls by about 160 million crowns. The reason for this is that very few households have incomes above 2.5 times the subsistence minimum, and so the numbers affected by the income limit are quite small.

In Tables 2.9 and 2.10 we show some of the distributional consequences of the reforms. In order to properly evaluate the distributional impact we must take into account the overall impact on government finances, by making the reform revenue neutral. As we have seen, the reforms produce a small increase in government revenue. The amount is enough to allow a fall in the basic rate of income tax of about 1% (0.88% to be exact), so we assume that this adjustment is also made.

Table 2.9 Gains and losses of benefit reform package by income range.
Units: crowns per month

Income range	Average gain	Losers (%)	No change (%)	Gainers (%)	Percentage of households
Less than 3 000	64	0	0	100	5
3 000–3 999	16	0	50	50	15
4 000–4 999	48	0	37	63	6
5 000–5 999	48	8	17	75	5
6 000–6 999	52	7	62	32	9
7 000–7 999	64	12	44	45	9
8 000–8 999	80	25	11	64	7
9 000–9 999	24	38	1	61	7
10 000–10 999	-27	49	0	51	8
11 000–11 999	-72	46	0	54	7
12 000–14 999	-67	42	0	58	15
More than 15 000	-111	39	0	61	9
All	0	23	20	56	100

Source: Authors' tax benefit model, CZ.

Table 2.10 Gains and losses of benefit reform package by household type.
Units: crowns per month

Household type	Average gain	Losers (%)	No change (%)	Gainers (%)	Percentage of households
Single unemployed	70	0	38	62	0.1
Single employed	30	0	0	100	3
Single parent	69	50	1	49	4
Unemployed couple	513	0	0	100	0.1
SE couple without children	34	0	1	99	2
SE couple with children	-26	53	1	46	7
TE couple without children	64	0	0	100	9
TE couple with children	-119	61	0	39	25
Single pensioner	34	0	39	61	25
Couple pensioner	47	4	59	37	17
MFU without children	145	0	3	97	4
MFU with children	-34	45	0	55	3
All	0	23	20	56	100

Source: Authors' tax benefit model, CZ.

Notes: SE = Single earner; TE = Two earner; MFU = Multiple family unit

In Table 2.9 we show the gains and losses according to the income range to which each household belongs. The first column shows the average change in net household income, while columns two, three and four show the percentage of households in each income range that lose from the reform, that are unaffected, and that gain. Column 5 shows the percentages of households in each income range.

We can see from the table that the reforms are progressive, as we would expect from the previous discussion. Up to an income range of 10 000 crowns per month households gain on average, while households above that range lose on average. Moreover, none of the households in the bottom three income ranges lose at all. However, the pattern is not entirely uniform: even among the highest income range a majority of households gain from the reforms; the largest average gain is found among the 8 000 to 8 999 income range; while households in the 10 000 to 10 999 range are most likely to be losers.

Table 2.10 shows the same information for households grouped according to family type. We can see that the losses are overwhelmingly concentrated among families with children, while the vast majority of childless households gain from the reforms. Even so, a substantial number of families with children also gain from the reforms.

We can make sense of these patterns by considering carefully the combined distributional impact of the reforms. Note that the fall in income tax will benefit the majority of households (about 73%) who pay income tax. The largest absolute gain will be received by better-off households, however, while lower income households who pay no tax will not benefit.

By far the most important change, in revenue terms, is the abolition of the compensation benefit, however. We have assumed that pensioners are fully compensated for this, but families with children will not necessarily be compensated. Some families on higher incomes will also lose the parents' allowance or the child allowance. Lower income families may receive the new social additional allowance, and the average payment of this allowance is slightly greater than for the compensation benefit, so that we would expect the overall impact of the benefit changes to be progressive.

The impact of the housing contribution is particularly interesting, since it is payable to childless households as well as pensioners and families with children – the groups traditionally favoured by the benefit system. This, in addition to the cut in income tax, explains why childless households do so well from the reforms.

Overall, the majority of households (56%) gain from the reforms, compared with only 23% who lose, the rest being unaffected. Since the reform is revenue neutral, this implies that the losers must lose far more, on average, than the gainers gain. We find that this is the case: the average gain is about 109 crowns per month, while the average loss is 458 crowns per month.

In Tables 2.11 and 2.12 we show the effects of the reforms on marginal tax rates, by household income range. The first column of Table 2.11 shows the average marginal tax rate under the current system, while the second, third and

Table 2.11 Pre-reform marginal tax rates by income range and the effect of benefit reform package on marginal tax rates

Income range (crowns per month)	Average rate	Reduced (%)	No change (%)	Increased (%)
Less than 3 000	36	24	20	56
3 000–3 999	37	71	3	26
4 000–4 999	37	80	3	18
5 000–5 999	34	37	11	52
6 000–6 999	35	44	45	11
7 000–7 999	37	42	34	24
8 000–8 999	41	57	21	22
9 000–9 999	42	59	14	27
10 000–10 999	42	59	22	19
11 000–11 999	53	70	21	9
12 000–14 999	42	57	37	6
More than 15 000	42	34	65	0.4
All	41	54	27	19

Source: Authors' tax benefit model, CZ

Table 2.12 Change in average marginal tax rates by income range

Income range (crowns per month)	All	Reduced	Increased
Less than 3 000	6.7	-0.6	12.2
3 000–3 999	2.6	-0.6	11.7
4 000–4 999	1.7	-0.6	12.5
5 000–5 999	5.5	-0.6	11.0
6 000–6 999	1.9	-0.6	20.2
7 000–7 999	4.6	-0.6	20.0
8 000–8 999	2.4	-4.6	22.2
9 000–9 999	5.7	-0.9	23.1
10 000–10 999	1.5	-4.9	23.7
11 000–11 999	-3.5	-8.1	24.0
12 000–14 999	-0.7	-3.8	24.6
More than 15 000	6.6	-0.6	1622.1
All	2.4	-2.8	20.3

Source: Authors' tax benefit model, CZ

fourth columns show the percentages with reduced marginal tax rates, no change, and with increased marginal tax rates respectively. The first column of Table 2.12 shows the average change in marginal tax rates for all households in the income range, while columns two and three show the average change for those with reduced and with increased marginal rates respectively.

Table 2.12 shows that the overall average marginal tax rate rises by 2.4 percentage points. However, we can also see from Table 2.11 that, for the majority (54%) of households, the marginal tax rate falls, while it only actually rises for 19% of households.

We can see from Table 2.12 that the explanation for this is that, among those households with reduced marginal rates, the fall is quite small (2.8% on average), while, among those households with rising marginal rates, the rise is large (20.3% on average). In some cases the rise in marginal tax rates can be very large indeed: one married couple in the top income range have an income just below the point where they would lose the child allowance, and so would face a marginal tax rate of 1600% for one additional hour of work. This explains the very large average marginal tax rate recorded for those households with increased marginal tax rates in the highest income range in Table 2.12.

Even apart from dramatic cases such as this, there are substantial numbers of households that face large increases in their marginal tax rates. This is particularly true for the lower income range, and it seems likely that many lower income households will face a substantial disincentive to increase their hours of work as a result.

As our earlier discussion indicated, the benefit reforms are highly progressive. It is a general consequence of any revenue neutral and progressive tax and benefit reform that marginal tax rates rise. The reason for this is that, if we give more generous benefits to the poor, these must then be taxed at a higher rate in order to maintain a fixed budget. The average rise in marginal tax rates that we observe, therefore, is entirely to be expected. The interesting feature in this case, though, is the fact that the increased marginal rates are heavily concentrated on particular groups, and may have a distinctly adverse effect on the incentive to work among these groups.

There are two reasons for these large increases in marginal tax rates. First, higher income households may be in the position where increasing hours of work will result in the loss of the child or parents' allowance. Second, lower income households that receive the social additional allowance or the housing contribution will be affected by the withdrawal of these means-tested benefits as hours of work are increased.

Finally, we consider the effectiveness of the reforms in reducing poverty. As we have for the first time benefits specifically targeted on families with lower incomes, we would expect the reforms to result in a reduction in poverty.

Tables 2.13 and 2.14 show the distribution of disposable income relative to the subsistence minimum for families with children and for all households, respectively. The definition of income used in the tables includes: all income from employment, self-employment and other non-state sources, plus all cash benefits, and net of income tax and employee's insurance and health fund contributions. The first column in each table shows the percentage of households with income in each range under the current system, while the second column shows the cumulative percentages. The same information for the new system is shown in the third and fourth columns.

We can see that, both for families with children and for all households, the reforms do appear to reduce substantially the numbers with very low incomes. The percentage of families with children with incomes below 1.25 times the subsistence minimum falls from 4.0 to 2.2%, while for all households it falls from 8.0 to 4.2%. These

Table 2.13 Incomes relative to subsistence minimum under current and new system for families with children

Multiple of subsistence minimum	Current system		New system	
	Percentage	Cumulative percentage	Percentage	Cumulative percentage
0.0 to 1.0	0.5	0.5	0.2	0 .2
1.0 to 1.25	3.5	4.0	2.0	2.2
1.25 to 1.5	17.2	21.2	20.3	22.5
1.5 to 1.75	21.8	43.0	22.0	44.5
1.75 to 2.0	18.2	61.2	17.7	62.2
2.0 to 2.25	13.2	74.4	11.4	73.6
2.25 to 2.5	7.8	82.2	8.0	81.6
2.5 to 2.75	5.7	87.9	6.1	87.7
2.75 to 3.0	3.9	91.8	4.0	91.7
More than 3.0	8.1	100[1]	8.2	100[1]

Source: Authors' tax benefit model, CZ.

[1]Do not sum to 100% due to rounding

Table 2.14 Incomes relative to subsistence minimum under current and new system for all households

Multiple of subsistence minimum	Current system		New system	
	Percentage	Cumulative percentage	Percentage	Cumulative percentage
0.0 to 1.0	1.1	1.1	0.3	0 .3
1.0 to 1.25	6.9	8.0	3.9	4.2
1.25 to 1.5	14.4	22.4	21.4	25.6
1.5 to 1.75	20.4	42.8	21.2	46.8
1.75 to 2.0	19.5	62.3	18.4	65.2
2.0 to 2.25	18.2	80.5	14.7	79.9
2.25 to 2.5	8.1	88.6	8.6	88.5
2.5 to 2.75	4.4	93.0	5.2	93.7
2.75 to 3.0	2.4	95.4	2.7	96.4
More than 3.0	4.5	100[1]	3.7	100[1]

Source: Authors' tax benefit model, CZ.

[1]Do not sum to 100% due to rounding

households, however, appear to be gaining largely at the expense of those slightly better off rather than those at the top of the income distribution, because the proportion with incomes below 1.5% of the subsistence minimum increases, from 21.2 to 22.5% for families with children, and from 22.4 to 25.6% for all households. We can also see from the tables that the proportion of households with very high incomes, above 2.5 times the subsistence minimum, appears to increase slightly.

Table 2.15 shows the points of the Lorenz curves for the current and the new systems. This shows the cumulative shares of total disposable income received by each decile of households. In this table income has been adjusted to take account of differences in household needs using the equivalence scales implicit

Table 2.15   Cumulative decile shares under the current and reformed systems

Decile	Current system	New system
Bottom	6.2	6.5
2nd	13.3	13.6
3rd	21.1	21.2
4th	29.4	29.4
5th	38.2	38.2
6th	47.8	47.7
7th	58.0	57.9
8th	69.4	69.3
9th	82.5	82.5
Top	100	100

Source: Authors' tax benefit model, CZ.

in the subsistence minimum. If it were the case that the cumulative decile shares were higher for all deciles under the new system (that is, the Lorenz curves did not intersect), we could say unambiguously that inequality had decreased. In fact the results confirm the impression that the reforms reduce poverty, but at the cost of greater inequality among households higher up the income distribution. The cumulative shares in total income are higher under the new system for all deciles below the 6th, but at this point the Lorenz curves cross, implying that the share of total income received by high income households increases.

2.6   Conclusions

In Czechoslovakia, as in most CEECs, tax reforms have sought to create tax systems similar to those in Western European market economies. The 1993 reform of the federal tax system in former Czechoslovakia, introduced in both the Czech and Slovak Republics as the country split, created a Western European type system of direct and indirect taxation.

The key priority in tax reform has been to make a transition from the arbitrary and negotiable tax structures characteristic of centrally planned economies to a more uniform and rule-based taxation system, as in the economies of Western Europe. The tax reforms successfully achieve this objective, in principle at least, although questions may remain about the application of the new rules in practice. We have suggested that a higher priority should have been given than would be normal in Western Europe to avoiding taxes which require administrative judgement and discretion, in order to ensure that a decisive break is made with past traditions of negotiation and bargaining over enterprise tax payments; the 'soft' budget constraint that results when tax payments can be negotiated to reflect *ex post* profitability or social and employment objectives would seriously undermine enterprise incentives for efficiency in a market economy.

A second priority, to which higher weight may appropriately be given than in Western Europe, is to design the system in such a way as to minimize the requirements for the limited administrative resources which are available. We believe that this could have been given greater consideration in the Czechoslovak reforms; greater use of administratively straightforward taxes, even rough-and-ready systems, might have been appropriate.

One case in point is the design of the VAT system, where the choice of a single rate would have reduced the administrative burden. Our analysis has shown that the adverse distributive consequences of such simplification can be eliminated by altering other taxes and benefits, but only at the cost of increasing the overall marginal tax rate.

Finally, we have looked at an issue that faces all the countries of Central and Eastern Europe, and also many established market economies: the targeting of social benefits. We have shown that the proposed reforms in the Czech Republic will both reduce poverty and slightly reduce government expenditure, but at the inevitable cost of increasing marginal tax rates.

Notes

1. For 1989, comparisons may be made on the basis of an exchange rate of 25 Czechoslovak crowns (Kcs) to the pound sterling; in 1993 the market exchange rate averaged some 45 Czech crowns (Kc) to the pound.
2. This was equivalent to about 4% of the average industrial wage, of some Kcs 3 400 per month.
3. As in other socialist countries, the convention with the turnover tax was to express the rate as a percentage of the tax-inclusive price rather than the tax exclusive price. Thus, a turnover tax rate of 20% (on the tax-inclusive price) corresponds to a tax rate of 25% on the basis usually employed in western Europe.
4. In May 1991, each of the turnover tax rates was reduced by 10%, to reflect the unanticipated buoyancy of public revenues; the rates thus became zero, 11, 20 and 29%.
5. As Hussain and Stern (1993) point out, the most unsatisfactory aspect of current Western European practice is in regard to property taxation. Hussain and Stern argue persuasively for introducing effective property taxes in transition economies, starting with a simple definition of the tax base, and increasing in sophistication as the property market develops. Governments should, they argue, retain some equity in housing, perhaps through significant capital gains taxes applied to property transactions, since the initial prices at which property is privatized are likely to understate severely long-term values. Property taxes were not part of the initial bundle of fiscal reforms enacted in Czechoslovakia in 1992, and it is still unclear whether Czech and Slovak legislation on the taxation of housing and other property will be able to improve on Western European practice.
6. Equivalent to some £453 at the current market exchange rate; the allowance is equivalent to about 30% of the current average industrial wage.
7. The threshold is equivalent to some £33 000 at the market exchange rate, similar to the UK VAT registration threshold of £36 600 at the start of 1993. Given the much lower wage and price levels in the Czech Republic, however, the VAT registration threshold in the Czech Republic represents a significantly larger business than the threshold in the United Kingdom.
8. It should be noted that the income ranges are for total household income rather than equivalized income, which adjusts for household composition. The impact of tax changes on different demographic groups is shown in the lower part of the table. We have found that this method of

presentation makes it easier to devise tax reforms with specific distributional goals.
9. It does not, however, include the employer's contributions to the social insurance funds. As these contributions are a constant proportion of wage income, their inclusion would simply raise the marginal tax rates without altering their pattern.
10. The material in this section is discussed more fully in Coulter *et al*. (1995).

References

Atkinson, A. B. and Stiglitz, J. E. (1976), 'The design of tax structure: direct versus indirect taxation', *Journal of Public Economics*, **6**, 55–75.

Coulter, F., Heady, C., Lawson, C. and Smith, S. (1992), 'The effects of raising child tax allowances on the incomes of households in Czechoslovakia and Slovakia', *Informator*, 1992(7), 89–105.

Coulter, F., Heady, C., Lawson, C. and Smith, S. (1993), 'Simplifying the Czechoslovak personal income tax', *Prague Economic Papers*, **II**, No. 2, 131–46.

Coulter, F., Heady, C., Lawson, C. and Smith, S. (1995), 'Social security reform in the Czech Republic', mimeo.

Coulter, F., Heady, C., Lawson, C., Smith, S. and Stark, G. (1994), 'Microsimulation modelling of personal taxation and social security benefits in the Czech Republic', OECD, forthcoming.

Deaton, A. and Stern, N. (1986), 'Optimally uniform commodity taxes, taste differences and lump-sum grants', *Economics Letters*, **20**, 263–6.

Dorsett, R. and Heady, C. (1991), 'The take-up of means-tested benefits by working families with children', *Fiscal Studies*, **12**, No. 4, 22–32.

Ebrahimi, A. and Heady, C. (1988), 'Tax design and household composition', *Economic Journal*, **98**, No. 390, 83–96.

Gray, C. W. (1990), 'Tax systems in the reforming socialist economies of Europe', The World Bank, Country Economics Department, Policy Research and External Affairs Working Papers, WPS 501.

Heady, C., Pearson, M., Rajah, N. and Smith, S. (1993), 'Czechoslovakia's taxes on goods and services', *International VAT Monitor*, Volume 3 1993, 9–13, The International Bureau of Fiscal Documentation, Amsterdam.

Hussain, A., and Stern, N. (1993), 'The role of the state, ownership and taxation in transitional economies', *Economics of Transition*, **1**, No. 1, 61–87.

Kamenickova, V. (1990), 'Tax system in Czechoslovakia', paper prepared for the first joint workshop on tax structure and public finance, Institute of Economics, Prague, 17 September.

Kopits, G. (1990), 'Fiscal reform in European economies in transition', paper presented at an OECD conference on 'The transition to a market economy in Central and Eastern Europe', 28–30 November.

Kornai, J. (1986), 'The soft budget constraint', *Kyklos*, **39**, 3–30.

Mervart, J. and Vavrejnova, M. (1992), 'Indirect taxes reform in the CSFR', *Prague Economic Papers*, **I**, No. 3, 221–240.

Vostatek, J. and Vaskova, D. (1990), 'Tax system and public finance transformation in the period of the transition to a market economy in Czechoslovakia', paper prepared for the first joint workshop on tax structure and public finance, Institute of Economics, Prague, 17 September.

3

Redistributive Policy in a Transition Economy: The Case of Hungary[*]

Sarah Jarvis and Stephen Pudney

3.1   Introduction

The process of economic transformation in the former socialist countries of
Eastern Europe has inevitably involved radical social, economic and institutional
change in the countries concerned. Market-oriented reforms including the
removal of state control of wage levels, extensive privatization and the
liberalization of prices coincided with the collapse of COMECON trading
arrangements, leading to a substantial drop in output accompanied by the
emergence of large-scale unemployment, inflation and a large fiscal deficit.
Inevitably there have been both gainers and losers from this process and, as
inequality has increased, the redesign of the tax–benefit system has become one
of the key issues facing policy-makers.

This chapter explores the scope for redistributive policy by pursuing two
lines of analysis. We examine the distributional properties of successive variants
of the progressive personal income tax (PIT) system that have been introduced
in Hungary since 1988, using simulations based on data from the 1991 Household
Budget Survey. Whilst the PIT is clearly progressive, the results suggest that
successive tax reforms have tended to reduce the redistributive impact of the
system. Given the relative ineffectiveness of the income tax system as an anti-
poverty device and the obvious political reluctance to use the tax system for
active redistribution, it is clear that it is the benefit system rather than the direct

[*] We are grateful to the Hungarian Central Statistical Office for access to official surveys and for
their helpful advice. Tamas Révész gave valuable research assistance. This work is supported
by the European Commission under the PHARE initiative and by the Economic and Social
Research Council (grant no R00023 3787).

tax system that has the most significant role to play. We then go on to paint a rather more impressionistic picture of the redistributive properties of various types of direct income transfer, using the technique of optimal targeting. The intention here is to give a rough indication of the relative potential for redistribution of transfer policies corresponding to industrial, regional and conventional social protection policies. Using poverty measures as the main criterion, we find that industrial and regional policy has relatively little potential for poverty alleviation compared to income transfers based on demographic characteristics. The results cast some doubt on Hungary's current emphasis on child benefits, and identify pensioners as the main group for concern.

3.2 Developments During Transition

3.2.1 Pre-1988 Trends in Inequality

The strictly regulated system of wage determination that existed under state socialism led to a pre-transition distribution of earnings in Hungary that was much less dispersed than in Western Europe. Atkinson and Micklewright (1992) compare the earnings distribution in a number of Eastern European countries with that of the United Kingdom in 1986/7. The decile ratio (i.e. the ratio of earnings at the top decile to those at the bottom decile) was equal to approximately 3.2 in the United Kingdom as compared to 2.6 in Hungary in 1986, and the Gini coefficient was 4.5 points higher in the United Kingdom than in Hungary at this time. The 1980s had seen a marked rise in earnings inequality in Hungary following a period in the 1970s in which the trend had been towards a more equal distribution.

This pattern is reflected in the changes in income inequality over the same period. According to data based on the quinquennial household income surveys, the trend in income inequality in the 1970s and 1980s in Hungary followed a U-shaped pattern (Atkinson and Micklewright, 1992; Szivos, 1993). During the period from 1972 to 1982 the distribution of per capita household income became somewhat less dispersed, but from 1982 to 1987 there was a notable increase in income inequality, reflected in a three and a half point increase in the Gini coefficient. As Atkinson and Micklewright suggest, this may have in part been due to the effect of various market-oriented reforms that were introduced during the 1980s, and in particular to the considerable growth in the second economy during this period.

3.2.2 Inequality since 1988

Given the removal of much of the control previously exercised by the state over wage levels, one would expect there to have been a significant increase in earnings inequality since 1988. Pudney (1994a) addresses this question using data from the 1989 and 1991 household budget surveys and the biennial earnings surveys. He finds statistically significant evidence of an increase in earnings inequality between 1988 and 1992 to a level comparable with the situation found in a market economy such as the United Kingdom. This increase, however, was not of the magnitude predicted by some observers and, more importantly, the data suggest that this had not (yet) had a considerable impact on consumption inequality. Szivos (1993) analyses the trend in income inequality over the same period, using data from a CSO microsimulation model based on the 1987 household income survey. In terms of the Gini coefficient, these data show an increase in inequality between 1987 and 1992 of approximately the same magnitude as that which occurred between 1982 and 1987. It is notable that the introduction of the personal income tax in 1988 (which was initially steeply progressive) led to only a temporary reduction in inequality.

3.2.3   Self-employment and Part-time Work since 1988

The period since 1988 has seen a significant growth in self-employment. At the end of 1989 the number of registered private entrepreneurs in Hungary was 320 000. By the end of 1992 this figure had virtually doubled, reaching almost 700 000 by the end of 1993. As Szivos (1993) notes, the distribution of this form of income is considerably more dispersed than earnings – in 1991 more than 47% of income from self-employment was found in the top income decile and only 1.5% in the bottom decile.

The nature of part-time work under state socialism differed from that commonly found in market economies. Jobs in the state sector were almost exclusively full time, and the low level of wages meant that few people could have afforded to work part time even if they had been given the choice. Part-time jobs were concentrated in the second economy and tended to be carried out in addition to full-time work in the state sector. One example of this was the 'work partnerships' formed by groups of workers within state enterprises. These were semi-autonomous units which produced goods or services after hours using factory equipment. Other forms of part-time work in the second economy included small-scale agricultural production, repair services and house building. According to Sik (1992) the effect of the transition process has been to transform this part-time second economy into a full-time informal economy. This is supported by rising unemployment which 'increases the number of those who are forced to make their living doing casual work that used to be their part-time auxiliary job. In other words, losing a full-time (formal) economy job leads to full-time involvement in the informal economy' (Sik, 1992). In 1990 only 6% of women were working part time, of whom approximately two-thirds were working pensioners. The number is reported to have decreased still further since then

(Frey, 1994). This can be compared with rates of around 40% of working women in part-time jobs in the United Kingdom and Sweden, and 25% in the United States in 1990 (OECD, 1991).

3.2.4   Female Labour Force Participation

The high labour force participation rate of women was a distinctive feature of state socialist economies. Women were encouraged to join the labour market by the widespread availability of heavily subsidised child care and the scheme which enabled those who wished to leave their jobs temporarily in order to have children to take paid child-care leave (for a maximum of three years). The participation rate[1] of women in Hungary steadily increased throughout the 1980s, rising from 82% in 1980 to 85.7% in 1990. Since 1990 the rate has begun to fall and by 1993 the percentage of women participating in the labour market had dropped to 79.7%. This pattern differs considerably from that of males over the same period. The male labour force participation rate decreased throughout the 1970s and 1980s, a process that has continued into the 1990s. In 1993 the female participation rate fell below that of males for the first time.

3.2.5   Labour Force Participation of the Young and Old

The period since 1988 has seen a substantial decrease in the labour force participation rate in the upper and lower parts of the age distribution. In the case of young people this is partly explained by the increase in the size of the student population. The number of full-time students as a percentage of the population of the relevant age (as defined by the CSO) rose from 10.4% in 1990 to 12.5% in 1992.

The pattern of labour force participation has also changed for the older section of the population. Particularly notable has been the fall in the number of working pensioners (from 473 200 in 1988 to 223 000 in 1993). This has been accompanied by an increase in the proportion of those retiring from employment before reaching the official retirement age of 55 for women and 60 for men. In 1989 5% of the working age population had retired, a figure which had increased to 6.5% by 1992 (ILO, 1994). The introduction of an 'early pension' scheme which entitles the unemployed who are within three years of retirement to retire early has provided an added incentive for older people to withdraw from the labour market. These changes have implications for the dependency ratio and if the trend continues will lead to a greater burden on an increasingly smaller section of the working population.

3.2.6   Unemployment

The appearance of large-scale unemployment is one of the most significant changes that has occurred in Hungary during the transition period. Registered unemployment rose from less than 1% of the labour force at the beginning of 1990 to approximately 14% in the first quarter of 1993. The phenomenon of long-term unemployment has been cited as a major contributor to the rapid rise in the unemployment rate as the increase seems to have been driven by a very small outflow from unemployment rather than a rise in the inflow rate (see Micklewright and Nagy, 1992 chapter 6). The highest rate of unemployment is found among young people. In the first quarter of 1993 the unemployment rate of young people between the ages of 15 and 24 was 18.9%, more than twice that of the adult population. There has also been a clear regional pattern to unemployment. The rate of unemployment in the north eastern counties (where there was a high concentration of heavy industry) in December 1993 was three times as high as that in Budapest. The capital had the lowest regional rate of unemployment in the country. It is notable that women in Hungary have been less seriously affected by unemployment than men. In the last quarter of 1993 the rate among women was 8.9%, compared to 12.6% among men. The main reason for this unusual situation lies in the fact that women are under-represented in the sectors which have suffered most during the transition (e.g. heavy industry and manufacturing), tending to be concentrated in the service sector, which has performed relatively well. Women also form the large majority of workers who take up child-care leave, which (at least in some cases) provides protection against unemployment.

Since February 1993 the number of unemployed has slowly been decreasing. A number of reasons have been put forward for this reversal of the previous trend. One is that an increasing number of benefit recipients are exhausting their period of entitlement, which has been halved from two years to one since the introduction of the scheme. Those who lose entitlement to benefit and are not entitled to means-tested unemployment assistance (this applied to half of those losing eligibility at the end of 1993) have no reason to remain on the unemployment register. There has also been a slowdown in the flow of people into unemployment and an increase in the number of unemployed who are taking part in active labour market programmes which remove them from the register. While the rate of unemployment is falling the problem clearly remains, and the increasingly large number of unemployed people no longer eligible for benefit is beginning to place significant pressure on resources for social assistance provided by local governments (see section 3.3.6 below).

3.2.7   Urban and Rural Incomes

The relationship between rural and urban incomes has been heavily affected by net changes in employment. Agriculture suffered a 41.2% drop in the number of jobs between January 1990 and January 1993 (ILO, 1994) whereas the respective figure for industry was 23.6%. According to Szivos (1993) the income level in Budapest and other towns tends to be substantially higher than in the villages. This observation is supported by data from the 1990 income tax returns which showed that in Budapest average incomes were 37% higher than the average in rural areas (Ministry of Finance, 1992).

3.3   Changes in the Tax–Benefit System since 1988

The process of market-oriented tax reform in Hungary began in the late 1980s under the so-called 'reform Communist' government. The personal income tax (PIT) and value added tax (VAT) were introduced in 1988, followed by the corporate income tax and enterprise profit tax in 1989. Since its introduction a number of changes have been made to the structure of the PIT. Table 3.1 gives the schedules of tax rates for 1988–94. Employees are required to pay 10% of gross earnings in the form of a social insurance contribution. Tax is assessed on the basis of gross income.[2] As of 1991, employees also had to contribute to the Solidarity Fund which was set up to finance unemployment compensation. In 1991 this contribution was set at 0.5% of gross earnings. It was raised to 2% in 1992 and subsequently reduced to 1.5% in 1994.

The main changes to the benefit system since 1988 have included the introduction of unemployment compensation and more recently the reform of the local government social assistance scheme. In terms of existing benefits, such as those awarded to families with children, the government has avoided politically unpopular benefit cuts but has nevertheless allowed the real value of such benefits to be eroded by inflation. The debate concerning the future of the benefit system continues to be dominated by the need to reduce social expenditures whilst ensuring that those in most need continue to receive state support. Improving the targeting of benefits has become a key issue, but by 1994 had not been translated into concrete policy proposals for benefit reform.

3.3.1   Direct Taxation

Hungary was one of the first of the former socialist countries to tax individual incomes directly. The personal income tax (PIT) is an individual-based tax such that the income of each member of the household is taxed independently. When introduced in January 1988 the PIT had a steeply progressive structure (at least

Table 3.1 Rates of PIT 1988–94

Taxable income (Ft/year 000s)	1988	1989	1990	1991	1992	1993	1994
0–48	0	0	0	0	0	0	0
48–55	20						
55–70		17	15	12			
70–90	25	23					
90–100	35	29	30	18			
100–110					25	25	
110–120							20
120–150	39			30			
150–180	44	35		32			25
180–200							
200–220					35	35	
220-240							35
240–300	48	42					
300–360			40	40			
360–380	52	49					
380–500							40
500–550			50	50	40	40	
550–600							44
600–800	56	56					
800+	60						
Price level (1988=100)	100	115.5	135.1	174.1	235.3	289.4	354.5

by Western European standards), with ten positive marginal rates ranging from 20% to a top rate of 60%. The tax threshold was set at approximately 45% of average earnings. Incomes from state sector jobs were grossed up so as to leave net incomes from this source unchanged when the tax was introduced. As no adjustment was made to secondary incomes and overtime earnings the net income of those with additional earnings outside of their main job was reduced. However, the overall impact of the tax on household incomes was lessened by the large number of exemptions (such as fringe benefits and virtually all social incomes) and favourable treatment received by those with incomes from small-scale agriculture or so-called 'intellectual activities'. Semjen (1993) reports that in 1988 the PIT was levied on only 40% of total household incomes.

The PIT has been modified considerably since its introduction. It was claimed that the steeply progressive structure of marginal rates 'undermined tax compliance from the very beginning and did not serve the interests of the emerging market economy' (Semjen, 1993). In 1989 the number of tax brackets was reduced to eight and the top and bottom rates decreased to 56 and 17%, respectively. A further reduction in the top rate was made in 1990 (to 50%), and the number of brackets was reduced to just five. The newly elected democratic government decided to increase the number of tax brackets to seven and lower the bottom rate of tax to 12% in 1991, but this step was quickly reversed in 1992 when a system of just four tax brackets (0, 25, 30 and 40%) was introduced. This system survived until the end of 1993, but in 1994 the top rate was raised to 44% and an additional lower rate of 20% was introduced. Given that these numerous changes were not accompanied by a full adjustment of the tax brackets for the effects of inflation it is not clear what the impact has been in terms of changes in effective tax rates. This issue is investigated in section 3.4.

In addition to changes to the structure of marginal rates, the government has also tightened the tax regulations in an attempt to capture sources of 'invisible income', and has reduced the number of tax exemptions so as to increase the size of the tax base. In 1992 the range of tax-free allowances was narrowed, and this was followed in 1993 by a move which made one-third of the estimated fringe benefits taxable and increased the tax liability of agricultural producers and 'intellectuals'.

The PIT as introduced in 1988 was heavily criticized for being 'punitive to individuals with families and children' (Hethy, 1991), on the basis that there were no allowances for married or cohabiting couples and the only concession for children was a child tax allowance restricted to families with at least three children. The government succumbed to pressure to extend the child tax allowance, and in January 1992 it was extended to cover all children (irrespective of family size) and increased from 1 000 to 1 300 Forints (£10) per month per child. This move was aimed to 'ensure that the incomes required to ensure the conditions of existence will not be taxed' (Ministry of Finance, 1992). Since, however, the tax allowance was deducted from the section of income on which the highest marginal rate of tax was paid it was worth progressively more as income increased. In 1993 child tax allowances were replaced by a more progressive system of tax credits under which all tax-paying households with children receive the same deduction from tax paid, rather than taxable income. This is effectively a system of tax allowances with a single rate. Since, however, non-tax-paying households are still not covered by this form of support the redistributive impact of this policy is confined to those with incomes high enough to be liable for income tax.

3.3.2   Indirect Taxation

Value added tax was introduced in Hungary in 1988. Initially there were three VAT rates: 15%, 25% and a zero rate. The zero rate was applied to basic foods, household fuel, sewage and water, public transport, books, newspapers and pharmaceutical products. All other industrial products including alcohol, tobacco and clothes (including children's clothes) were taxed at the highest rate of 25%. The 15% rate was applied only to certain services such as hotels, hairdressing and repair services. The introduction of VAT was accompanied by an adjustment of prices so as not to lead to an overly large increase in the price level. Nevertheless, the size of the difference between the two main rates tended to exacerbate the already existing differential between agricultural and industrial products, with the former being undervalued and the latter overvalued.

In 1992 the government proposed a radical reform of the VAT system in which the zero rate would have been replaced by an 8% rate. This was strongly opposed by trades unions, the public and political parties (even within the coalition). A compromise was reached such that on 1 January 1993 VAT on all previously zero-rated goods and services (excluding medicines and household electricity) was increased to 6%. The 15% rate was abolished and VAT on hotel services was reduced to 6%. VAT on all other services previously taxed at the 15% rate was increased to 25%. Due to budgetary pressures the government found it necessary to raise VAT again just eight months later. In August 1993 the 6% rate was increased to 10%, and the rate of VAT on domestic electricity rose from zero to 10%. Only medicines remained zero rated. As a result, the Hungarian population faces VAT rates that are notably high by international standards, and cover virtually all of purchased consumption.

3.3.3   Subsidy Reduction

In 1988 production and consumption subsidies (including housing subsidies) accounted for approximately 15% of GDP in Hungary (Abel, 1990). The most important consumer subsidies in 1989 (as a percentage of the total) were housing investment (46.7%), heating (14.9%), medicine (11.0%) and public transport (10.2%) (Kupa and Fajth, 1990). Some reductions had been made during the early 1980s, but it is the period since 1988 that has seen the most dramatic subsidy cuts. An important 1991 budget measure gave holders of pre-1989 housing loans the choice between paying back the loan in instalments (higher but still subsidized (15%) fixed interest payments) or having half of the outstanding debt 'written off' and paying market interest rates on the remainder. Semjen (1993) reports that a majority opted for the second option and paid the remaining debt back immediately. By 1991 the share of total subsidies in GDP had fallen to just less than 7% and in 1993 was estimated to have reached just 4.6% (Semjen, 1993).

In their analysis of the impact of the subsidies in place in 1989 Atkinson and Micklewright (1992) note that, while contributing to an overall reduction in inequality, in the case of housing subsidies the value of the subsidy tended to rise with income. The importance of consumer subsidies varied considerably across household types, largely reflecting life-cycle differences in consumption patterns. Szivos (1993) notes that the ratio of total subsidies to income was 20.1% for households with three or more children, 13.9% for all active households and 17.7% for inactive households. The net effect of VAT changes and subsidy reductions superimposed on underlying price changes has proved to be surprisingly neutral in terms of its distributional impact, as Newbery's (1995) analysis shows.

3.3.4   Unemployment Compensation

Unemployment benefit was introduced in Hungary in January 1989. Whereas under state socialism the government had guaranteed employment for all citizens of working age, in a market economy this guarantee could no longer hold and a system of income support for the unemployed was required. The scheme is employment and earnings related, and as of 1991 (when the rate of unemployment began to rise considerably) has been financed on a contributory basis. Major changes were made to this system in 1991, 1992 and 1993 and are described in Nagy and Micklewright (1994) and Chapter 6 below. The overall direction of change has been towards a less generous system of unemployment benefit and in March 1992 two-thirds of claimants received benefits not exceeding the minimum level. Furthermore, of those receiving unemployment benefit in March 1992, an estimated 82% were receiving an amount below the per capita subsistence minima for a household of two active adults (Nagy and Micklewright, 1994). While in terms of the replacement ratio and length of entitlement the Hungarian system might appear to be relatively generous, in practice the majority of recipients receive payments that do not cover subsistence expenses.

In addition to changes to the original unemployment benefit, a number of other types of unemployment assistance have been introduced. In 1991 a flat-rate 'career beginners' benefit was introduced, which was aimed at young people joining the labour market who failed to qualify for unemployment benefit because of their lack of an employment record. As of 1992 those exhausting entitlement to unemployment benefit can apply to their local council for means-tested assistance. The level of the benefit is set at the rate of the lowest old age pension. This scheme is administered by the local governments who are also expected to provide 50% of the funding for the scheme. Given the rapidly increasing numbers of long-term unemployed who are no longer entitled to the insurance-based unemployment benefit the demand for this form of assistance can be expected to increase in the near future.

3.3.5 Family Benefits

Family benefits have traditionally formed a very important part of social policy in Hungary, both in terms of the share of government expenditure that they represent and their contribution to the incomes of families with children. Under state socialism the government provided a comprehensive set of employment-related benefits including generous family allowances, maternity benefits and paid child-care leave. Government spending on family and maternity allowances accounted for 4% of GDP in 1989.

The system of child-care and maternity allowances enabled women to receive maternity pay for a period of up to 24 weeks during confinement at a rate of 100% of previous earnings, followed by two years of child-care pay at a rate of 75% of previous earnings and a further year of child-care aid paid at a fixed rate. Mothers who were ineligible for child-care pay were able to claim the fixed-rate child-care aid for up to three years. In addition, family allowance was paid in respect of all dependent children. This benefit had come to play an increasingly important role in the late 1980s – between 1987 and 1989 payments were increased substantially in a move which was designed to compensate families with children for the effects of the introduction of the PIT and in particular for cuts in price subsidies to children's commodities. In effect part of the in kind benefit previously given in the form of subsidies was converted into a cash transfer. In 1989 the family allowance payment for families with two parents and two children was equal to approximately 40% of average earnings.

During the transition the government has continued to pursue a pro-natalist family policy and relatively few changes have been made to the system of benefits in place in 1988, despite pressure for cuts in social spending. One important change was introduced by one of the last Acts passed by the outgoing Communist government in April 1990. This replaced the existing employment-related family allowance with a universal family allowance awarded to all children as an individual right. Eligibility for family allowance was further extended by the change to the Abortion Act in 1993, which gave women the right to receive family allowance from their fourth month of pregnancy. This replaced the maternity grant which was previously payable as a lump sum at birth. The financing of the new programme was taken over by the state budget (previously it had been a part of social insurance). The future of the allowance has been the subject of much debate, but despite widespread calls for means testing and/or taxation of the allowance it has so far survived intact. However, failure to index fully the benefit to inflation since 1990 has led to a fall in its real value. There is some evidence to suggest that in spite of the existence of this relatively generous system of family benefits children were over-represented amongst the poor in pre-transition Hungary, particularly those living in urban areas. Szalai (1989) reports that in 1987 the risk of being in poverty was 28% for urban children, compared to a rate of 15% in the population as a whole. This kind of conclusion may be very sensitive to the particular choice of poverty line or method of equivalizing family income. Furthermore, it remains an open question whether child benefits are the most cost-effective way of reducing poverty. We return to this in section 3.5.

3.3.6   Social Assistance

In pre-transition Hungary social assistance was limited to a system of means-tested benefits awarded entirely at the discretion of local councils. The two main problems with this scheme were that (i) there was no legal entitlement to social assistance and (ii) the local councils had extremely limited funds which could be used for this purpose. The World Bank (1992) reports that in 1990 most councils had exhausted their funds earmarked for social assistance by the end of August. This partly reflected the increase in demand for social assistance as a result of the growing number of individuals in need of state support. The government has only recently introduced a new Social law which outlines the criteria which should be used by local governments in allocating social assistance funds. The range of benefits includes unemployment assistance for those who have exhausted their entitlement to unemployment benefit, a child-raising benefit[3] and a form of housing benefit. It is not yet possible to gauge exactly how well this new system is working in practice, but unofficial reports from the Ministry of Finance suggest that the problem of inadequate funding (particularly in those areas facing very high unemployment) has so far hampered the efforts of local councils to implement the law fully so as to award benefits according to the recommended criteria.

3.4   The Personal Income Tax (PIT) 1988–94

The section looks in greater detail at the Hungarian PIT since 1988, concentrating mainly on the redistributional character of the different versions of the tax system that were in place during this period. The frequent changes made to the structure of tax brackets during a period of high inflation make it difficult to assess the impact of tax reform in terms of the change in the progressivity of the system without using household level data. In the absence of a time series of survey data covering the whole period (the most recent Household Budget Survey (HBS) data available is from 1991) some form of simulation is required. The approach adopted here is to simulate the effect of other years' PIT systems on the 1991 distribution of earnings, using micro-data from the 1991 HBS. Thus the gross earnings distribution is held constant and the effect of alternative tax systems is then analysed. We focus only on the direct impact of reform, without attempting to incorporate any behavioural responses. As Pudney (1991) stresses, the nature of the transition process is such that it is unlikely that any stable behavioural relationships could be identified.

3.4.1   Data: The 1991 HBS

The Hungarian Central Statistical Office (CSO) conducts a household budget survey (HBS) every two years. A detailed description of the survey design and methodology is given in Pudney (1991). Two aspects of the survey data are particularly relevant to the use of these data for tax modelling. First, as is the case in all surveys which rely on voluntary participation, the pattern of response is not uniform. Non-response is relatively low when compared to Western surveys (see Atkinson and Micklewright, 1992) but the CSO notes that high income and elderly households have low response rates. This means that the survey population will inevitably fail to represent fully the tax-paying population, and in particular will under-represent higher rate taxpayers. The CSO have a policy of replacing non-respondents with households from the same geographical area with broadly similar characteristics and are therefore able to achieve the target sample size of approximately 12 000 households. However, this substitution policy does not solve the problem of differential response since the substitute households will also fail to represent the population of uncooperative households.

Second, although the data provide detailed information concerning expenditures, incomes, which are taxed in different ways under the rules of the PIT, are not always separately identified in the survey. For example, the PIT gives special tax treatment to incomes from 'intellectual activities', but it is not possible to identify these incomes in the survey. Another problem arises with the treatment of income from small-scale agriculture, which for tax purposes is shared between household members participating in the farm, but in the data is recorded only as a household total. This makes it difficult to carry out a full-scale tax simulation using recorded gross income as a base and applying the PIT rules, as the calculation of tax allowances requires more detailed information on income sources. It is largely for this reason that in this simulation we use taxable income rather than gross income as a base for simulating the impact of alternative tax systems. Taxable income in 1991 can be calculated from the reported total amount of tax paid by each individual during the survey year. This variable is obtained from data collected in the second wave of interviewing which takes place at the end of the year. The use of year end data for this purpose (as opposed to data collected in the first wave which involves a two-month period of diary keeping) has the advantage of producing data which cover the whole of the tax year.

The analysis is conducted using the full sample of 11 813 households from the HBS. Tax-payers are defined here as all earners who reported any form of labour income, including those on paid child-care leave and paid sick leave

62   *S Jarvis and S Pudney*

Table 3.2   A comparison of the 1991 HBS with Ministry of Finance tax records

Tax bracket (Ft/year)	Marginal tax rate (%)	Percentage of taxpayers each bracket	
		Ministry of Finance	HBS 1991
0–55 000	0	7.5	9.8
55 001–90 000	12	10.7	14.2
90 001–120 000	18	29.0	13.6
120 001–150 000	30		14.1
150 001–300 000	32	36.1	36.4
300 001–500 000	40	11.9	9.3
500 001+	50	4.8	2.6
Total		100.0	100.0
Sum of tax paid (million Ft)		156 200	123 000
Total number of tax payers		3 978 052	3 934 833

Sources: 1991 HBS micro-data.
Unpublished data provided by the Ministry of Finance .

Notes: HBS data are re-weighted to correct for non-uniform sampling design.
In 1991 £1 = 132 Forints (yearly average).

(both of which are subject to income tax). Pensioners are only included if they reported earnings in addition to their pension. Table 3.2 compares the pattern of tax payments recorded in the 1991 HBS with the Ministry of Finance (MoF) tax records. When the survey is weighted to give population totals, the number of tax-payers in the HBS sample is almost identical in size to the total number of employees reported by the MoF. However, the survey fails to capture approximately 20% of the total PIT paid. This shortfall may be partly accounted for by under-reporting, but it also reflects the tendency of those with very high incomes to be under-represented in the survey sample as a whole due to a relatively high rate of non-response (see Révész, 1994). This is illustrated by the difference between the distributions of marginal tax rates in the survey and MoF data also given in Table 3.2. Whilst the MoF records 18.2% of tax-payers in the lower two tax brackets, 24% of the survey sample fall into this category. Conversely, at the upper end of the distribution only 11.9% of earners in the survey are recorded as paying a marginal rate of more than 40% whereas according to the MoF these rates applied to approximately 16% of taxpayers.

3.4.2   Simulating Alternative Tax Systems

The analysis focuses on the impact of changes in the structure of marginal tax rates. For the purposes of this analysis the only changes to the system of tax

Table 3.3   Employee and child tax allowances and credits 1988–94

Year	Child tax allowance (per child/per month)	Child tax credit (per child/ per month)	Employee tax allowance (per month)	Employee tax credit (per month)
1988	1 000 Ft (where 3+ children)	-	1 000 Ft	-
1989	as 1988	-	1 000 Ft	-
1990	as 1988	-	1 000 Ft	-
1991	as 1988	-	-	250 Ft
1992	1 300 Ft (extended to cover all children)	-	-	-
1993	-	300 Ft (1–2 children) 400 Ft (3+ children)	-	200 Ft
1994	-	400 Ft (1–2 children) 600 Ft (3+ children)	-	-

allowances and credits included in the simulation are those awarded to all employees and to households with children. The major changes to this system of tax allowances and credits are given in Table 3.3.

Tax allowances are worth more in absolute terms to higher rate tax-payers since they are set against the tax-payers' highest marginal rate. Under a tax credit system all earners receive the same deduction from tax paid. The replacement of the employees' tax allowance with a tax credit in 1991 and switch to child tax credits in 1992 was therefore a move towards a more progressive tax system. Table 3.1 summarizes the changes in the tax schedule between 1988 and 1994, along with the rate of inflation in each year. As was described in section 3.2 above, the system has been gradually simplified, with a reduction in the number of tax brackets. This has been accompanied by a fall in the top rate of tax and numerous changes to the structure of the lower tax rates. The level of earnings at which earners begin to pay a positive rate of tax (i.e. the top of the zero-rate bracket) has also been adjusted, but not in every year, and, more importantly, by considerably less than the rate of inflation. Whereas the price level in 1991 had increased by 74% with respect to 1988 the top of the zero-rate tax bracket had risen by less than 7% over the same period. The effects of inflation and the change in the level of the tax brackets becomes far more difficult to separate at positive rates of tax, especially since none of the marginal tax rates are common to all seven years of the PIT. A far clearer picture of the impact of the various changes to the PIT can be gained by simulating these changes in tax at the household level.

In order to simulate the impact of alternative versions of the PIT we adjust the tax brackets in Table 3.1 by the relevant change in the price level for each year so as to produce a series of tax schedules expressed in 1991 prices. These schedules are then applied to the 1991 distribution of taxable incomes and the tax paid by each individual under the alternative tax regimes is then calculated. Using these simulation results we measure the distributional impact of the alternative versions of the PIT in a number of ways.

3.4.3   Results

First we consider the distribution of total tax paid. Table 3.4 gives the estimated share of the total PIT paid by each quintile of the distribution of household equivalized expenditure for the seven alternative tax systems. The OECD equivalence scale is used throughout. The table clearly illustrates the progressive nature of the PIT. Taking 1991 as an example and comparing the two extremes of the distribution, the bottom quintile of households contain 11.6% of all earners and accounts for 2.3% of the total amount of PIT paid whereas the top quintile contains 28.2% of earners and accounts for 58.1% of the total. In terms of the change in the distribution of total tax paid as the tax system is changed the general picture is of an increase in the share of the total tax burden borne by the lower half of the income distribution relative to the upper part of the distribution. The only exception to this pattern occurs in 1991, when there is a slight shift in the opposite direction. This may reflect the switch from employee tax allowances to a more progressive system of tax credits (see Table 3.3). Particularly notable

Table 3.4   The distribution of PIT paid by quintiles of equivalized household expenditure: a comparison of alternative versions of the PIT 1988–94

Quintile (% of earners)	Simulated distribution of total PIT paid under alternative tax regimes						
	1988	1989	1990	1991	1992	1993	1994
1 (11.6)	1.8	1.8	2.4	2.3	2.7	2.7	2.8
2 (15.8)	5.2	5.3	6.3	6.1	6.7	6.7	6.8
3 (20.0)	10.3	10.4	11.5	11.2	12.0	12.1	12.2
4 (24.4)	21.7	21.7	22.6	22.3	22.8	22.9	22.9
5 (28.2)	61.0	60.8	57.2	58.1	55.8	55.7	55.3
Total (100)	100.0	100.0	100.0	100.0	100.0	100.0	100.0
Total tax Ft millions 1991 prices	93 200	94 500	108 000	113 000	127 000	135 000	153 000

Source: 1991 HBS micro-data.

Note: The calculations are based on the distribution of equivalized total household expenditure using the OECD equivalence scale. The figures in brackets in column 1 give the percentage of the total number of earners found in each quintile of households.

is the change in the share of total tax paid by households in the top quintile as the tax system is altered. If the 1988 version is applied this decile accounts for 61% of total tax paid, while under the 1993 and 1994 systems this figure falls to approximately 55%. This change is mirrored by an increase in the percentage of total tax paid by the bottom quintile from 1.8% under the 1988 PIT to 2.8% in 1994. Households in the second and third quintile also bear a greater part of the tax burden under the later PIT structures.

The steady increase in the sum of total tax paid shows the increase in the size of the overall tax burden implied by the successive versions of the tax system. Thus the total tax burden is seen to rise at the same time as the relative size of the tax burden of the lower quintiles increases. The impact of this at the household level can be investigated further by looking at the simulated average tax payments per household in each quintile of the distribution of expenditure.

Table 3.5(a) compares the average amount of total tax paid per household across the whole range of tax regimes. In Table 3.5(b) the amounts are expressed relative to the tax paid in 1991 and finally table in 3.5(c) the payments are given relative to the average tax payment in the top quintile.

These tables illustrate how the impact of imposing alternative systems of marginal tax rates differs across the distribution of expenditure. The average amount of tax paid increases for all quintiles moving across the table from left to right. Table 3.5(b) shows how this difference in the amount of tax paid is proportionately greater for those in the lower quintiles as compared to the upper quintiles. Whereas the 1994 tax system implies an average payment more than two and a half times higher than the 1988 system for households in the bottom quintile, the average payment of households in the top quintile is just less than 50% higher.

Table 3.5(c) further illustrates the difference in progressivity of the alternative tax systems by expressing the amount of tax paid in each of the lower four quintiles as a percentage of that paid in the upper quintile. Overall the results suggest that the successive reforms to the tax system have reduced its progressivity – whereas under the 1988 system the average amount of tax paid per household in the second quintile is estimated to have been 14% of that paid in the top quintile, under the 1994 system the equivalent estimate is 19.8%. Particularly notable is the marked difference between the relative amounts of tax paid under the 1989 and 1990 systems. The 1990 system appears to reduce the gap between the top and bottom quintiles (in terms of tax paid) considerably and, with the exception of 1991, successive reforms narrow the gap still further.

We have attempted to show using a simple simulation model how the redistributive character of the PIT has been changed by the frequent reforms of the tax schedule since its introduction in 1988. The aim has not been to simulate how each tax system performed in the year in question, but to try to compare the systems by examining the different impact of each one on a fixed earnings distribution. The results suggest that the changes made to the PIT have tended

Table 3.5   Simulated amounts of tax paid by quintile of the equivalized distribution of expenditure: a comparison of alternative versions of the PIT 1988–94

(a)   Tax paid in Forints

Quintile of household equivalized expenditure	Simulated average annual amount of tax (Fts) paid per household (1991 distribution of taxable earnings)						
	1988	1989	1990	1991	1992	1993	1994
1	1 795	1 884	2 794	2 826	3 710	3 970	4 688
2	8 301	8 754	11 612	11 773	14 535	15 492	17 858
3	15 096	15 425	19 533	20 055	23 904	25 678	29 274
4	27 015	27 403	32 481	33 735	38 533	41 352	46 720
5	59 182	59 733	64 188	68 682	75 340	78 412	87 892

(b)   1988 tax paid = 100

Quintile of household equivalized expenditure	Simulated average annual amount of tax paid per household (1991 distribution of taxable earnings, 1988 tax paid = 100)						
	1988	1989	1990	1991	1992	1993	1994
1	100.0	105.0	155.7	157.4	206.7	221.2	261.2
2	100.0	103.3	139.9	141.8	175.1	186.6	215.1
3	100.0	102.2	129.4	132.8	158.3	170.1	193.9
4	100.0	101.4	120.2	124.9	142.6	153.1	172.9
5	100.0	100.9	108.5	116.6	124.3	132.5	148.5

(c)   Tax paid by top quintile = 100

Quintile of household equivalized expenditure	Simulated average annual amount of tax paid per household (tax paid by to quintile = 100)						
	1988	1989	1990	1991	1992	1993	1994
1	3.0	3.2	4.4	4.1	5.0	5.1	5.3
2	14.0	14.4	18.1	17.1	19.8	19.8	19.8
3	25.5	25.8	30.4	29.2	32.5	32.7	33.3
4	45.6	45.9	50.6	49.1	52.4	52.7	53.2
5	100.0	100.0	100.0	100.0	100.0	100.0	100.0

Source: 1991 HBS micro-data.

to reduce its progressivity and shift the overall burden of taxation towards those at the lower end of the distribution of expenditure (which has been used to proxy welfare). If it is the case that the redistributive power of the tax system has been weakened by these reforms (which have tended to be driven by a concern to improve incentives) then the redistributive role of the benefit system becomes relatively more important.

3.5   An Exploration of Directions for Reform

The CEECs have seen an avalanche of economic reform in the last five years. The Hungarian legislation summarized in section 3.3 above is typical of the sort of measures that have had a direct bearing on family incomes in these countries. It is hard to escape the feeling that this programme of change has been undertaken without a clear strategy, and particularly without a foundation of research to establish that the areas chosen for policy reform are indeed the areas that really matter in terms of the ultimate objective. In this section we illustrate the way this type of research can be done, adopting as an objective the reduction of poverty. Without attempting to address the fine details of policy design, we seek to identify the broad directions in which policy reform might usefully proceed.

3.5.1   The Use of Optimal Targeting Algorithms

The device we use to achieve this is an optimal targeting algorithm, similar to those proposed by Kanbur (1987) and Ravallion and Chao (1989). (See also van de Walle *et al.* (1993) for an application to 1987/89 Hungarian data.) As developed by these authors, optimal targeting requires us to:

* define a formal quantitative measure of poverty;
* divide the population up into a set of non-overlapping sub-groups;
* find the level of transfer payment to all the families within each group which will reduce to a minimum the measured level of poverty subject to some government budget constraint.

These algorithms have been proposed as serious techniques for policy design. However, they have several shortcomings when used in this way:

* the system of non-means-tested transfers determined by the algorithm has few similarities to the systems of government transfer payments found in practice, and are unlikely to be politically feasible;
* the population groups used to underpin the optimal transfer system are usually not exogenous (at least in the long run), so there is a possibility of the optimum being disrupted by second-round behavioural responses;
* the system of transfers is usually modelled with an assumption of perfect take-up, which in practice may not be feasible.

Most previous implementations of the optimal targeting idea have also suffered from some more technical drawbacks:

* existing targeting algorithms are based on the implicit assumption that full population information is available; in practice, survey samples must be used, and the results are therefore subject to sampling error; no standard error formulae have previously been derived for the estimated optimal transfers;

- a detailed decomposition of the population (for example location x household structure x age group) leads to a very large number of population subgroups, with correspondingly small numbers of observations in the cells of an analogous breakdown of the survey sample to be used for the targeting calculations; detailed results may therefore be very imprecise.

These drawbacks may be serious, but they do not completely destroy the usefulness of the optimal targeting idea. We can re-interpret the targeting algorithm as an approach analogous to the decomposition of poverty measures, where the object is to estimate the proportions of poverty originating within and between population subgroups. Instead, the targeting algorithm characterises the incidence of poverty in terms of the income transfers[4] between groups that would be necessary to reduce total poverty to a minimum, subject to restrictions on the scale and form of the income transfers. When seen in this light, optimal targeting is a way of understanding the nature of poverty in the population (and thus identifying fruitful avenues for policy reform), rather than a means of designing a policy that could be immediately implemented in practice. Under this interpretation, the neglect of second-round behavioural responses is no more important for the analysis than implicitly it is for the use of conventional poverty decompositions as a guide to policy.

The technical drawbacks related to sampling variability can be addressed in two ways. In Pudney (1994b) we have proposed a change in the form of the hypothetical transfer system to one which involves a sum of a series of benefits each related to some observable characteristic, rather than a system involving a separate lump sum transfer to each of a series of distinct population subgroups. By using additive non-mutually-exclusive transfers rather than mutually-exclusive group-specific transfers, we can overcome the problem of small sample sizes in individual cells. Although it appears not to have been done before, there is no difficulty in deriving approximate standard errors for the calculated optimal transfers, and these can be used to give an idea of the degree of statistical reliability of the results. See Pudney (1994b) and Pudney and Sutherland (1994) for the details of this.

The analysis is based on two elements: a formal measure of poverty (or inequality); and a specification of the types of transfer that are to be considered. In technical terms, these are expressed as follows. The poverty index is written $I(\tau)$, where τ represents a set of transfer rates (i.e. levels of the benefits) to be determined by the algorithm. Define y to be the variable describing a household's welfare after the addition of the hypothetical transfers. A variable s records the household's size, in terms of equivalent adults. A formal poverty line, L, is then defined as minimum required income per equivalent adult. We use two alternative poverty measures:

Headcount

$$I_{H}(\tau) \quad = \quad \text{percentage of households below poverty line}$$

Foster, Greer and Thorbecke (FGT)

$$I_{FGT}(\tau)= \quad \text{average value of } [1-(y/s)/L]^2 \text{ for households below poverty line} \times \text{ proportion of households below poverty line}$$

Thus the headcount index simply counts the number of 'poor' households, while the FGT index gives each poor household a weight equal to the square of the amount by which it falls below the poverty line. Foster *et al.* (1984) and Kanbur (1987) discuss these and other indices in detail. Note also that these measures define poverty on a household rather than individual basis; large families receive the same social weight as small families, and this necessarily moves the optimum away from size-related family benefits to some extent. They also make no distinction between adult poverty and (arguably more important) child poverty. The analysis can easily be extended in these directions, and section 3.5.5 below reports the results of some sensitivity analyses.

When we use the headcount index in practice, we implement it in 'smoothed' form. Rather than counting a household as 1 if it is below the line and 0 if it is above it, the smoothed headcount gives it a value varying smoothly from 0 to 1 over a short range centred on the poverty line (see Pudney (1994b) for further details of this). This is done mainly for technical reasons, but it can be defended as an attempt to avoid the inherent arbitrariness of a sharp poverty line.

The transfer structure we use is as follows. If y_0 is the household's initial level of resources, its post-transfer resources are

$$y = y_0 + \beta_1\tau_1 + ...+\beta_J\tau_J$$

where β_J is the household's entitlement to the Jth transfer, which is assumed to depend in some way on the household's structure and characteristics and τ_J is the (positive or negative) amount of the jth type of transfer which is payable to a household with eligibility level $\beta_J = 1$.

Thus, for example, if we decide to examine the scope for transfers between childless households and households with children, we might take $J = 2$ and define β_1 as the number of children in the household and β_2 equal to 1 if the household is childless and 0 otherwise. In this case, τ_1 would be a fixed-rate child benefit and τ_2 would be a fixed amount per household paid to (or from) every childless household. If, at the optimum, τ_1 were positive and τ_2 were negative, this would suggest that poverty could be reduced by introducing some form of transfer from childless households to households with children (particularly large numbers of children). Many other child-related transfer structures are possible.

The analysis has to be constrained by at least one government budget constraint, since otherwise poverty could be reduced to an arbitrarily low level at sufficiently high cost. The total cost to the government of the hypothetical transfer system must be constrained and, if we insist on revenue neutrality, this implies

$$\text{Net revenue} = \tau_1\mu_1 + \dots + \tau_J\mu_J$$
$$= 0$$

where μ_J is the average value (in the whole household population) of the eligibility, β_J, for the Jth transfer.

We can also work with more than one budget constraint. For example we might analyse a set of transfers for employees classified by gender (representing the distributional impact of policy on male–female pay differentials) jointly with a set of transfers related to family structure (representing child benefits, pensions, etc.). In this case, we might wish to assume that net transfers between employees in different industries are internally revenue neutral and that demographic transfers are separately revenue neutral. Imposing these two constraints separately is equivalent to ruling out transfers from the employed sector to the non-employed sector, which we might wish to do in order to avoid policies implying a major increase in labour costs.

We use household survey data to estimate statistically the poverty index, $I(\tau)$, and the mean eligibilities, $\mu_1 \dots \mu_J$. The optimal targeting algorithm then chooses the values for $\tau_1 \dots \tau_J$ that minimize the estimated poverty index subject to the estimated budget constraint(s). The results are only estimates of the true levels of optimal transfer for the whole population, and we calculate standard errors to give an indication of the degree of statistical reliability of the results.

3.5.2   Implementation

The 1991 Household Budget Survey (HBS) has been described in section 3.4 above. We use a basic household resources variable, y_0, defined as the household's total consumption expenditure. Because inflation during 1991 was high and interviewing was done in six waves throughout the year, we revalued expenditure to constant 1987 prices. The equivalized household size variable, s, is defined to be 1 for the first adult plus 0.7 for each additional adult plus 0.5 for each child. Consumption rather than income is used for two reasons: consumption expenditure appears to be less vulnerable to short-term fortuitous fluctuations that are unrelated to the household's sustainable level of welfare; and the intertemporal behaviour of households implies that current consumption is more closely related to the household's perception of its long-term command over economic resources than is current income.

To give some idea of the robustness of the conclusions with respect to the underlying definition of poverty, we use two poverty measures: the (smoothed) headcount with an (annual) poverty line of 35 000 Ft per equivalent adult; and the FGT index with a poverty line of 40 000 Ft per equivalent adult; both poverty lines are expressed in 1987 prices. Roughly 14% and 24% of households are in poverty by these two criteria. Note that the poverty lines used here differ considerably from the complex official poverty line used by the CSO and also used in the study of van de Walle *et al.* (1993).

The forms of income transfer we consider are of three broad types: transfers related to employment in a set of 18 industrial sectors; transfers related to location in terms of the 20 counties of Hungary and an urban/rural distinction; and transfers related to a range of demographic categories. These three classes of income transfer can be thought of loosely as capturing the redistributive potential of industrial policy, regional policy and conventional welfare or social security policy. They can be analysed either as separate alternative transfer systems or simultaneously, so that their relative potential as redistributive policy can be judged directly. We first consider the industrial and regional dimensions as alternatives, and then concentrate separately and in greater detail on the more conventional avenue of demographic transfers.

When interpreting the results for location-related transfers it is important to bear in mind that the HBS is designed only to be a nationally representative survey, and the subsamples drawn from particular counties may not be as representative of the population of that county as we might like.

3.5.3 Industrial and Regional Income Transfers

Our aim here is to estimate the degree to which measured poverty could be influenced by income transfers related to location and sector of employment of household members. If either of these could be identified as major dimensions of poverty, then it might be possible to make a strong case for active regional or industrial policy on distributional grounds.

The two sets of eligibility variables, β_r, are as follows:

- 18 variables indicating the number of household members employed in each of 18 industrial sectors;
- 20 dummy variables indicating the county of residence and a 21st dummy identifying households located in rural areas.

Note that these eligibility variables imply a fixed industry-specific transfer payment to or from each employed *person*, and a fixed location-specific payment to or from each *household*. The estimated optimal transfers should be interpreted in the context of a mean level of base resources (y_0) equal to 120 000 Ft consumption expenditure per household per year. We do not explore the estimated optimal transfers for the industrial/regional case in detail, since transfers of this type turn out to be much less effective in reducing poverty than the demographic transfers discussed in the next section.

Table 3.6   Targeting gains from combinations of industrial and locational income transfers (standard errors in parentheses)

Transfer system	Headcount criterion (%)	FGT criterion
Base (no transfers)	14.49	1.31
	(0.35)	(0.05)
Gain from targeted transfers:		
20 counties + rural addition	0.64	0.06
	(0.16)	(0.01)
Budapest + 19 counties (urban) +	0.89	0.09
19 counties (rural)	(0.16)	(0.01)
18 industries	0.57	0.04
	(0.11)	(0.01)
20 counties + rural addition +		
18 industries (separate industrial	1.15	0.10
and locational neutrality constraints)	(0.18)	(0.01)
20 counties + rural addition +		
18 industries (single neutrality	4.38	0.53
constraint)	(0.28)	(0.03)

Table 3.6, however, summarizes the estimated gains from optimal targeting, using a number of different industrial/regional implementations.

In the case of industrial transfers, the gain from optimal targeting can be interpreted as an estimate of the component of measured poverty which is accounted for by the combined effect of inter-industry pay differentials and the industrial distribution of employment among poor households. The estimated potential targeting gain is modest: about 3–4% of the initial poverty measure in both cases. In absolute terms this amounts to about half of a percentage point by the headcount index. Given this result, it is hard to see a major role for an active selective industrial policy purely on distributional grounds.

Selective industrial support is often seen as fulfilling a similar role to regional policy in terms of income maintenance. Optimal targeting allows a simple comparison of the two policy approaches by allowing for both forms of transfer simultaneously, thus generating an estimate of their relative distributional significance. The degree of substitutability of industrial and regional transfers as redistributive devices turns out to be surprisingly low, since the total reduction in measured poverty is roughly equal to the sum of the reductions produced by separate targeting. Combined industrial and regional targeting (with separate neutrality constraints imposed on each) produces a modest gain of around 8% of initial poverty by either measure. Regional targeting is responsible for a little more than half of the total gain.

The third row of the table gives the results for an extended regional transfer system, involving full interactions between county and area type, in effect allowing the rural subsidy to vary by county. This increases the regional targeting gain significantly, but to a level that remains moderate. The final row of Table 3.6 brings out the most important message: it shows the result of removing the revenue neutrality constraint on industrial transfers, thus allowing net transfers from the employed to the non-employed sectors. The result is a four- or five-fold increase in the targeting gain, and all industrial transfers change to large negative amounts. This puts into proportion the scope for industrial and regional policy from the distributional point of view: the extent of measured poverty depends, above all else, on the scale of transfers from economically active to inactive households. In terms of immediate distributional impact, it is social security policy, rather than regional or industrial policy, that really matters.

3.5.4 Demographic Transfers

In this section we examine the potential role for redistribution by means of transfers related to simple observable attributes of households that are mainly demographic in nature. There are 11 hypothetical transfer types, and the eligibility variables are defined as follows:

(i)   the number of male earners in the household;
(ii)   the number of female earners;
(iii)   the number of unemployed household members (defined as those receiving any unemployment benefit during the year);
(iv)   dummy variable equal to 1 if the household is a public tenant and 0 otherwise;
(v)   dummy variable equal to 1 if the household is not a public tenant and 0 otherwise;
(vi)   the number of male pensioners in the household;
(vii)   the number of female pensioners;
(viii) the number of children aged under 3 years;
(ix)   the number of children aged 3–5 years;
(x)   the number of children aged 6–14 years;
(xi)   the number of non-pensioner, non-earner adults in the household.

It is important to bear in mind that we are using actual consumption as the base resources variable. This implies that we are starting from the status quo (including the consumption made possible by existing social benefits) and considering poverty-reducing movements from that base position. Thus the estimated optimal transfers should be interpreted as desirable additions to households' disposable resources: they are *not* gross cash payments like existing benefits and they do not replace existing benefits. In practice, there may be many different tax–benefit reforms that could be used to generate something like the estimated pattern of optimal consumption transfers.

The relationship between unemployment and poverty is of particular interest, and this presents a problem, since our 1991 data show a relatively low incidence of unemployment. Overall, 5.2% of the sampled households experienced some unemployment during 1991. However, if we consider the six interview waves, the figure rises smoothly from 3.2% in January/February to 7.6% in November/December, reflecting the rise in the aggregate unemployment rate. To allow us to take full account of unemployment, we report two sets of results: one for the original sample weighted only to correct for the non-uniform sample design; and a second, where we give a higher weight to unemployed households to produce a weighted unemployment rate of 12% in the sample.

We also experiment with three different financial constraints. The first case involves an overall revenue neutrality constraint plus an additional neutrality constraint covering male and female earners. This allows net transfers from employed men to employed women, but not from employees to inactive household members. The second case also involves an additional neutrality constraint covering employees, but this time unemployed individuals are included in the same category. This allows for unemployment-related transfers to be financed by people in employment, but no other net transfers are permitted between employed and non-employed people. The third variant involves only the overall revenue neutrality constraint, and thus permits unrestricted transfers between workers and others.

We include the third variant only to illustrate the importance of the limitations one chooses to place on the source of finance for a transfer system, not as a serious policy option. As the results will show, one could in principle generate a very large reduction in measured poverty by permitting a major transfer of resources from employed to non-employed people. However, such a policy would obviously entail enormous disincentives for employment and therefore be unattractive on grounds of economic efficiency (as well as political feasibility). This observation re-emphasizes the point that our analysis is purely distributional in nature, and is designed only to highlight possible directions for reform of the social safety net. Whether one wishes to proceed in these directions and, if so, using what particular policy measures, are separate questions that need to be answered with broader criteria in mind. Our analysis is designed to be a complement, rather than an alternative, to conventional policy analysis that emphasizes economic efficiency but ignores distributional considerations.

The results are reported in Table 3.7 for the headcount index and Table 3.8 for the FGT index. Each table has two blocks of three columns, relating respectively to the results with and without reweighting to increase the sample unemployment rate. We concentrate mainly on the first two columns of each block: in other words the two cases involving separate neutrality constraints for employment (or employment plus unemployment) related transfers.

Table 3.7   Optimal transfers and the incidence of unemployment: household-level headcount poverty index (Ft; standard errors in parentheses)

Transfer	Original sample			Re-weighted (unemployment rate = 12%)		
	Additional revenue neutrality constraint within employed sector	Additional revenue neutrality constraint within employed and unemployed sector	Single revenue neutrality constraint	Additional revenue neutrality constraint within employed sector	Additional revenue neutrality constraint within employed and unemployed sector	Single revenue neutrality constraint
Male earners	-295 (333)	-660 (358)	-16 217 (433)	-589 (317)	-1 647 (376)	-15 380 (543)
Female earners	286 (323)	-488 (348)	-15 082 (357)	574 (308)	-1 156 (356)	-14 240 (308)
Unemployment	3 415 (1 142)	12 306 (650)	405 (71)	3 099 (1 219)	12 218 (652)	816 (1 026)
Public sector tenants	1 104 (340)	1 759 (340)	14 458 (533)	989 (373)	2 472 (363)	16 575 (422)
Other tenures	500 (505)	1 318 (457)	13 891 (500)	505 (578)	2 476 (430)	15 194 (381)
Male pensioners	6 888 (474)	6 787 (433)	-1 041 (348)	7 078 (548)	6 574 (418)	-576 (349)
Female pensioners	8 481 (378)	8 052 (352)	-1 520 (315)	8 667 (424)	7 790 (351)	-1 201 (328)
Children under 3 years	-9 485 (1 392)	-8 820 (1 906)	7 044 (1 334)	-9 674 (1 209)	-8 550 (2 062)	13 045 (1 029)
Children 3–5 years	-16 224 (1 495)	-17 136 (1 575)	-4 586 (1 398)	-15 609 (1 259)	-17 390 (1 573)	-15 099 (1 639)
Children 6–14 years	-17 906 (626)	-17 762 (671)	-592 (714)	-17 273 (688)	-17 173 (765)	-1 567 (734)
Other individual types	336 (415)	-490 (479)	3 827 (429)	529 (398)	-1 098 (476)	2 880 (497)
Initial poverty level (%)	14.49 (0.35)	14.49 (0.35)	14.49 (0.35)	14.99 (0.37)	14.99 (0.37)	14.99 (0.37)
Targeting gain (percentage points)	3.31 (0.30)	3.40 (0.30)	4.96 (0.31)	3.13 (0.30)	3.33 (0.31)	4.74 (0.32)

Table 3.8 Optimal transfers and the incidence of unemployment: household-level FGT poverty index (Forints; standard errors in parentheses)

Transfer	Original sample			Re-weighted (unemployment rate = 12%)		
	Additional revenue neutrality constraint within employed sector	Additional revenue neutrality constraint within employed and unemployed sector	Single revenue neutrality constraint	Additional revenue neutrality constraint within employed sector	Additional revenue neutrality constraint within employed and unemployed sector	Single revenue neutrality constraint
Male earners	-512 (194)	-1 081 (200)	-10 613 (269)	-1 439 (212)	-2 857 (231)	-11 727 (306)
Female earners	497 (188)	-639 (203)	-12 125 (283)	1 401 (206)	-1 137 (250)	-11 389 (335)
Unemployment	9 823 (960)	18 413 (813)	3 801 (930)	8 741 (938)	17 350 (724)	3 029 (937)
Public sector tenants	-3 088 (372)	-2 009 (376)	11 083 (372)	-4 063 (394)	-1 746 (405)	10 350 (399)
Other tenures	-4 259 (324)	-3 066 (333)	10 837 (314)	-5 604 (349)	-3 042 (358)	9 850 (343)
Male pensioners	7 189 (339)	6 854 (332)	-442 (270)	7 424 (348)	6 691 (340)	-336 (294)
Female pensioners	9 157 (327)	8 284 (333)	-582 (278)	10 020 (340)	8 173 (352)	19 (306)
Children under 3 years	-5889 (1 091)	-5 393 (1 058)	2 156 (936)	-3 245 (1 157)	-2 116 (1 132)	4 532 (1 045)
Children 3–5 years	-891 (1 144)	-1 643 (1 090)	627 (966)	56 (1 254)	-1 463 (1 146)	1 619 (1 074)
Children 6–14 years	-9 261 (484)	-8 754 (478)	-2 360 (452)	-8 331 (538)	-7 184 (521)	-2 044 (502)
Other individual types	650 (293)	12 (283)	3 630 (269)	924 (321)	-377 (299)	3 591 (303)
Initial poverty level (%)	1.310 (0.046)	1.310 (0.046)	1.310 (0.046)	1.377 (0.051)	1.377 (0.051)	1.377 (0.051)
Targeting gain (percentage points)	0.304 (0.026)	0.329 (0.027)	0.522 (0.034)	0.276 (0.026)	0.333 (0.028)	0.511 (0.035)

The two tables paint a generally coherent picture. The main difference between them is that the FGT criterion weights very poor households more heavily than the headcount criterion, and consequently generates a more 'targeted' set of optimal transfers. In particular, the FGT results produce transfers that are more favourable to the unemployed, pensioners and women, and the optimal transfers away from children are smaller. The headcount criterion involves a nearly uniform basic transfer to all households irrespective of housing tenure, while the FGT criterion implies a transfer from all households, with a more substantial discount for public sector tenants.

Perhaps the most striking point to emerge is that targeting in these demographic dimensions is capable of producing a far greater poverty reduction that regional or industrial targeting. By either criterion, measured poverty is reduced by one quarter if transfers between employees and non-employees are ruled out or one third if they are permitted; this compares with a gain of around 8% if full regional and industrial targeting is allowed.

The estimates are interesting and surprising in some respects. The optimum entails a small (and not always statistically significant) transfer from male to female employees: male–female wage differentials may be large, but they are not a significant contributor to family poverty. A second notable result is that there is only a modest (and often statistically insignificant) transfer from non-public tenants (mostly owner-occupiers) to public tenants, particularly for the headcount criterion. This stems from the fact that public rental subsidies are not very well targeted (see Pudney, 1995) in the sense that the proportion of public tenants who are poor is quite modest. However, the difference between the estimates for the headcount and FGT poverty measures indicates that a greater proportion of the *very* poor are public tenants.

The biggest recipients of transfers are pensioners, with a significantly higher optimal transfer for females than for males. Thus pensioners are identified as the most distributionally sensitive group, and the results give little support to the current pro-natalist Hungarian family policy. At the optimum, families with children lose significantly, and their net contribution finances a transfer to pensioners (also a modest general household transfer in the headcount case). The vulnerability of the pensioner population is of particular concern at a time when pension reform is being contemplated and doubts are being expressed about the capacity of countries like Hungary to maintain existing pension levels in the medium term (see, for example World Bank, 1994). The identification of pensioners rather than children as the vulnerable group is the result of a complex set of factors, and we discuss this issue in more detail in the next section.

The role of unemployment is interesting. The optimal transfer to the unemployed is among the largest of the estimated individual-specific transfers, so there is certainly no support here for any reduction in the generosity of the unemployment insurance system. Unsurprisingly, if we allow transfers from the employed to the unemployed, we find a much larger net transfer (of around

10% of average household consumption) to each unemployed household member. The warranted unemployment transfer is much smaller if it must be financed from within the system of non-employment transfers. When we re-weight to capture the effect of increased unemployment, there is little change to the optimal unemployment transfer, although the implied number of recipients is much larger, and the necessary levy on the (now reduced) group of workers rises considerably.

When we permit large net transfers from the employed sector by imposing only a single neutrality constraint (a very implausible prospect in the real world), the pattern changes considerably, with large net contributions from all employees and an almost equally large general transfer to all households. The unemployment-, pensioner- and child-related modifications to that general transfer are then quite modest, so the optimum in fact involves very little targeting in the normal sense.

3.5.5   Sensitivity Analysis

In the previous section we identified pensioners rather than children as the vulnerable group in terms of poverty. In the 1991 HBS data, the proportions of pensioners and children who live in 'poor' households (using $L = 35\,000$ Ft) are 19.2% and 9.6%, respectively. There are many factors contributing to the identification of pensioners as the vulnerable group. An important influence is the relative level of current earnings and pension and child benefit payments. Equally important is the fact that a high proportion of pensioners live in households without an earner, whereas children mostly have earners to support them (in our sample, the correlation between the numbers of pensioners and earners is -0.7, compared with +0.4 for the number of children and earners).

Other factors relate to the conventions we have used in conducting the analysis, rather than the nature of the underlying population. The household-based poverty measures used to construct Tables 3.7 and 3.8 give less weight to large households (which generally contain children) than would be the case for individual-based measures. The HBS is known to under-represent children (the proportion aged 0–14 was roughly 18% in the 1991 population statistics, compared with 15% in the 1991 HBS). A third consideration is that the equivalence scale used in this analysis gives children a weight of only 0.5 in constructing the 'needs' of the household. If this were raised, then the proportion of children in poverty would be increased and the results pushed more in favour of families with children.

The aim of this section is to explore the sensitivity of our results to the assumptions embodied in the analysis. In particular, we investigate in Tables 3.9, 3.10 and 3.11 the separate effects of: switching to an individual-based poverty measure; re-weighting the HBS to bring it more in line with the known demographic structure; and using an equivalence scale that gives all household members equal weight. We give results only for the first two financing options (neutrality within the set of employees or within the set of employed plus unemployed). The headcount index is used as the basis for this sensitivity analysis and no re-weighting is done to raise the sample unemployment rate. The individual-based poverty index is the percentage of sampled individuals living in households below the poverty line (i.e. with $y/s < L$). Again, it is implemented in 'fuzzy' form.

The results of optimizing this criterion are shown in Table 3.9. Comparison with Table 3.7 reveals a more obviously targeted result. There is now a large transfer from male to female earners, and the transfers away from children are reduced and partly replaced as a source of finance by a general household levy. However, the latter is now much smaller for public tenants than for other tenures.

Table 3.9 Optimal transfers: individual-level headcount poverty index (Forints; standard errors in parentheses)

Transfer	Additional revenue neutrality constraint within employed sector	Additional revenue neutrality constraint within employed and unemployed sector
Male earners	-4 109	-4 533
	(423)	(438)
Female earners	4 137	2 802
	(426)	(463)
Unemployment	9 407	18 034
	(1 324)	(982)
Public sector tenants	-5 199	-3 886
	(629)	(617)
Other tenures	-9 029	-7 720
	(575)	(457)
Male pensioners	11 111	10 627
	(483)	(507)
Female pensioners	14 843	13 765
	(542)	(490)
Children under 3 years	-2 759	-595
	(1 233)	(1 279)
Children 3–5 years	-12 473	-13 821
	(1 821)	(1 242)
Children 6–14 years	-2 942	-2 707
	(953)	(608)
Other individual types	4 307	3 870
	(418)	(413)
Initial poverty level (%)	13.09	13.09
	(0.36)	(0.36)
Targeting gain (percentage points)	2.16	2.27
	(0.26)	(0.27)

Table 3.10 Optimal transfers: demographic re-weighting; household-level headcount index (Forints; standard errors in parentheses)

Transfer	Additional revenue neutrality constraint within employed sector	Additional revenue neutrality constraint within employed and unemployed sector
Male earners	-5 220	-5 859
	(416)	(419)
Female earners	5 072	4 410
	(404)	(406)
Unemployment	5 007	13 835
	(1 419)	(1 489)
Public sector tenants	-4 074	-3 707
	(557)	(494)
Other tenures	-4 350	-4 041
	(712)	(632)
Male pensioners	7 384	7 347
	(479)	(521)
Female pensioners	13 860	13 504
	(556)	(540)
Children under 3 years	-10 266	-8 781
	(878)	(1 283)
Children 3–5 years	-7 236	-7 155
	(1 638)	(1 430)
Children 6–14 years	-13 672	-13 026
	(1 097)	(895)
Other individual types	3 914	3 465
	(500)	(515)
Initial poverty level (%)	14.30	14.30
	(0.34)	(0.34)
Targeting gain (percentage points)	3.26	3.34
	(0.29)	(0.29)

The additional revenue now finances larger transfers to pensioners (especially females) and the unemployed.

Table 3.10 shows the results of a very simple attempt to re-weight the sample to match better the known demographic structure of the 1991 sample. To achieve this in a simple way, we add to the weight for each household an amount proportional to the number of children aged 0–14 in the household. This amount is chosen so that the weighted proportion of children agrees with the proportion taken from population statistics. Again the result is to produce a slightly more 'targeted' pattern of transfers, financed partly by a general household levy, and with a moderate reduction in the scale of transfers away from children. Nevertheless, there remains a substantial transfer in favour of pensioners.

Finally, Table 3.11 shows the results of switching from the OECD equivalence scale used in the previous section to a simple per capita scale that gives all

Table 3.11 Optimal transfers: per capita equivalence scale; household-level headcount index (Forints; standard errors in parentheses)

Transfer	Additional revenue neutrality constraint within employed sector	Additional revenue neutrality constraint within employed and unemployed sector
Male earners	-550	-964
	(147)	(165)
Female earners	534	93
	(143)	(157)
Unemployment	88	9 189
	(976)	(1 066)
Public sector tenants	-6 704	-6 340
	(206)	(216)
Other tenures	-6 071	-5 647
	(257)	(245)
Male pensioners	7 609	7 590
	(305)	(294)
Female pensioners	9 451	9 201
	(235)	(238)
Children under 3 years	1 605	2 280
	(1 193)	(1 357)
Children 3–5 years	-7 210	-8 280
	(1 594)	(1 540)
Children 6–14 years	-6 415	-6 428
	(623)	(671)
Other individual types	4 233	3 740
	(316)	(372)
Initial poverty level (%)	11.67	11.67
	(0.31)	(0.31)
Targeting gain (percentage points)	1.05	1.09
	(0.18)	(0.19)

household members equal weight. To keep the poverty line constant in equivalized form, the new scale is constructed in such a way that it has the same weighted mean as previously. As expected, the effect of giving all individuals equal weight within the household is to reduce the scale of the predicted transfers away from children. The required transfer to children under 3 years now becomes positive (although not statistically significant), and the transfers away from older children are halved. Pensioners and the unemployed remain the main beneficiaries of the optimal transfers, although the latter group figures less strongly than before. The size of transfers to pensioners is almost unaffected, but they are now financed partly from a general household transfer of around 6 000–7 000 Ft (for both public tenants and households with other tenures). Previously, the increased transfers to pensioners were financed exclusively from a reduction in child benefit.

3.6   Conclusions

This chapter has examined in some detail the scope for redistribution in one transition economy – Hungary. We have examined the changing redistributive character of the personal income tax since its introduction in 1988 and found a clear tendency for its structure to become less progressive through time. Moreover, the PIT is quite irrelevant to many of the families who might be seen as living in poverty (and who are non-tax-payers), so the main burden of redistribution must be borne by the benefit (or 'social income') system.

The remainder of the study has used the technique of optimal targeting in a deliberately impressionistic way, to try to give some indication of the most fruitful directions for future development of the benefit system. If we look at this system purely as an anti-poverty mechanism, our calculations suggest quite strongly that the present pro-natalist design certainly goes far enough (and possibly too far) in devoting resources to families with children. In general, pensioners and the unemployed are identified as more important target groups, and this is particularly so in the light of some current opinion in favour of a reduction in the generosity of existing unemployment insurance and pension arrangements. Our evidence suggests a less important role for male/female earnings equalization and public housing subsidy as anti-poverty measures. We have also examined the scope for using regional and industrial policy as a redistributive device. These policies turn out to be much less distributionally sensitive than conventional demographic transfers.

We have experimented with a range of alternative specifications of the poverty measure and poverty line, and with alternative assumptions about the scale of unemployment. The general character of our conclusions seem quite robust. However, we conclude with a word of caution. Optimal targeting used in this way is not a technique for designing social policies that could be implemented in practice. However, it is useful as a rough-and-ready method of identifying which, from the very large range of different *types* of policy available, might be the most effective. Whether, for example, our results are used to support an increase in the state pension, or an age-related demogrant, or (say) an age-related heating and food subsidy, is a quite separate matter requiring much more detailed analysis.

Notes

1. This rate is expressed in terms of the number of female participants as a percentage of the total 'labour force resources' which includes the working age population plus earners over working age.
2. In 1994, PIT was levied on income *not* on the social insurance contribution.
3. This benefit is awarded to families with three or more children (the youngest of whom must be under eight years old) who have a per capita income below the minimum old age pension.

4. We refer to income transfers in a loose sense: in the empirical application, we are in fact considering direct consumption transfers. Any other measure of household resources or welfare could be used instead.

References

Abel, I. (1990), 'Subsidy reduction in the Hungarian economy', *European Economy*, **43**, 21–34.

Atkinson, A. B. and Micklewright, J. (1992), *Economic Transformation in Eastern Europe and the Distribution of Income*, Cambridge University Press, Cambridge.

Foster, J., Greer, J. and Thorbecke, E. (1984), 'A class of decomposable poverty measures', *Econometrica*, **52**, 761–5.

Frey, M. (1994), 'The role of the state in employment policy and labour market programmes: the Hungarian case in international comparison', ILO/Japan report on employment policies for transition in Hungary, Research Institute of Labour, Budapest.

Hethy, L. (1991), 'Structural adjustment and changes in income distribution in the 1980s in Hungary', World Employment Programme Working Paper, ILO, Geneva.

ILO (1994), 'Labour market developments in Hungary', ILO-CEET report No.3, Budapest.

Kanbur, R. (1987), 'Measurement and alleviation of poverty', *IMF Staff Papers*, **34**, 60–85.

Kupa, M. and Fajth, G. (1990), 'Incidence study '90: The Hungarian social policy systems and distribution of incomes of households', Central Statistical Office and Ministry of Finance, Budapest.

Ministry of Finance (1992), 'New Act on Personal Income Tax – PIT', Public Finance in Hungary series No. 94, Budapest.

Nagy, G. and Micklewright, J. (1994), 'How does the Hungarian unemployment insurance system really work ?', *Economics of Transition*, **2**(2), 209–32.

Newbery, D. M. (1995), 'The distributional impact of price changes in Hungary and the UK', *Economic Journal*, July.

OECD (1991), *Employment Outlook*, OECD, Paris.

Pudney, S. E. (1991), 'Economic transformation and income distribution in Hungary: can the tax benefit system cope ?' Working paper DPET No.9201, Department of Applied Economics, Cambridge.

Pudney, S. E. (1994a), 'Earnings inequality in Hungary: a comparative analysis of household and enterprise survey data', *Economics of Planning*, **27**, 251–76.

Pudney, S. E. (1994b), 'On the use of algorithms for optimal targeting of income transfers', *Leicester University Discussion Paper*.

Pudney, S. E. (1995), 'Income distribution and the reform of public housing in Hungary', *Economics of Transition*, forthcoming.

Pudney, S. E. and Sutherland, H. (1994), 'How reliable are microsimulation results? An analysis of the role of sampling error in a UK tax–benefit model', *Journal of Public Economics*, **53**, 327–65.

Ravallion, M. and Chao, K. (1989), 'Targeted policies for poverty alleviation under imperfect information: algorithms and applications', *Journal of Policy Modelling*, **11**, 213–24.

Révész, T. (1994), 'An analysis of the representativity of the Hungarian Household Budget Survey samples', Discussion Paper on Economic Transition No. DPET 9403, Department of Applied Economics, Cambridge.

Semjen, A. (1994), 'Some fiscal problems during economic transition in Hungary' in K. Mizsei (ed.), *Developing Public Finance in Emerging World Economies*, Institute for East–West Studies/Westview Press, Boulder, CO.

Sik, E. (1992), 'From the second to the informal economy', *Journal of Public Policy*, **12**, 2.

Szalai, J. (1989), 'Poverty in Hungary durimg the period of economic crisis', background paper prepared for the 1990 World Devlopment Report, World Bank,Washington DC.

Szivos, P. (1993), 'Vertical and horizontal inequality in Hungary in the early 1990s', paper presented at the 7th annual meeting of the European Society for Population Economics, Budapest.

van de Walle, D., Ravallion, M. and Gautam, M. (1993), 'The incidence of cash benefits in Hungary', unpublished mimeo, World Bank.

World Bank (1992), *Hungary: Reform of Social Policy and Expenditures*, Washington, DC.

World Bank (1994), 'How to rejuvenate a greying pension system in transition economies', unsigned article, *Transition*, **5**, No 7, September.

4

The Taxation of Entrepreneurial Income in a Transition Economy Issues Raised by Experience in Poland*

Maciej Grabowski and Stephen Smith

This chapter considers one aspect of tax policy in a transition economy: the design of taxation arrangements for small businesses and entrepreneurial incomes. The chapter sets out the range of major issues involved in taxing entrepreneurial activities in transition economies and considers how these problems have been addressed in Poland.

What should tax policy in relation to entrepreneurial activities seek to achieve? Broadly, there would seem to be two potential objectives, both of which are reflected in aspects of Western practice. The first is the achievement of neutrality in taxation between entrepreneurship and other activities and income sources; in other words, the tax treatment of entrepreneurs should be designed so as to cause as little damage as possible to the allocation of resources between different activities and types of organization. The second is the active promotion of some aspects of entrepreneurial activity, such as small firms, to reflect and offset possible market obstacles to the efficient development of this type of activity. The major conceptual issues arise in the definition of policies to achieve the first of these objectives. Such a 'neutral' system should in any case be taken as the baseline against which policies to promote entrepreneurial activities should be framed and assessed.

Even in established market economies, the neutral taxation of entrepreneurial incomes presents particular difficulties, partly due to the absence of clearly defined 'borderlines', for example between labour and capital incomes, and

* This chapter is based on research supported by the Commission of the European Communities under the PHARE Programme. The authors are grateful to David Newbery, Mark Schaffer and Marysia Walsh, and to seminar participants in Brussels, Mannheim and Warsaw, for comments on an earlier draft. However, the views expressed in the chapter, and any errors, are those of the authors alone.

between business expenses and private consumption. The treatment of income volatility, of social insurance contributions, and of inheritance by the tax system can easily have a non-neutral impact on the balance between entrepreneurial investment and other investments. These problems are magnified in transition economies by the rapid expansion of the small business sector, the fluidity of business structures and contractual relationships, by the lack of established institutional relationships between government and business, and by the limited administrative resources of the tax authorities. At the same time, efficient taxation of small businesses is of particular importance in guiding the development of the economy; tax factors may affect both the overall level of entrepreneurial activity, and also the structure and financing of small business.

4.1   Scale and Characteristics of Entrepreneurial Activity

4.1.1   Evidence of Changes in the Private Enterprise Sector in 1989–93 in Poland

One of the features of the planned economy in Poland – as in other countries in Central and Eastern Europe – was the small number of enterprises, and the highly concentrated structure of production. Private firms, to the extent that they were tolerated, were restricted in their development by rules which discouraged growth beyond a certain size. For instance, Polish private firms were not permitted to employ more than 50 workers per shift. Private firms which grew beyond this limit were at risk of nationalization. As a result, the structure of enterprises consisted of a very small number of large state-owned enterprises and, at the other extreme, some small private firms. The latter group was not very numerous, and was economically weak.

This structure of enterprises is unlikely to be consistent with efficiency in a market economy. The small- and medium-sized enterprise sector is regarded as having considerable importance in a modern market economy, due to its potential contributions to innovation, flexibility and employment growth.[1] In the transition of the Polish planned economy to a market economy, changes in the enterprise structure would be expected, in which the small- and medium-sized enterprise sector would grow in relative importance.

The Economic Transformation Programme in Poland, which was launched with the 'big bang' in January 1990, opened the economy to greater international competitive pressure, and freed the majority of prices. In some respects, the effects of the economic transformation programme have been different to those anticipated; the social costs of transformation have been higher, and the pace of privatization slower, than previously expected (or, at least, than politicians had promised). The private sector responded quickly, and the number and economic activity of private businesses boomed, however.

Table 4.1   The development of the non-agricultural private sector in Poland, 1989–93 (thousands)

	1989	1990	1991	1992	1993
Total private sector					
Number of firms	857.4	1 201.9	1 473.3	1 717.8	1 888.6
Employment	3 360.7*	3 738.1*	4 161.9*	4 675.3	4 977.0
Trade					
Number of firms	77.8	382.3	609.6	654.5	795.0
Employment	938.6*	1 198.8	1 493.4	1 466.7	1 915.6
Manufacturing					
Number of firms	291.2	346.1	363.6	364.7	363.3
Employment	1 221.0*	1 374.0	1 440.6	1 577.7	1 538.4
Construction					
Number of firms	146.7*	172.4	182.3	200.6	209.5
Employment	414.4*	459.8	628.3	775.3	638.1

Sources: *Rocznik Statystyczny* 1992, pp. XIV, XXII, XXIII, LI, *Rocznik Statystyczny* 1991, pp. XIV, XV, XX i XXI, *Rocznik Statystyczny* 1990, pp. 93, 96, 274, 312, 314, 290, 418, 419, *Maly Rocznik Statystyczny* 1994, pp. 312, 313 and own calculations, *Praca* 1990, pp. 23, 31, 42, 48, 49, 54 and own calculations.

Notes:
(1) Private sector jointly with cooperative sector. The state statistical system included the latter in figures for the public sector until 1991, and thereafter in the private sector. There were 16 691 cooperatives in 1989, employing 1.85 million people; in 1990 there were 18 575 cooperative firms employing 1.73 million. At the end of 1993 there were 19 746 cooperatives, but their employment was not published.
(2) 296 000 persons worked in privatized enterprises by the end of 1993.
(3) Except where otherwise indicated by *, figures relate to December in each year.
* Average in the year.

This rapid growth in private business surprised both the statistical and fiscal authorities, and, as a result, official statistical and administrative data, especially those based on fiscal records, may not give an accurate picture of the current scale of the private sector in Poland. Due to the difficulties experienced by the fiscal authorities in controlling private sector business, many small firms have been able to under-record their profit margins, turnover and value added in order to pay less tax. Data on employment and the number of firms would appear to be the best available indicators of the development of this sector, while data on turnover, profits or value added is likely to be much more unreliable, especially where it has been derived from fiscal records.

Evidence on the growth in the number of firms and employment in the non-agriculture private sector in Poland over 1989–93 is shown in Table 4.1. It shows very rapid growth, especially in the trade sector, which consists principally of firms engaged in wholesale and retail trade and catering. Growth was much less rapid in manufacturing and construction. Overall, the number of firms in the private sector increased by 120% over the period 1989–93, with especially rapid growth in the first year of the economic transformation programme. Employment in the private sector grew by some 48% over the same period. In the trade sector, however,

Table 4.2   Development of non-agriculture micro-enterprises in Poland in 1990–93 (thousands)

	1990	1991	1992	1993
Total				
Number of firms	636.4	882.1	1 131.6	1 382.0
Employment	898.6	1 538.1	2 011.2	2 427.1
Trade`*`				
Number of firms	77.6	209.9	327.2	656.8
Employment	115.7	445.3	639.0	1 335.2
Manufacturing				
Number of firms	260.4	314.8	321.4	265.1
Employment	436.0	608.8	574.0	477.4
Construction				
Number of firms	134.9	159.1	173.7	157.5
Employment	189.5	255.8	281.7	227.7

Source: (1) *Podstawowe dane statystyczne o dzialalnosci gospodarczej jednostek malych o liczbie pracujacych do 5 osob,* GUS Warszawa 1994, p. 18 *(Main statistical data on economic activity of small entities employing up to 5 persons)*

Notes: Data are not fully comparable due to different definitions of micro-enterprises in different years. Micro-enterprises are defined throughout as firms with no more than five employees; however, in 1992 and 1993 the owner of the enterprise was counted as one of the employees, but not in the earlier years. The number of micro-enterprises recorded in 1990 and 1991 would have been lower if the criteria used in 1992 and 1993 had been applied. This implies that growth in the number of micro-enterprises is higher than the table suggests. Note, however, an offsetting effect for the trade sector in note `*`.
`*` Trade data includes travelling salesmen in 1993 only.

the number of firms increased roughly ten-fold between 1989 and 1993, while employment roughly doubled. The average size of firms in the private sector is, however, small, and has declined significantly since the start of the transformation programme, from 3.9 employees in 1989 to 2.6 in 1993.

In order to explore these trends further, Table 4.2 presents details of the development of micro-enterprises, defined in Polish data as firms with five employees or fewer. We can observe that the increase in employment in the micro-enterprise sector was higher than the increase for the private sector as a whole. While employment in micro-enterprises grew by some 1.52 million between 1990 and 1993, employment in the total private sector grew by only 1.24 million. This suggests that the structure of the Polish private sector is evolving in an unbalanced way. Micro-enterprises employing less than five persons are growing rapidly, but medium-sized firms are not yet numerous.

4.1.2   International Comparisons

A comparison of the structure of enterprises in Poland and in the European Union helps to bring out certain features of private enterprise development in

Table 4.3 Employment in micro-enterprises in the European Union and Poland as percentage of total employment, totals and sectoral breakdown

	EU (1988)	Poland (1990)	Poland (1993)
Total	**30**	**8**	**22**
Trade	45	7.9	65.2
Manufacturing	14	9.9	13.2
Construction	44	17.4	27.0

Sources: EU data: *The European Observatory for SMEs, First Annual Report* 1993, p. 64.
Poland: sources as in Table 4.2 and own calculations.

Notes:
Data for Poland covers enterprises employing no more than five persons, and for EU enterprises employing less than ten persons.
Share of employment of micro-enterprises to total employment in non-agricultural sectors in Poland.
Total employment in non-agricultural sectors was 11.6 million in 1990 and 10.9 million in 1993.

Poland. Although European countries differ widely in terms of enterprise structure,[2] the role of small- and medium-sized enterprises is important in all sectors.

Table 4.3 shows data on employment in micro-enterprises in the EU, and similar data for Poland. It should be noted that the definitions of micro enterprises are not the same in Poland and the EU, and the figures shown in Table 4.3 are not therefore wholly comparable. Micro-enterprises are defined in Poland as firms employing up to five persons, while in the EU data micro-enterprises are defined as firms employing less than ten persons.

Although the data for Poland and EU are not fully comparable, the evidence is clear that the Polish trade sector consists of too many small firms, while Polish manufacturing and construction sectors better reflect European standards. Second, the trade sector definitely has changed its structure the most. This can be supported by the average size of trade firms in 1989 and 1993, which was 12.1 and 2.4 persons, respectively.

Although the size of the micro-enterprise sector may be close to (or, in the case of trade firms, exceed) Western European standards, the position looks worse if the entire small- and medium-sized enterprise sector in Poland is considered. Basic data on the small- and medium-sized enterprise sector, as defined in EUROSTAT[3], are given in Table 4.4.

By and large, employment in the small- and medium-sized enterprise sector in Poland is still below European standards. This suggests that further reconstruction is needed if the economic advantages of the small- and medium-sized enterprise sector, in terms of flexibility to market needs, competition and innovation, are to be fully exploited.

In summary, during the first years of the economic transformation programme, the numbers and employment of small- and medium-sized enterprises have changed relatively little in the construction and manufacturing sectors, while

Table 4.4   Employment in the small- and medium-sized enterprise sector in the European Union and Poland (percentages)

	EU countries			Poland	
	All	Poor*	Large**	1989	1992
Trade	86	96	84	n.a.	n.a.
Manufacturing	63	84	58	34	47.7
Construction	91	94	89	47.7	70.7

Sources: EU data: *The European Observatory for SMEs, First Annual Report* 1993, p. 64.
Poland: Sources as in Table 4.1, and own calculations.

Notes:
Small- and medium-sized enterprises defined as non-agriculture firms, employing less than 500 persons.
* Portugal, Spain, Greece, Ireland.
** France, Germany, Italy, United Kingdom.
n.a.: not available.

there has been rapid expansion of small- and medium-sized firms in the trade sector. The above figures, however, suggest that the current position is one in which there are probably too many micro-enterprises in trade, and a shortage of medium-sized firms. The situation of manufacturing and construction firms is different. Large construction enterprises dominate and probably will await privatization to be split and reconstructed. Micro-enterprises in construction are, by contrast, already quite numerous. Manufacturing has a better balance in the micro-enterprise sector, but worse in the entire small- and medium-sized enterprise sector than construction.

The average size of private sector firms in Poland is 2.6 persons per firm. This number, while lower than the EU average, is broadly similar to the average private sector firm size in EU countries with low levels of GDP per capita. There is a clear correlation between average private sector firm size and per capita GDP within the EU countries; the average firm size across all EU members is six employees, but only three for Greece, and four for Italy, Spain and Portugal.

A comparison of the enterprise structure of Poland and other CEECs can only be made on a very limited basis, due the lack of available data. Table 4.5 presents data on the number of private enterprises, both incorporated and unincorporated, for Hungary, Czechoslovakia and Poland.

It may be observed that there are relatively more incorporated private firms in Hungary and Czechoslovakia than in Poland. Calculation of the number of incorporated firms per 1000 inhabitants yields the following ratios: 1.4, 4.2 and 5.6 for Poland, Czechoslovakia and Hungary, respectively.[4] Presumably, incorporated firms are bigger and have better chances for development than unincorporated. This suggests that probably there are relatively more medium-sized firms in Hungary and Czechoslovakia than in Poland. This is, however, hard to prove due to the lack of data on employment in the small- and

Table 4.5 Numbers of incorporated and unincorporated private firms in Poland, Hungary and Czechoslovakia, 1989–92 (thousands)

	Poland	Hungary	Czechoslovakia
1989			
Incorporated	11.7	4.5	0.2
Unincorporated	813	186.3	86.8
1990			
Incorporated	29.6	18.3	12.2
Unincorporated	1 135	234.0	468.4
1991			
Incorporated	45.1	41.2	39.0
Unincorporated	1 420	300.0	1 175
1992			
Incorporated	51.2	57.3	43.5
Unincorporated	1 523	n.a.	1 262

Sources: Webster, (1992a, 1992b, 1992c). Grabowski and Kulawczuk (1992). *Statisztikai havi Kozlemenyek*, Dec 1992, Budapest 1993. *Biuletyn statystyczny*, 11/1992, GUS Warszawa 1992. *Short-term economic statistics Central and Eastern Europe*, OECD, Paris 1992.

Notes:
(1) Incorporated firms defined as Limited Liability Companies and Joint Stock Companies, including privatized companies.
(2) Unincorporated firms defined as sole proprietors and partnerships.
(3) Data on incorporated firms for Hungary refer only to limited liability companies. Most limited liability companies, however, are privately owned, and most of joint stock companies are state owned. In Hungary there are about 35 times more limited liability companies than joint stock companies.
(4) For Czechoslovakia, data includes state-owned incorporated firms. According to Webster (1992a, p.13) about two-thirds of all incorporated firms are privately owned in Czechoslovakia, so the probable number of private incorporated firms in September 1992 is some 33 000.

medium-sized enterprise sector. Some evidence from empirical surveys supports this hypothesis. In Czechoslovakia, the main competitor for private firms was the state sector, in Hungary both the state and private sectors, and for Polish firms it was the private and informal sectors.[5] Since the state sector consists mainly of large enterprises, private firms competing with the state sector are probably bigger.

The evidence of Polish private sector development in the first years of economic transformation proved that micro-enterprise growth dominates the small- and medium-sized enterprise sector. The under-representation of medium-sized firms is still significant. The trade sector experienced the largest shift towards micro-enterprises. This is a rather unexpected result of economic transformation. The trade sector was underdeveloped before transformation, however. Capital and skill requirements to start trade firms were low and it is easy to find a place in the market place in the first stage of economic transformation. The question then arises, did tax reform play any role in the transformation of enterprise structure during economic transformation?

4.2   Taxation of Entrepreneurial Activity – General Issues

The tax system existing in Poland prior to the start of economic transition was not designed to tax entrepreneurs. Entrepreneurs were, on the one hand, unimportant, but those tax provisions which did relate to entrepreneurs reflected the negative view of their role in the economy, and taxed them punitively. It is important that the new tax system be carefully designed if an appropriate basis for entrepreneurial activity is to be created, in which the creative economic potential of entrepreneurs can be put to work, while at the same time the entrepreneurial sector does not simply become a refuge for tax evaders.

The start of a new tax system offers the opportunity to get things right in a way not usually available to existing market economies. Business practices in market economies already reflect the tax systems in place; tax privileges and concessions may be capitalized into asset values, and reforms then lead to consequential capital gains and losses which may be undesired, and which almost certainly have a political cost. This is likely to be particularly true of the taxation of the small business sector.

But getting the taxation of entrepreneurs right is not an easy matter. There are a number of reasons for this, which are set out below. A number of these difficulties concern 'boundaries' between activities with different tax treatments – for example, the boundary between labour and capital income, or between industrial inputs and private consumption. In small firms these boundaries are often much more difficult to observe, and, therefore, to draw than in larger firms; fewer observable transactions occur, and the roles of manager, worker and supplier of capital are frequently combined in the same individual. Where 'arms length' transactions occur between a large firm and, for example, its investors, these can generally be taken for tax purposes as an accurate reflection of the income flows accruing to investors; however, where no such transactions take place, they may have to be imputed for tax purposes, and such imputation is likely to be imprecise and unsatisfactory.

4.2.1   Labour and Capital Incomes

The self-employed and small businesses combine two factors of production – labour and capital – which are, quite often, taxed elsewhere in the tax system very differently from each other. Some countries levy higher taxes on capital incomes than labour incomes (as in the United Kingdom in the 1950s and 1960s); other countries levy lower taxes on capital incomes than labour incomes (as the United Kingdom now). Because these two types of incomes are combined in the small business sector in a way which may be difficult to disentangle, small businesses will, almost inevitably, have to be taxed more favourably than the constituent factors would be, and the small business structure may become a route for evasion of tax on incomes more generally.

Moreover, like most businesses, small businesses have the option of manipulating their flows of capital income to their owners so that they are received in the form either of income or of capital gains. Many tax systems tax capital gains at a different (often lower) rate compared to capital income. However, the potential for large businesses to make use of this by paying out profits in the most tax-efficient form may be limited by differences in the interests of different shareholders; small businesses can tailor the choice between income and capital gains in a way which suits the precise circumstances of their proprietor.

4.2.2   *Transaction Evidence and Enforcement*

Quite apart from the problems of defining the appropriate boundary between capital and labour incomes, it is usually more difficult to enforce taxes on small business incomes than on other income flows. One of the ways in which the tax authorities can restrict evasion of taxes on incomes is by requiring both sides of the transaction to report the payments; for evasion to work, both sides then have to be willing to make a false report, and large enterprises will usually be unwilling to do so. (A large enterprise which keeps false records to back up false reports to the revenue authorities will often find it difficult to prevent similar methods being used by its employees to defraud the company for their own gain.) The proprietors of small businesses are able to control both sides of the information flow to the revenue authorities (i.e. payments to themselves, as owner or employee, and their receipt of these payments).

Employee tax-payers can be taxed through a deduction-at-source mechanism, which provides greater certainty of tax payment than if tax payments were made by the individual employee, on the basis of periodic declared statements of income. The system works because there are two parties to the deduction-at-source arrangements, the employer and the employee. For evasion to be possible, it would normally be necessary for both these parties to have an interest in the evasion. However, large companies, at least, are unlikely to wish to get involved in collusive fraud of this sort.

In the case of the self-employed, however, payments of income involve only one, rather than two, parties, and a deduction-at-source mechanism would contribute no improvement to the certainty of tax payment. Indeed, as argued above, the very notion of an income payment to the proprietor of a small business may often be blurred or meaningless; the 'income' of the proprietor may be something that can only be ascertained as the result of detailed *ex post* accounting and audit.

4.2.3   Individual and Business Consumption

It may also be difficult to define the boundary between individual and business consumption sufficiently tightly to prevent abuse. Many commodities which individuals consume are also used as business inputs, and some activities which can count as business expenses may often have a large consumption element (business entertaining, travel, etc.). The tax authorities may often be unable to tell the difference.

Ideally, where business expenditures reflect consumption by individuals they should be subject to consumption and income taxes in the same way as if equivalent income payments were made to the individuals concerned, and consumption purchases were made out of this income. Also, it is desirable that business input uses of similar goods should not be taxed (a reflection of the general rule of Diamond and Mirrlees (1971) that – under certain restrictive conditions – intermediate goods should not be subject to taxation).

4.2.4   Income and Expenditure Tax Strategies and 'Borderline' Problems in Taxation of Entrepreneurial Incomes

The problems which are posed for the attainment of a neutral treatment of entrepreneurial activities by the 'borderline' problems described above vary depending on the underlying decisions made about the treatment of income, savings and consumption in the fiscal system. Depending on the general tax treatment of income, saving and consumption, some of the problems which arise because of the difficulty of distinguishing the boundaries between capital and labour income, and between business inputs and consumption, in entrepreneurial activities may be eased, although generally at the cost of accentuating the problems associated with other borderlines.

This may be illustrated by considering the choice between three general 'philosophies' of the taxation of income, saving and consumption:

- A 'comprehensive income tax' regime, in which both labour and capital incomes are taxed at the same rate, while individuals' investments are made out of taxed income.
- A 'direct expenditure tax' regime, in which tax liability is based on income minus net saving in any period; individual investments are thus made out of untaxed incomes, while the returns to investments, in the form of capital incomes, are taxed when consumed.
- A 'deferred expenditure tax' regime, in which labour incomes are taxed but capital incomes are not; individual investments are made out of taxed income, but the returns to these investments are not taxed.

Broadly speaking, most Western countries have in the past operated systems closest to the first of these regimes; in this system, the tax system acts to discourage savings (a problem sometimes referred to as the 'double taxation' of savings). The second and third systems avoid the double taxation of savings, in two different ways; in the case of the direct expenditure tax by allowing savings to be made out of untaxed income while taxing the resulting capital incomes, and in the case of the third regime, by exempting capital incomes from tax. Direct expenditure taxes have rarely been applied (although extensively advocated in academic literature), partly because of the major transitional difficulties which would arise. On the other hand, in recent years many Western economies have taken steps which have moved them closer to the third system, partly because increased international capital mobility has increased the pressure of international tax competition. The measures taken have included either reductions in the rates of capital income taxes, or the establishment of special regimes permitting certain investments to be made without taxation of the returns (e.g. PEPs and TESSAs in the United Kingdom).

The borderlines which matter in achieving neural taxation of entrepreneurial activities depend on which of these regimes is in force.

- Under a comprehensive income tax regime, there is no need to try to distinguish the capital and labour incomes of business proprietors. Since both such incomes are taxed at the same rate, there is little to be gained[6] by changing the 'mix' between capital and labour incomes in the incomes paid to the proprietor. There is, on the other hand, a strong incentive to misrepresent individual consumption as business expenditure, since by doing so it is possible to reduce income tax liability as well as any liability to consumption taxes.
- Under an expenditure tax regime, capital and labour incomes are again taxed on the same basis, and so the borderline between the capital and labour incomes of proprietors is not sensitive for tax purposes.[7] There is, however, a need to identify resources invested by the proprietor in the business, since, for neutrality with other forms of investment, these should be made out of untaxed income. This potentially creates particular difficulties with enforcement of the distinction between individual and business consumption; not only is it possible for business proprietors to avoid tax on their business incomes by channelling individual consumption through the business, but they can also avoid paying tax on consumption expenditures made out of earlier incomes, if money invested in the business is used to supply their personal consumption.
- Under the 'deferred expenditure tax' regime, acute problems arise in achieving a neutral tax treatment of entrepreneurial activities compared to other forms of investment. Since capital incomes are untaxed, while the full burden of taxation is borne by labour income, there is a substantial gain to a business proprietor if most or all of the income from a small business can be treated as

capital income. In this case, the tax exemption also, in effect, applies to (much or all of) the proprietor's labour income as well as capital income. On the other hand, the gain from misrepresenting individual consumption as business consumption is small, since it will only save any consumption taxes which would be levied on personal consumption but not on business inputs.

For these reasons, most countries which operate systems of this sort confine them to defined classes of assets; incomes from these assets only are exempted from tax, while other sources of capital income, including entrepreneurial incomes, remain taxed. However, while this is a solution to the problem of achieving neutrality between the labour and capital incomes of small business proprietors, it creates further possible non-neutralities between small and large businesses, if the shares or other sources of finance to large businesses can benefit from the capital income tax exemption. Large businesses then have access to tax-privileged sources of investment finance denied to small businesses, and the tax system may thus distort the enterprise structure in the direction of large businesses, financed from tax-privileged funds.

What conclusions should be drawn from this discussion for the design of the tax system? It would clearly be inappropriate for the choice between these fundamental bases for taxing consumption, savings and income to be made solely in order to facilitate tax enforcement among small businesses and independent entrepreneurs. Nevertheless, this is one consideration which would need to be evaluated in assessing the choice between, for example, comprehensive income taxation and its alternatives, and is, perhaps, one of the stronger arguments favouring comprehensive income taxation over systems which do not involve double taxation of savings. Where, however, these alternative systems are adopted, it is clear that particular difficulties will need to be addressed in designing tax systems for small business. In particular, countries which adopt regimes in which the returns from certain classes of assets are exempted from tax (PEPs, etc.) will need to bear in mind that, because this treatment cannot feasibly be applied to own-capital investments in small businesses, the tax system will substantially accentuate any existing distortions in the economic system against entrepreneurial activities. There will then be a strong case for substantial offsetting compensation, either in the rather rough-and-ready form of tolerating tax distortions in favour of small business elsewhere in the tax system, or in the form of explicit subsidy or support schemes.

4.2.5   Timing of Tax Payments

Tax payments by the self-employed are therefore usually made on the basis of an income statement ('tax return') to the authorities, as a result of which liability to tax is assessed, and payment demanded. In this process, tax payments need no longer be made at the same time as the incomes to which they relate. Payments might be made in arrears (i.e. in relation to incomes earned at some time previously), although estimated payments 'on account' could be demanded earlier. There are a number of possibilities, and international practice varies. Where tax payments by the self-employed are on average made later than tax payments by employees, there is a potential gain in terms of postponed tax payments which can be made by being treated as self-employed.

4.2.6   Social Security Contributions

There are often issues about the social security taxes levied on the self-employed and small business proprietors. In principle, self-employed individuals should pay both the employer's and employee's element of social security taxes. However, given the combined rates at which such taxes are levied this may often prove impractical. Moreover, if capital income is not subject to social security taxes, such taxes may simply encourage small business proprietors to take as much income as possible in the form of capital income rather than labour income.

On the other hand, there may be perfectly valid reasons for levying lower social security taxes on the self-employed. Since the concept of unemployment may be difficult to define for someone who is self-employed, it may be difficult to define circumstances under which the self-employed can be allowed to benefit from unemployment insurance. If – as in many Western systems – the entitlements of the self-employed to unemployment benefits are severely restricted, it may then be inappropriate to require the self-employed to pay that part of social security taxes which represents a premium for unemployment insurance.

As Table 4.6 shows, rates of social security contributions paid by the self-employed in Western Europe are generally substantially lower than the combined rate in respect of employees paid by employers and employees.

4.2.7   Restricting Access to 'Self-employment'

If there are significant fiscal advantages to being taxed as self-employed rather than as an employee, it may be necessary for the fiscal authorities to control the ability of individuals to choose to be taxed as self-employed.

The UK system restricts eligibility for the self-employment tax regime tightly, and refuses the 'privilege' of being taxed as self-employed to certain groups of tax-payers who, it is believed, wish to class themselves as self-employed purely for the purposes of evasion. The rule employed is one which confines the self-employed income tax regime ('Schedule D') to individuals who have substantial control and discretion over major aspects of the performance of their

Table 4.6 Compulsory social security contributions as a percentage of pre-tax incomes of self-employed and employees compared, for income level of the average production worker

	Contribution of self-employed	Wage employment: employee contribution	Wage employment: employer contribution
France	41.5	18.0	38.0
Germany	–	17.8	17.8
Italy	–	8.5	50.1
Netherlands	17.3	29.1	11.5
Spain	–	6.0	30.3
Sweden	20.5	–	32.2
United Kingdom	5.5	7.7	10.4

Source: OECD *Economic Outlook*, (1992).

work.[8] Considerations such as the time and manner in which work is done, the location of the work, ownership of tools and equipment, and the extent of individual control are regarded as relevant in identifying genuine self-employment. Over and above this test, however, the UK tax authorities also require certain groups of borderline self-employed individuals to be taxed according to deduction-at-source arrangements equivalent to those applying to employees; such rules, for example, apply to labour-only subcontractors in the building industry and to agency workers.

4.2.8   Income Volatility

Entrepreneurial incomes are likely to fluctuate more widely than earned incomes, for two reasons.

First, they may be more sensitive to the economic cycle and other aspects of business conditions. For example, in the United Kingdom, a comparison of annual percentage changes in aggregate employment income and aggregate self-employment income over the years 1970–90 shows considerably greater volatility in self-employment income. The standard deviation of the annual percentage change in aggregate self-employment income, adjusted for inflation, is 6.65, compared to 2.65 for the standard deviation of the annual percentage change in aggregate employment income. In addition to this aggregate volatility, reflecting the greater exposure of self-employment incomes to the overall macroeconomic situation, the self-employed tend to face greater individual year-on-year volatility in incomes, reflecting specific factors relating to each individual.

Ideally, the tax system should not penalize or advantage the self-employed simply because their incomes are more sensitive to economic conditions, and some system of income averaging would then appear appropriate. This may then create non-neutrality with employees who may not have opportunities for income averaging for tax purposes, however.

Second, entrepreneurial activity usually involves a period of initial investment, followed by subsequent receipts of income. Part of the initial investment may take the form of profits of the business immediately re-invested in the business (ideally, such incomes should be taxed in the same way as incomes which were paid to the proprietor and then explicitly re-invested, but this may be impractical). The time profile of individual taxable incomes may then be very uneven.

4.2.9 Impact of Taxation on the Incorporation Decision

The tax system may be one of a number of factors influencing the choice of legal form – in other words, the decision whether to incorporate. In most countries, unincorporated small businesses are taxed through the application of the personal income tax system to the income of their proprietor, while a separate corporate tax regime applies to incorporated businesses. Depending on the relationship between the personal income tax and corporate income tax systems, there may be a fiscal incentive or disincentive to choose incorporation in preference to operating as an unincorporated small business.

Calculating the scale of the fiscal incentive to incorporate a small business is complex, and requires account to be taken of a number of factors, including:

- The 'headline' rates of tax applied to profits earned in businesses of each legal form. Where the personal income tax is progressive, but corporate profits are taxed at a single percentage, the incentive to incorporate may differ depending on the income of the proprietor.
- The definition of taxable profits under each regime, including the basis of depreciation, and the types of costs allowable.
- The corporate tax system employed. This will determine the extent to which corporate profits taxes can be offset against the personal income tax liability of shareholders, avoiding 'double taxation' of both company profits and shareholder incomes. The extent of such double taxation may vary depending on the source of business finance.
- The level and timing of taxation of capital gains earned by incorporated and unincorporated businesses.
- The availability of special tax regimes for small firms, in either incorporated or unincorporated form. To the extent that such special regimes may either reduce the tax burden, or the burden of tax compliance, they may influence the decision to incorporate.

In addition to tax considerations, other relevant considerations in deciding whether to incorporate a small business include the possible benefits of limited liability status which incorporated firms may obtain, implications for the proprietor's ability to maintain personal control, differences in administrative requirements and costs, effects on the availability of capital, and possible attractions of incorporation in easing the process of business disposal through sale or inheritance. Evidence on the extent to which tax considerations are likely in practice to influence the choice of legal form by small firms is mixed. As OECD (1994) discusses, even in countries where there appears to be a clear fiscal advantage to one particular legal form, not all businesses appear to select this form. However, there are also cases where fiscal incentives do appear to have influenced the incorporation decision; for example, OECD (1994) cites the case of Belgium, where the tax system provides strong incentives for incorporation and where a high proportion of small businesses choose this form.

4.2.10 Beyond Neutrality: Arguments for Active Promotion of Small Businesses Through the Tax System

Small businesses suffer a number of potential disadvantages in competition with larger enterprises in the economic system – for example, where economies of scale are significant, or where financial institutions only provide resources to small firms on less favourable terms than to larger businesses. However, as a recent discussion of the issue in OECD (1994) emphasizes, the existence of these disadvantages is no immediate reason to provide a rationale for special treatment of small businesses, whether through the tax system or more direct assistance, since some at least of these disadvantages reflect genuine inefficiencies connected with small-scale enterprise. A case for intervention requires identification of market failures which impede efficient development of small business.

OECD (1994) identifies sources of market imperfection which could warrant government intervention. These include the possibility that small businesses may contribute to stabilization or equity objectives, possible managerial limitations which could be addressed by centrally provided management advice and information, financing obstacles, and government-imposed costs bearing particularly heavily on small businesses. The last two probably constitute the core of any justification for differential fiscal treatment to promote small businesses.

As regards access to finance, problems experienced by small firms include both problems of the availability and cost of finance. Financial resources may be rationed due to informational asymmetries between lender and borrower; for example, financial resources may not be available to small firms without collateral, while larger firms may be able to raise finance for the same project by using existing assets as collateral. Also, the cost of finance to smaller firms may be higher than to larger firms for a number of reasons. While some of these reflect genuine underlying differences in situation which would imply differences

Table 4.7 Average income tax compliance cost for
self-employed (Schedule D) taxpayers in the United Kingdom,
1993–4

Income band	Mean compliance cost	Mean compliance cost as percentage of income
under £7 500	£274	6.8%
£7 500–£15 000	£411	3.9%
£15 000–£30 000	£618	2.9%
£30 000–£50 000	£513	1.5%
over £50 000	£1 397	1.7%

Source: OECD (1994), p.14.

in risk, small firms may be disadvantaged if the market takes an excessively short-term view, or because of certain effects of the tax system on the relative cost of the sources of investment finance available to small and large firms (OECD, 1994).

As regards government-imposed costs, it is clear that the cost of tax compliance bears disproportionately heavily on smaller firms. Data for the United Kingdom shows that the compliance cost of income tax for the self-employed rises less than proportionately with income; compliance costs are nearly 7% of income for the lowest income band of self-employed ('Schedule D') tax-payers, but only 1.5–1.7% of income for tax-payers in the top two income bands (Table 4.7).

While the disproportionately high compliance costs for small businesses would seem good grounds[9] for some form of compensation, however, it should be noted that there may be possible benefits to small businesses from some of the requirements of the tax system, such as the need to keep proper accounts. These may in part compensate for the initial higher compliance cost burden.

There is clearly an issue as to whether any compensation for the disadvantages experienced by small firms should take place through the tax system or should be provided in other ways. The forms of explicit promotion of small businesses which have been used in recent years in Western countries have included lower tax rates on small companies or capital gains tax exemptions for shares. The arguments for using the tax system in this way include the gains from using existing administrative apparatus, the automaticity of subsidies delivered through the tax system; arguments against include lack of transparency, poor targeting (direct payments may achieve greater 'additionality' per dollar from the resources spent), and inability to aid unprofitable firms (some of which will be new firms most in need of the assistance).

4.3   Taxation of Entrepreneurial Activity – Particular Issues in Transition Economies

Some of the issues set out in the previous section arise in very similar form in transition economies and in established market economies. Others pose particular difficulties in the case of economies in transition. In addition, there are a number of considerations specific to the position of transition economies.

4.3.1   Problems of Valuation Evidence

Where the tax system requires valuations to be made of assets, either in the form of capital goods or stocks, transition economies may face particular difficulties in non-arbitrary tax administration, reflecting the lack of good market data on which to base valuations.

Market evidence on values may be deficient for either of two reasons. One is that in the early stages of transition, markets may be unusually thin (for example, if restitution disputes limit the amount of real estate with clear ownership title). In these conditions, it may be difficult to identify appropriate market valuations to use for tax purposes; there may be insufficient evidence based on genuinely competitive market valuations.

A second source of problems with valuation evidence is that during transition there may be substantial disequilibrium in markets, resulting in large temporary rents accruing to particular assets, goods or individuals. These rents reflect lags in supply responses, either of a physical nature (for example, the time required to build new transport or telecommunications infrastructure) or a non-tangible nature (the time required for individuals to acquire certain skills valued in a market economy). Over time these rents may be eliminated, but for a period during the process of transition the scarcity rents for particular assets may be substantial and rapidly changing over time. Current market values may thus be a poor guide to long-run market values and, if current values are changing rapidly, it may indeed be difficult to find uncontroversial evidence of the current level of market values in any period.

This suggests that transition economies should, as far as possible, avoid the use of tax systems requiring valuation evidence, and should be based as far as possible on tax bases which relate to current transactions values alone. Among the practical implications which might be drawn are that systems of business taxation based on assessed asset values – such as, for example, business rates, which are the largest single business tax in the United Kingdom – are unworkable and should be avoided during transition. Better taxes – even though they might involve some inherent risk of inefficiency – would be taxes levied on unambiguous quantity bases, such as floorspace, rather than asset values.

A second implication of the unreliability of valuation evidence during transition is that it will generally be difficult to operate indexation arrangements for any system of business taxation. This perhaps points in the direction of cash-flow taxation of business enterprises, rather than taxation on the basis of inflation-adjusted accounting profit, although, as discussed in section 4.2.4 above, there are quite alarming risks associated with applying to small business proprietors a cash-flow consistent expenditure tax treatment for individual incomes.

4.3.2 Administrative Limitations

One of the most severe limitations on tax policy in transition economies is the lack – and cost – of administrative manpower. Tax administration in a planned economy required few staff and little enforcement, few existing trained staff are therefore available to operate tax systems in the new market economy. The financial skills and training required of newly recruited staff are initially in short supply, but in strong demand in the new private sector; consequently a rapid build-up of an appropriately-staffed tax administration will be costly and difficult. The implication of this is that the tax system should be designed to minimize the administrative resources required; initially at least, sophistication must give way to practicality. This is a particularly acute requirement in the context of the taxation of small businesses, which absorb a disproportionately high proportion of the administrative resources consumed in operating income taxation in Western economies.

A second, and somewhat distinctive, administrative limitation in transition economies is the 'hangover' from past administrative traditions of extensive negotiation in taxation, in which taxes were simply one element in a wide-ranging bargain struck between production units and the state, over the achievement of both production and social objectives. As many commentators (including Gray, 1990; Bolkowiak *et al.*, 1991) have observed, this tradition of negotiation introduced into the system an element of *ex post* taxation, which is incompatible with the requirement in a market economy that enterprises face hard budget constraints. To make a decisive break with this past tradition, it is probably desirable that the tax systems employed during transition should involve the minimum possible ambiguity, so as to ensure that little scope is left for administrative discretion and negotiation to continue. Thus, over and above the arguments in section 4.3.1 for avoiding valuation-based tax systems, these are probably among the most exposed to administrative flexibility, and should also be avoided for this reason.

4.3.3   *Positive Opportunities*

While there are difficulties in operating a tax system in a transition economy which do not arise in existing market economies, there are also certain opportunities which are available to transition economies, which are in some respects unavailable in more established market economies. Initially, decisions regarding taxation begin – at least partly – with a clean sheet (albeit subject to constraints imposed by the expectations and past experiences of both tax administrators and subjects). Decisions regarding the tax treatment of assets can initially be made freely, without imposing the major capital gains and losses to existing asset holders which are one of the consequences of reforms to taxation affecting asset values in established economies. This freedom to make efficiency-improving changes without imposing arbitrary gains and losses on asset holders will diminish over time as private sector decisions adjust to the structure of taxation, and taxes are capitalized into asset values.

How far might tax policy towards entrepreneurial incomes in transition economies such as Poland be able to respond to this opportunity? Clearly, there are some potential gains from choosing a tax system which is expected to be durable in its broad structure. If initial policy can move immediately to the long-run structure of taxation, then there will be reduced uncertainty about future taxation, and less need for subsequent reforms with arbitrary distributional effects. If, on the other hand, an explicitly transitional tax regime is chosen, there is a danger, either that the expected costs of later reform will deter efficient current behaviour, or that the reform will become permanent, as subsequent governments prove unwilling to accept the costly move from the transitional regime.

If it is possible to identify, therefore, an underlying 'philosophy' to the intended long-run tax system which can be implemented at once, albeit subject in certain areas to *ad hoc* compromises to reflect particular difficulties during the transition, this may be expected to impose a lower long-run cost on the economy than choosing an initial tax system which will require costly reform later. This is of particular concern in the tax treatment of capital incomes and assets, both of which bear on the regime to be applied to small business and entrepreneurial incomes.

One way of approaching this issue is to identify the likely characteristics of the desirable long-run capital tax system for Poland. This will involve the considerations relevant to such decisions in market economies more generally, such as the extent to which the efficiency arguments for an expenditure-tax-type system should be accepted, the degree of integration of corporate and individual income taxes, and the implications of increasing international capital mobility for the sustainability of any taxation at all on capital income. In addition, given Poland's declared intention of ultimately joining the European Union, it will be appropriate to select solutions – where a range of options exist – which are compatible with those adopted elsewhere in the European Union.

The difficulty of this line of approach is that it provides relatively few practical guidelines. Certainly, a trend can be identified towards a reduced tax burden on individual incomes from capital. This may partly reflect the growing internationalization of the capital market, but also probably reflects changing political preferences in many economies, and the role of the market pressures in leading to this outcome can perhaps be overstated. Beyond this, there is little observable international convergence regarding the basic philosophy of capital taxation in market economies. Foreseeing what the likely tax requirements for EU accession would be in 2000 or beyond is thus difficult, and subject to a large margin of error.

A better approach may be to try to design the tax system in a way which retains as much scope to accommodate future change as possible. While the long-term European (or global) structure of taxes on capital is unclear, it may be reasonable to suppose both that it will continue to leave considerable scope for tax competition between countries (which, for political reasons, if not for efficiency reasons, may point in the direction of lower taxation on more 'exposed' assets), and that it will involve relatively limited discrimination in the treatment of different assets and asset types (partly because major tax discrimination will be undermined by mobility, but also because both national and international policy is likely to be based on some broad principles of neutrality). This, in practice, may well avoid the greatest pitfalls of badly-designed 'transition' tax policy, since the unwinding of tax privileges given to specific sectors or assets (e.g. housing in the United Kingdom) is likely to prove one of the most difficult and costly obstacles to efficient long-run adjustment.

4.3.4 Transition Compromises

In the shorter term, administrative constraints are likely to impose severe limits on the ability of transition economies to operate tax systems with the degree of complexity of those employed in the West. Some compromise of efficiency in the interests of administrative practicality is necessary if legislated taxes are to be collected, and the enforcement of the tax system is clearly desirable if long-run tax compliance is not to be undermined by a general acceptance of evasion. Short-term pursuit of the 'ideal' system may be not only unrealistic, but from a longer run perspective, positively damaging.

The general principles for targeting limited resources are perhaps obvious – to concentrate on those revenue sources which can yield large amounts of revenue at low administrative cost per dollar raised. What should then follow is that other sources should either be exempted from tax, or should be made subject to special transition taxes which raise revenue without excessive administrative requirements.

In practical terms, it would seem appropriate to make the maximum possible use of VAT exemption, both through exempting sectors of economic activity which contribute low revenues per dollar of administrative input (the food sector would seem an obvious candidate), and through continued use of a high VAT registration threshold.

It would also seem appropriate to make the maximum possible use of presumptive and lump-sum taxes, set broadly in line with the average tax burdens that the activities covered would incur if taxed 'properly'. Such taxes are in general relatively easy to collect and enforce, and so long as they are not too far out of line with the provisions of the main tax system, may not severely distort competition between enterprises and activities subject to the presumptive tax and those taxed under the main system. There will of course be some distortion; particular enterprises may find that they benefit, or lose, from the presumptive tax compared to the main system, and may therefore choose to arrange their affairs so that they remain taxed under the more favourable regime. There is also likely to be some economic damage from heavy lump-sum taxes, which may push weak enterprises into bankruptcy more rapidly than would be desirable.

Nevertheless, taxes raising little revenue should not simply be discarded without regard to the potential implications for other parts of the system. For example, capital gains taxes can play a beneficial role in maintaining the integrity of taxes on capital incomes, even if they, themselves, raise little revenue.

4.4 Tax Policy in Poland, and the Treatment of Entrepreneurial Activity

4.4.1 Taxation of Small- and Medium-sized Enterprises in Poland after 1990

At the outset of the economic transformation programme, different taxation regimes applied to the private sector and to the state-owned sector. Turnover tax rates were set differently for the two sectors. The excess wage tax which was levied on enterprises in the state sector did not apply to private firms. Private firms were, however, subject to other taxes, not levied on firms in the state sector. Incorporated firms were subject to a Corporate Income Tax (CIT), levied at a rate of 40%. Unincorporated micro-enterprises (with less than five employees) were subject to a 'lump-sum tax', at a level which depended on the type of activity, the number of employees and the size of the town or city in which they were located.

As part of the economic transformation programme three major changes were introduced into the Polish tax system. Personal Income Tax (PIT) was introduced in January 1992, a new law on Corporate Income Tax was passed in 1992 and the Value Added Tax was introduced in July 1993.

Besides these changes to the general system of taxation, two other tax policy measures introduced by the Ministry of Finance have had a major impact on the fiscal treatment of small- and medium-sized enterprises in Poland. In May 1990 the Balcerowicz government granted tax holidays for newly established firms in the 'trade' sector (mainly retail and wholesale trade and catering). In January 1994, as part of a modification of the personal income tax law, a new 'revenue lump-sum tax' was introduced, to apply to small businesses.

4.4.1.1   Tax Holidays for Trade Firms

Conditions for the establishment and operation of small firms were liberalized from 1989, when the Law on Economic Activity was introduced. In May 1990 the Ministry of Finance granted tax holidays for unincorporated businesses. Firms in the 'trade' sector were entitled to a three-year exemption from income and turnover taxes, and a two-year tax holiday applied to some services. This regulation applied only to firms established between May 1990 and the end of December 1990.

The tax holidays granted to private firms in the 'trade' sector had the effect that most of the private sector was, in practice, exempted from taxation, since it created scope for relatively straightforward routes to tax avoidance. So-called 'transactional prices' were used by non-trade firms (for example, firms in manufacturing) dealing with tax-exempt trade firms, to shift profits to the tax-exempt firm; the exaggerated profit recorded by the tax-exempt trade firm was then shared under the table with the non-exempt firm.

The number of unincorporated trade firms increased more than five-fold during the course of 1990, from 71 800 in December 1989 to 368 800 in December 1990. It seems probable that at least part of this rapid growth can be attributed to the decision to grant tax holidays to unincorporated trade firms. Certainly, it is generally believed that many new entrepreneurs were attracted by this regulation. Athough these tax holidays may have increased the number of small firms, however, they may at the same time have had a significant cost, in that they may have encouraged the development of informal economic relationships among firms, in order to take advantage of the opportunities for evasion which were presented by the differences in the tax treatment of firms in different sectors.

4.4.1.2   Personal Income Tax and Corporate Income Tax

The legislation governing the new Personal Income Tax (PIT) was passed in 1991 and the tax was introduced in January 1992. The Personal Income Tax applies to personal incomes, including incomes from unincorporated business (except in agriculture which is exempted from the Personal Income Tax). The marginal rates of the personal income tax were set at 20, 30, and 40% for successive bands of income.[10] Taxable income was calculated as revenue minus costs, so there were incentives both to under-declare revenues and to inflate the costs of running a business, for example by recording personal consumption expenditures as business costs. Surveys, such as that by Grabowski and Kulawczuk (1992), have shown that there was relatively little discontent among businessmen about the Personal Income Tax, which suggests that they may have found it comparatively straightforward to find ways of manipulating the tax in order to reduce their tax liability.

The 1992 Act which sets out the Corporate Income Tax follows certain features of the previous regulation from 1988. As far as the small- and medium-sized enterprise sector is concerned, it is probably the least controversial tax in the present Polish tax system, despite the fact that its flat rate of 40% is not low. It allows losses to be carried forward for three years, and accelerated depreciation. The Polish income tax system, however, does not provide a deduction in the personal income tax for distributed corporate profits. This double taxation almost certainly discourages the development of small-scale incorporated firms.

4.4.1.3   Value Added Tax

The Polish VAT was introduced in July 1993, and is claimed to be a big success. Due to careful preparation work, the impact of the introduction of VAT on inflation was limited, and spread over time. Some turnover tax rates were increased to a higher level before VAT was introduced, thus avoiding a large, and perceptible, jump in prices as the time that VAT was introduced, and this strategy appears to have been successful in reducing the inflationary effect of VAT. There are three VAT rates, of 0, 7 and 22%. Several goods are exempt from VAT, including milk, meat, eggs, fish and domestic fruits.

The VAT has been introduced with a high turnover threshold for VAT registration, in order to limit the burden of administration; enterprises are required to register for VAT only if their annual turnover exceeds 1.2 billion zloty, or about US$50 000. In comparison, VAT registration is required from a considerably smaller turnover in most EU countries. The registration limit in 1992 in France was the equivalent of $12 200, in Germany $15 900, and in Denmark only $1 500; in Italy all businesses, regardless of size, are subject to VAT (OECD, 1994). While the registration threshold in the United Kingdom, the equivalent of $66 300, was higher than in Poland, the maximum size of enterprise covered by the Polish concession was considerably greater than in the United Kingdom, given the very much higher wage rates in the United Kingdom than in Poland.

The high turnover requirement for registration has meant that about three-quarters of small businesses in Poland are not registered for VAT. Detailed data on the number of VAT tax-payers in Poland and their structure are not available. However it can be estimated that there are about 460 000 private firms in the VAT system, some 25% of the total number of private firms.

With effect from the start of 1995, the limit for VAT has been reduced by 50% in real terms; this is likely to have the effect of doubling the number of firms within the VAT system, to a total of about 900 000 firms. This strategy, of introducing VAT with a high initial VAT registration threshold, and then decreasing the threshold over time, is in principle consistent with the severe administrative constraints in introducing VAT. It should keep the initial administrative burden of VAT within reasonable bounds, but, at the same time, avoid businesses becoming accustomed to VAT evasion. Initial enforcement resources can be concentrated on the largest firms, from which the bulk of VAT revenues would in any case be derived, while spending little time in the administration of the VAT system for smaller firms. The revenue foregone by not taxing smaller firms may be limited; while their output is not directly taxed, it may bear a certain effective VAT burden, since unregistered firms also forego the opportunity to reclaim the VAT paid on their purchased inputs. Questions arise, however, about the appropriate pace at which the VAT registration among small firms should be extended. The decision to reduce the real threshold by 50% after only a year of experience assumes that the learning process in the operation of VAT is very rapid.

Extending the coverage of VAT to include more small- and medium-sized firms will impose significant compliance costs on the firms concerned, as well as costs of administration on the fiscal authorities. Evidence on VAT compliance costs, discussed in OECD (1994), suggests that small firms experience higher compliance costs, in relation to turnover, than large firms. In the United Kingdom, firms with an annual turnover of between $30 000 and $75 000 (i.e. just above the VAT registration threshold) bear VAT compliance costs of the order of 0.8% of turnover, compared to less than 0.05% for firms with a turnover of $1.5–15 million. In Germany, VAT compliance costs are about 8% of turnover for firms with a turnover below $20 000, compared to less than 1% of turnover for firms with a turnover of $3 million or more (OECD, 1994, p. 107; see also Cnossen, 1994).

4.4.1.4 Revenue Lump-sum Tax

The limitations of the tax administration in dealing with a very high number of small tax-payers have also led to changes, enacted in December 1993, to the treatment of incomes earned in small businesses under the Personal Income Tax. In order to reduce incentives to declare exaggerated levels of business costs, the 'revenue lump-sum tax' was introduced in January 1994. Its main goal was to levy a simple and moderate tax on small businesses, with low compliance costs to business, and relatively straightforward administration and enforcement. An entrepreneur with annual turnover below 1.2 billion zloty is liable to revenue lump-sum tax, in place of the Personal Income Tax (described above).

Reflecting the objective of simplicity, the tax is levied as a flat percentage rate on turnover, although the rates levied vary according to the business sector. Firms in the retail trade pay revenue lump-sum tax at a rate of 2.5% of turnover, while firms in manufacturing and construction pay 5%, and firms in the service sector pay 7.5%. Some services, including accounting and audit services, are excluded from the requirement to pay the revenue lump-sum tax.

Table 4.8   Entrepreneurs according to taxes

	Number (thousands)		Average monthly tax per entrepreneur (thousand zlotys)		Average tax increase 1994/1993[d]
	Dec 1993	Apr 1994	1993	1994	(%)
Total	1 854	1 871	1 004	1 569	56
of which					
Lump-sum tax[a]	386	349	565	615	9
Revenue lump-sum tax[b]	Did not apply	1 043	–	545	–
PIT on business[c]	1 436	460	1 141	4 662	309

Source: Rzeczpospolitia, July 2–3, 1994 according to Ministry of Finance

Notes:

[a] The 'lump-sum tax' is paid by craftsmen, employing no more than four employees, operating in certain sectors. The tax due depends on the number of employees, size of city and profession, and is modified each year.

[b] The 'revenue lump-sum tax' is levied on businesses with annual turnover less than 1.2 billion zloty (around US $50 000).

[c] PIT (Personal Income Tax) on business activity is levied on unincorporated firms with an annual turnover in excess of 1.2 billion zloty.

[d] The inflation rate for 1994 is estimated at 30%.

Unlike the taxes paid on income by larger businesses, the revenue lump-sum tax takes no account of business costs in computing tax liability; the tax is levied on gross sales (turnover) rather than net income. The sectoral differentiation of the tax rate may be seen as a rough-and-ready reflection of the average cost structure of firms in particular sectors, however.

Table 4.8 shows the changes in the number of tax-payers subject to different taxes, and the average level of tax paid by different categories of tax-payer, following introduction of the revenue lump-sum tax. At the end of 1993, just prior to introduction of the revenue lump-sum tax, about 1.4 million businesses were subject to the Personal Income Tax, paying on average 1.1 million zlotys per month in tax in 1993. Total revenue in 1993 from the Personal Income Tax levied on entrepreneurs was some 19 700 billion zlotys (Table 4.9). Following the introduction of the revenue lump-sum tax, the number of small businesses subject to the Personal Income Tax fell by two-thirds, while the average personal income tax payment of those still subject to the Personal Income Tax rose to some 4.7 million zlotys per month, a rise in real terms (after allowing for 30% inflation) of some 300% compared to the average payment a year earlier. The reform has thus successfully concentrated the administrative resources on larger tax-payers, accounting for the bulk of the Personal Income Tax revenue; after allowing for 30% inflation, the total revenue from Personal Income Tax on small businesses in 1994 was in fact largely unchanged compared to the previous year. At the same time, significant additional revenues were derived from the

Table 4.9 Fiscal revenue from entrepreneurial income in 1993, and estimated revenues in 1994

	Tax revenue in 1993 (billion zloty)	Estimated tax revenue in 1994 (billion zloty)	Percentage increase in tax revenue
Total	22 337	35 201	58%
Lump-sum tax	2 617	2 577	-2%
Revenue lump-sum tax	Did not apply	6 817	–
PIT on business	19 668	25 749	31%

Source: As in Table 4.8

Notes:
The inflation rate for 1994 is estimated at 30%
See also notes to Table 4.8.

new revenue lump-sum tax applied to businesses with turnover below 1.2 billion zlotys. About one million businesses paid the new tax, with an average monthly tax payment of around 550 million zlotys, yielding a total revenue of 6 800 billion zlotys, equivalent to one-quarter of the total yield from Personal Income Tax paid by businesses.

Overall, tax revenues from small businesses subject to either of the two taxes are estimated to have risen between 1993 and 1994 by some 28%, after allowing for inflation. While the available data do not allow us to identify what proportion of the additional yield has been due to the larger payments obtained from tax-payers now subject to the revenue lump-sum tax, and what proportion reflects an increase in incomes, and hence taxable profits, of businesses still paying Personal Income Tax, the indications are that the reform has successfully targeted enforcement resources on the largest tax-payers, while also obtaining significant revenues through the administratively uncomplicated lump-sum tax.

Anecdotal evidence, however, suggests that many businesses subject to the revenue lump-sum tax have concealed part of their revenue, through collusive – and mutually profitable – action between seller and buyer. This evasion not only reduces the level of tax revenues, but also prevents the evolution of larger firms and a more concentrated business structure. Since collusive evasion of this sort requires tight control of information flows in the business, entrepreneurs do not willingly delegate their jobs, and the growth of micro-enterprises into larger firms is thus inhibited.

4.5   Conclusions and Policy Implications

The number of small businesses has grown rapidly in the past four years in Poland, with particularly rapid growth in the numbers of private restaurants and retail outlets; the number of small firms in manufacturing and construction grew much more slowly. However, it is unlikely that the current dimensions of this sector will prove a guide to its long-term significance in the economy; considerable further business restructuring is to be anticipated during the transition process.

Although very uneven, the level and pattern of small business activity in Western Europe may provide some guide to the direction of future trends in Poland and may therefore indicate the numbers likely to be involved, and the significance of the taxation of entrepreneurial activity for the economy as a whole. The small- and medium-sized enterprise sector in Poland is still underdeveloped by European standards. Also, limited comparisons with other Central and East European countries suggest that both Hungary and former Czechoslovakia have a more balanced structure of private enterprise than Poland. In particular, while micro-enterprises in the retail sector in Poland have developed at a high rate, the growth of medium-sized firms is still very weak.

Tax reforms for entrepreneurial income in Poland have affected the pace and pattern of growth of small business. The most important point is that tax holidays granted in 1990 for unincorporated firms in the retail sector were a major factor in the development of private retail trade firms, and in the structure of this sector. Different trade characteristics before the start of economic transition among the CEECs do not explain why Polish trade firms are so numerous and smaller than in other CEECs.

The chapter has set out the series of issues involved in taxing entrepreneurial incomes – many are common to policy both in Western Europe and in transition economies, although transition involves both new difficulties and new opportunities. The most severe transition difficulties concern the lack of good valuation evidence from market transactions (which suggests that floorspace taxes and other non-value measures should be preferred to real estate taxes, for example), and the shortage of administrative resources (which implies that resources should be concentrated on large revenue sources, leaving smaller firms subject to simply administered presumptive and lump-sum taxes). In this respect the Polish authorities' introduction of the 'revenue lump-sum tax' appears to be a beneficial measure in the context of transition.

Policy should also take account of longer-run objectives and constraints. The opportunity exists to make decisions now regarding the long-run structure of taxes on capital incomes and assets without the major adjustment costs that such decisions will involve later, once the private sector has adjusted to the existing tax regime. International competitive pressures (and the objective of EU entry) may dictate Poland's long-run tax system, but the form this will take is perhaps unclear. The most useful contribution to long-term efficiency in taxation which can currently be made is to avoid excessive discrimination in taxation between sectors or classes of activity. These tax privileges in Western European economies have proved among the most durable features of the tax system, and similar tax privileges in Poland could later prove costly to reform.

Notes

1. See, for example, Piore and Sabel (1984), Sengenberger *et al* (1990) and OECD (1989).
2. See The European Observatory for SMEs (1993), pp. 51–77.
3. See EUROSTAT and EC Directorate General XXIII (1992).
4. It is worth noting that the minimum capital required for a limited liability company was 100 000 KCS or approximately US $3 900 in Czechoslovakia, 1 000 000 HUF or approximately US $12 000 in Hungary and 40 000 000 PLZ or approximately US$2 600 in Poland. This suggests that unincorporated Polish firms are smaller.
5. Compare Webster (1992a, b, c) and Grabowski and Kulawczuk (1992).
6. As far as income taxation is concerned; in some tax systems, of course, there may still be tax reasons to channel labour incomes to the proprietor in a form other than direct income payments – for example as capital gains, if these are taxed at lower rates than income.
7. An expenditure tax has the further advantage of applying a consistent 'cash flow' treatment to business incomes, which ensures greater neutrality between the tax treatment of capital gains and income. The difficult issue of whether 'realized' or 'unrealized' capital gains should be subject to taxation is sidestepped by making the test the timing of consumption. If unrealized capital gains lead to higher current consumption, they are taxed, but not if consumption remains unchanged.
8. The borderline is based on the legal distinction between a 'contract of service' (the terms on which an employee is engaged) and a 'contract for services' (the basis on which a self-employed individual supplies services to the purchaser of these services).
9. This may at least partly be an issue of equity or perceived fairness, rather than efficiency. Given the need to raise tax revenues, small businesses impose a cost on society, in terms of the high level of public resources devoted to collecting comparatively-small amounts of revenue. Efficiency considerations on their own might suggest that if there were fewer small businesses, the costs of tax collection and enforcement would be much reduced.
10. The rates have been increased in 1994 to 21, 33 and 45%.

References

Bolkowiak, I., Lubick, D., Mieszkowski, P. and Sochacka-Krysiak, H. (1991), 'An evaluation of tax teform in Poland', Discussion Paper No 5. Polish Policy Research Group, Warsaw University.

Cnossen, S. (1994), 'Administrative and compliance costs of the VAT: A review of the evidence', *Tax Notes International*, June 20, p.1666.

Diamond, P. A. and Mirrlees, J. A. (1971), 'Optimal taxation and public production, I: Productive efficiency', *American Economic Review*, **61**, 8–27.

European Observatory for SMEs (1993), *First Annual Report 1993*, ENSR.

EUROSTAT and EC Directorate General XXIII (1992), *Enterprises in Europe – Second Report*.

Grabowski, M. and Kulawczuk, P. (1992), *Small- and medium-sized Enterprises in Poland – Analysis and Policy Recommendations*, Gdansk: The Gdansk Institute for Market Economics.

Gray, C. W. (1990), 'Tax systems in the reforming socialist economies of Europe', World Bank Country Economics Department, Policy Research and External Affairs Working Papers, WPS501, The World Bank, Washington, DC.

OECD (1989), *Les mécanismes de la création d'emplois*, OECD, Paris.

OECD (1994), *Taxation and Small Businesses*, OECD, Paris.

Piore, M. J. and Sabel, C. F. (1984), *The Second Industrial Divide*, Basic Books, New York.

Sengenberger, W., Loveman G. and Piore, M. J. (eds) (1990*), The Re-emergence of Small Enterprises*, ILO, Geneva.

Webster, L. (1992a), Private Sector Manufacturing in the Czech and Slovak Federal Republic: A survey of Firms, The World Bank, Washington DC.

Webster, L. (1992b), Private Sector Manufacturing in Hungary: A survey of Firms, The World Bank, Washington DC.

Webster, L. (1992c), Private Sector Manufacturing in Poland: A survey of Firms, The World Bank, Washington DC.

5

Government Subsidies to Enterprises in Central and Eastern Europe
Budgetary Subsidies and Tax Arrears*
Mark Schaffer

5.1   Introduction

This chapter looks at two very specific types of subsidies to enterprises in CEECs: budgetary subsidies and tax arrears. The purpose of the chapter is to document the scale of these subsidies, their distribution in the enterprise sector, and the mechanisms and principles by which they are allocated.

The first part of the chapter discusses budgetary subsidies, i.e. subsidies that go directly from the government budget to firms. I begin by looking at aggregate data on budgetary subsidies in the Visegrád countries (the Czech Republic, Hungary, Poland and the Slovak Republic). This is followed by a detailed analysis of the size and distribution of subsidies in Poland (in 1991) and the Czech Republic (in 1992) using comprehensive enterprise-level data. The main conclusions regarding budgetary subsidies are that they are relatively small in aggregate (of the order of 3–5% of GDP). They are highly sector specific, and derive in large part from the relatively few remaining price controls and regulations in these economies. The manufacturing sectors of the Visegrád economies are nearly budgetary-subsidy-free, because prices of manufactured goods are almost totally liberalized.

The second part of the chapter looks at the tax arrears of firms. Tax arrears are a significant and growing problem in the CEEC economies, and since eventual

*   The results in this chapter derive from a World Bank Research Project on Enterprise Behavior and Economic Reform (PRDTE). I am very grateful to Stanislaw Gomulka, David Newbery, Zosia Rutkowska, Jon Stern, András Vertés, and the PHARE workshop participants for comments and suggestions. The chapter was written when the author was a research fellow at the Centre for Economic Performance at the London School of Economics, Houghton Street, London WC2A 2AE. The Centre for Economic Performance is financed by the Economic and Social Research Council. The views expressed in this chapter are those of the author only and not of any of the aforementioned institutions or individuals.

repayment of most tax arrears is doubtful we may reasonably consider them to be a form of government subsidy. A rough estimate is that the flow of tax arrears in the transition period has averaged around 2% of GDP per annum. That is, the flow of tax arrears appears to be close to the same size as the flow of budgetary subsidies. Evidence is then presented on the distribution of the stock and flows of tax arrears based on surveys of manufacturing firms in Poland and Hungary. The survey evidence indicates that the flow of tax arrears to manufacturing firms amounts to very roughly 1–2% of GDP, i.e. much more than the flow of budgetary subsidies to manufacturing. Tax arrears appear to be quite concentrated in a relatively small number of low profitability firms; most firms, including most state-owned firms, do pay their taxes. Finally, I present some survey results on the flow of tax liabilities suggesting that a small number of severely financially distressed state-owned firms are running tax arrears in order to continue to survive.

5.2   Budgetary Subsidies

Under the socialist system, budgetary subsidies formed part of the complex system of price determination. Most prices were administratively determined, in the first instance, on the cost-plus principle. Budgetary subsidies and turnover taxes were the main instruments used by the centre to modify basic prices. Variations from the cost-plus price resulted for a variety of reasons. Prices of many consumer goods were set using 'social' or 'political' criteria. Prices of certain foodstuffs were set below cost; in this case a subsidy was given to producers to enable them to cover their costs. Prices of 'luxury' commodities or special goods such as alcoholic beverages would be set above cost; these goods would attract high turnover taxes. In the case of foreign trade, subsidies and taxes were used to implement prices for domestic producers or importers which differed from international prices.

In addition to these 'objective' criteria, planners used enterprise-specific criteria to set taxes and subsidies. Production costs varied from firm to firm, and firms were not allowed to accumulate losses nor to make 'unearned' profits. (Retained profit was sometimes used as an incentive to motivate firms to contain costs, but not very successfully, in part because of the centre's inability to commit to leaving the profits with the firm and not to ratchet up the firm's future targets.) Subsidies and taxes therefore contained enterprise-specific elements, and subsidy and tax rates would vary from firm to firm. Barbone and Marchetti (1994) argue convincingly that for this reason, profit taxes should also be considered as a key element of the price administration system along with turnover taxes and subsidies.

Table 5.1 shows the scale of subsidies and general government expenditure in the Visegrád countries prior to and after the start of transition. The scale of

Table 5.1 Government expenditure and subsidies in the Visegrád countries, pre- and post-reform (% of GDP)

	1986[a]	1992[b]	1993[b]
Former Czechoslovakia			
Expenditure of general government	65.9	60.1	
o.w., subsidies	25.4	5.0	
Czech Republic			
Expenditure of general government		47.5	47.5
o.w., subsidies		5.0	4.4
Slovak Republic			
Expenditure of general government		64.0	55.1
o.w., subsidies		5.4	4.8
Hungary			
Expenditure of general government	64.6	63.4	60.5
o.w., subsidies	16.6	5.8	4.8
Poland			
Expenditure of general government	49.7	50.7	48.4
o.w., subsidies	16.3	3.3	2.5[c]

Sources: (a) Barbone and Marchetti (1994); (b) IMF (1994); (c) author's estimate (subsidies in Poland 1993)

the cut in subsidies is dramatic: from 15–25% of GDP in 1986 to 3–5% in 1993, a level which is unexceptional by EU standards. This remarkable achievement was the direct result of the policy of price liberalization, which made most of the price administration system superfluous. When prices were liberalized, turnover taxes were rationalized (and subsequently replaced by VAT), profit tax rates were harmonized, *ad hoc* exemptions eliminated, and budgetary subsidies to producers of the price-liberalized goods were eliminated. This last measure was accomplished relatively straightforwardly precisely because prices were allowed to rise to market-clearing levels.

The budgetary subsidies which remain in place in the Visegrád countries are for the most part very sector specific. Table 5.2 presents some more detailed data on the scale of these subsidies in these countries (note that I have not attempted to make the data comparable across countries, nor are the data comparable to those in Table 5.1). Sectors which continue to receive some substantial subsidies are transport (in particular rail transport), housing, mining and agriculture. We can characterize the bulk of the budgetary subsidies that remain in the Visegrád countries as the result of remaining price controls (notably transport) and of social/political factors (notably housing). Nearly all of economic activity outside the sphere of general government and public services is budgetary-subsidy-free.

In the next section we look more closely at the distribution of budgetary subsidies in two leading transition economies – Poland and the Czech Republic – using enterprise-level data.

Table 5.2   Budgetary subsidies in the Visegrád countries by type (% of GDP)

Czech Republic	1993
Total current subsidies	4.2
Agriculture and foodstuffs	0.7
Forestry and water	0.1
Mining	0.4
Residential heating	0.6
Transportation	1.5
Other	0.9
Central investment subsidies	0.6

Hungary	1993	
Total current subsidies	2.3	
Production price subsidies	0.4	
Export subsidies to agriculture and food industry	0.7	
Agricultural market subsidy	0.5	
Consumer price subsidies	0.1	
Other	0.6	
Housing investment subsidies	0.9	

Poland	1992	(1993)
Total current subsidies	2.8	(2.3)
Product specific subsidies	0.4	(0.4)
o.w., transport	0.3	
o.w, coal	0.1	
Housing	0.7	(0.3)
o.w., to housing cooperatives	0.6	
Industrial restructuring	0.1	
Railway infrastructure	0.2	
Subsidies administered by local government	1.2	
Other	0.1	
Investment subsidies to firms	0.2	

Slovak Republic	1993 (based on budget forecasts)
Total subsidies	5.5
Agriculture and foodstuffs	2.9
Forestry and water	0.2
Mining and other industry	0.4
Residential heating	0.7
Transport	1.0
Other	0.3

5.3   Distribution of Budgetary Subsidies to Firms

The enterprise data we have come from the central statistical offices via a World Bank research project on enterprise behaviour and economic reform. The data are for the years 1991 (Poland) and 1992 (Czech Republic), the second full year of liberalized prices in each country. At these dates these countries had completed most of their subsidy cutting, but more subsidy cuts were still to come. The data cover virtually all business organizations excluding self-employed and very small firms. We will consider only firms in NACE sectors up to category 64: agriculture; mining; manufacturing; electricity, gas and water; construction; trade; transport; and post and telecommunications. The firms in our samples account for about 40% of total employment in the economy in Poland and about 70% in the Czech Republic (Table 5.3).

With respect to subsidies, the important sectors thus excluded from our sample are housing (subsidies to housing co-operatives are better thought of as subsidies to households rather than to firms) and the financial sector (a very special case altogether). Budgetary subsidies to the firms in the final samples amount to 2% of 1991 GDP in Poland and 4% of 1992 GDP in the Czech Republic (Table 5.3). It is also important to note that the sectoral data do not reflect aggregate patterns in sectors where small firms and self-employment are numerous – notably trade and agriculture (the latter especially in Poland, where in 1993 90% of agricultural employment was in small private farms; this is the main reason why the employment coverage of the sample is lower in Poland than in the Czech Republic).

Table 5.4 presents a classification of firms according to how much of their annual revenue was received in the form of budgetary subsidies:[1] first by the number of firms, then weighted by their employment,[2] then by their total revenue, and finally by the amount of budgetary subsidies they received. The pattern for

Table 5.3   Description of enterprise samples

	Poland	Czech Republic
Year	1991	1992
No. of firms	37 720	11 719
Employment		
Persons (thousands)	6 377	3 536
As % of employment in total economy	42	72
Subsidies		
In billion zloty/million crowns	16 071	35 858
As % of GDP	2	4

Firm coverage: All business entities excluding small firms and self-employed.
Sectoral coverage: NACE 01-64 (Agriculture, fishing and forestry; Mining; Manufacturing; Electricity, gas and water; Construction; Trade; Transport; Post and telecommunications).

Note: Polish figure for subsidies includes a small residual category for 'other income'.

Table 5.4 Distribution of budgetary subsidies, employment and revenue in enterprises by subsidy rate

Subsidies/revenue (%)	Poland (1991) Share of group in total (%)				Czech Republic (1992) Share of group in total (%)			
	No. of firms	Employment	Revenue	Subsidies	No. of firms	Employment	Revenue	Subsidies
0	91.0	74.7	83.8	0.2	78.0	67.7	68.2	0.2
0–1	2.9	7.7	6.3	2.1	5.4	9.2	9.1	1.9
1–5	2.8	4.4	3.8	8.9	9.9	10.9	11.8	9.6
5–25	2.6	11.2	5.2	60.1	5.0	10.8	9.1	51.3
>25	0.9	2.0	0.9	28.7	1.8	1.4	1.8	37.1
All firms	100.0	100.0	100.0	100.0	100.0	100.0	100.0	100.0
	(37 720 firms)	(6.4 million persons)	(1 473 trillion zloty)	(16 trillion zloty)	(11 719 firms)	(3.5 million persons)	(1 615 billion crowns)	(35 billion crowns)

Note: Totals do not sum to 100% due to rounding.

Table 5.5 Concentration of budgetary subsidies in the largest subsidy recipients

Recipients of largest subsidies	Poland (1991)			Czech Republic (1992)		
	Share of total subsidies (%)	Share of total employment (%)	Share of total revenue (%)	Share of total subsidies (%)	Share of total employment (%)	Share of total revenue (%)
5 firms with biggest subsidies	30.2	4.8	2.7	34.7	4.2	3.6
10 biggest	37.0	5.1	2.9	45.2	6.1	6.8
25 biggest	52.1	6.4	3.7	61.3	7.6	11.9
50 biggest	68.1	8.3	6.3	72.3	9.3	14.2
100 biggest	79.8	10.8	8.1	79.7	10.8	16.6

the two countries is very similar: about 85–90% of all firms in the samples, around 80% of total employment in the samples, and 75–90% of total revenues, are in firms receiving virtually no subsidies (i.e. firms where subsidies make up 1% or less of their total revenue). Close to 90% of total employment in both country samples is in firms where subsidies make up a small fraction of total income (5% or less of total revenues). The data confirm the pattern in government spending noted in the previous section: already by the second year of transition, most of the enterprise sector is budgetary-subsidy-free. The concentration of budgetary subsidies is actually even more marked than these figures indicate, as Table 5.5 shows. In both countries, the five firms receiving the biggest subsidies account for over 30% of total budgetary subsidies; the top 25 firms account for over half.

The sectoral distribution of budgetary subsidies is very uneven and is closely related to the pattern of remaining price controls, as expected (Table 5.6). In both countries, the transport sector receives about 35–40% of total subsidies. In Poland, mining was the other large subsidy recipient, receiving 37% of total subsidies in 1991 (mining subsidies were cut sharply in the fall of 1991 when coal prices were liberalized); in the Czech Republic the other large subsidy recipient was agriculture, with about one-quarter of total subsidies. The fraction of total revenues of firms in these subsidized sectors received in the form of budgetary subsidies ranges from 5 to 18%. The remaining sectors account for about 30% or so of total subsidies but 85% of total employment. A more detailed look at the enterprise-level data confirms the view that subsidies are closely linked to remaining price controls and/or provision of public services. In the Polish data, for example, of the top 25 subsidy recipients in the sample, 15 were coal mines, 3 were rail or municipal transport enterprises, and 6 were in the forestry sector.

In both countries, prices of manufactured goods were virtually all liberalized, and consequently manufacturing is almost budgetary-subsidy-free – manufacturing firms in the country samples account for only 10% of total

Table 5.6 Sectoral distribution of budgetary subsidies, employment and revenue in enterprises

	Poland (1991) Share of sector in total (%)				Czech Republic (1992) Share of sector in total (%)			
	Subsidies	Employment	Revenue[a]	Subsidies/ revenue (%)	Subsidies	Employment[a]	Revenue[a]	Subsidies/ revenue (%)
Agriculture, forestry and fishing	13.2	10.2	3.9	3.7	24.0	12.4	10.0	5.3
Mining	39.3	5.9	4.5	9.5	8.9	5.0	4.5	4.3
Manufacturing	6.9	43.6	36.6	0.2	10.7	57.3	55.2	0.4
Electricity, gas and water	1.8	3.6	8.7	0.2	12.8	3.9	8.9	3.2
Construction	0.7	10.9	6.8	0.1	0.3	5.5	6.7	0.1
Trade	3.1	14.0	33.6	0.1	1.2	7.8	7.7	0.3
Transport	35.0	9.2	4.9	7.7	40.6	5.8	5.1	17.6
Post and telecommunications	0.0	2.6	1.2	0.0	1.5	2.4	1.8	1.8

[a] Does not sum to 100% due to rounding.

Table 5.7 Distribution of budgetary subsidies, employment and revenue in enterprises by subsidy rate: manufacturing

	Poland (1991) Share of group in total (%)				Czech Republic (1992) Share of group in total (%)			
Subsidies/revenue (%)	No. of firms[a]	Employment	Revenue[a]	Subsidies	No. of firms[a]	Employment[a]	Revenue	Subsidies
0	94.3	83.7	86.0	1.3	87.3	81.4	79.4	1.2
0–1	2.5	11.5	10.6	18.9	6.7	13.1	13.4	14.1
1–5	2.0	3.3	2.6	27.3	3.9	4.3	5.8	22.0
5–25	0.9	1.4	0.8	32.4	1.5	0.9	1.1	19.2
> 25	0.2	0.1	0.1	20.1	1.6	0.4	0.3	43.5
All firms	100.0	100.0	100.0	100.0	100.0	100.0	100.0	100.0
	(11 112 firms)	(2.8 million persons)	(538 trillion zloty)	(1.1 trillion zloty)	(4 001 firms)	(2.0 million persons)	(891 billion crowns)	(3.8 billion crowns)

[a] Does not sum to 100% due to rounding.

subsidies (compared to about one-half of total employment) and receive less than one-half of one per cent of their total revenue in the form of subsidies. The total volume of budgetary subsidies to manufacturing firms is equivalent to less than one-half of one per cent of GDP in the years covered, and aggregate data indicate this figure would be lower still in 1994. The near absence of budgetary subsidies to manufacturing firms is worth stressing. Table 5.7 presents data on the distribution of manufacturing firms by subsidy rate (subsidy/total revenue in per cent). In both countries, in year 2 of liberalized prices about 95% of manufacturing firms, employment and revenues was accounted for by practically budgetary-subsidy-free firms (subsidy/revenue <1%). Again, 1994 figures would be higher still.

I now turn to the question of how budgetary subsidies are allocated to those few firms that do receive them. The key issue is whether subsidies are simply 'objective subsidies' meant to influence only the price of a good, or whether firm-specific characteristics, notably production costs, are used when setting subsidies. That is, are (the few remaining) subsidies to firms set according to 'market principles', or in the same fashion that subsidies were set under the socialist system? Unfortunately the enterprise data we have been using do not allow a simple answer to this question.

The data show quite clearly a negative relationship between pre-subsidy profit and subsidy rates, with a large clustering around a -45° line (Figures 5.1 and 5.2) where firms are receiving subsidies to match their losses. We have only

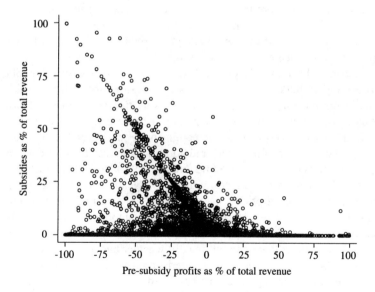

Figure 5.1 Subsidies and pre-subsidy profits: Poland 1991

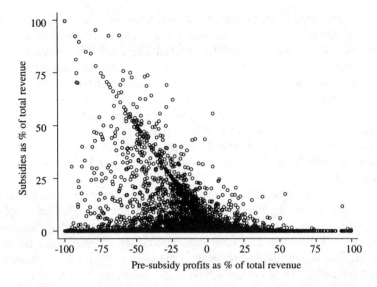

Figure 5.2   Subsidies and pre-subsidy profits: Czech Republic 1992

general industrial classification codes for what are for the most part multi-product firms, however. We simply cannot reliably distinguish in the data between average subsidy rates which are different across firms because production costs are different (and thus the more inefficient producers 'need' bigger subsidies or else they would have to shut down or lay off workers) and average subsidy rates which are different because subsidies are highly product specific and different firms produce different amounts of these products.

To summarize: firm-level data from Poland (1991) and the Czech Republic (1992) covering the bulk of their enterprise sectors confirm the view that nearly all firms in these countries are budgetary-subsidy-free or nearly so. Those budgetary subsidies which were distributed to firms were very sector specific and for the most part closely related to remaining price controls and/or provision of public services. Prices of manufactured goods in both countries were nearly all liberalized, and consequently we find that about 95% of the manufacturing sectors in both countries was already virtually budgetary-subsidy-free by the second year of liberalized prices. In these years the data indicate that total budgetary subsidies to manufacturing firms amounted to less than one-half of one per cent of GDP, and the figure is likely to be still lower in 1994. The enterprise data do not allow us to tell readily whether budgetary subsidies to firms are being set with firm-specific characteristics in mind (notably production costs), but even if this is taking place the very limited extent of remaining subsidies means this practice would not in aggregate be of much significance.

5.4 Tax Arrears

The rest of the chapter examines the problem of tax arrears of firms – tax liabilities accrued and known to the tax authorities, but unpaid – in the leading transition countries. Since most tax arrears are unlikely to be paid in full eventually (more on this below), we may reasonably consider the flow of tax arrears to be a form of government subsidy. I begin with estimates of the aggregate scale of tax arrears in the Visegrád countries. Basic data are presented in Table 5.8. To interpret these numbers we must first consider some measurement issues.

These figures are dominated by the overdue tax liabilities of enterprises; overdue personal income tax liabilities and other household/personal taxes will be small. Furthermore, most personal income tax and individual social security contributions are collected by firms in PAYE schemes. To the extent that these latter kinds of tax arrears exist, most will probably originate in taxes nominally 'paid' by employees but not passed on to the tax authorities by the firm.

An important measurement problem is whether interest on overdue taxes is included in the reported stock of tax arrears. The penalty interest rate in Poland and Hungary is linked to the central bank's interest rate, but the rates are not much higher than the going rate for bank credit, and the real interest rate on tax arrears in both countries is on the order of 20% p.a.[3] The Hungarian figure for tax arrears includes interest but the Polish figure consists of only the principal due. Both real interest rates and inflation have been high in Poland since the start of transition. According to one estimate, if interest were included, the figure in Table 5.8 for the stock of tax arrears in Poland would double, i.e. the true figure for total tax and social security arrears in Poland is of the order of 8–10% of GDP.

A second measurement problem concerns reschedulings. About half of the stock of (non-social security) tax arrears in Poland consists of tax liabilities

Table 5.8 Tax and social security arrears in the Visegrád countries (in percent of GDP; end-period values)

Country	end-1992	end-1993
Czech Republic	~2	~4
Coverage: interest/late penalties included (but see text).		
Hungary	5.8	6.9
Coverage: unrescheduled tax and social security arrears only; rescheduled arrears are not included. Interest/late penalties included.		
Poland	3.8	4.6
Coverage: all principal of tax and social security arrears, including rescheduled arrears. Interest/late penalties not included.	.	
Slovak Republic	n.a.	5.4
Coverage: not specified in source.		

Sources: National Bank of Hungary; Polish Central Statistical Office; Polish Social Security Fund; *Central European Business Weekly*; local press reports and sources; and author's estimates.

which went unpaid and were then subsequently formally rescheduled with the authorities (I have no data on reschedulings of social security arrears). The Hungarian figure includes only unrescheduled tax arrears and interest on these arrears; overdue taxes subsequently rescheduled, and the interest on these rescheduled arrears, are not included. The relatively low figure for the interest component of social security arrears in mid-1994 in Hungary suggests reschedulings may have been substantial.[4]

A rough estimate based on the above information and the data in Table 5.8 would be that the total stock of tax arrears in Poland and Hungary as of end-1993, including both interest and rescheduled overdue taxes, amounted to about 8–10% of GDP. Assuming the total stock of tax arrears at the start of transition in 1989–90 was near zero yields an estimate of an average annual flow of tax arrears in these countries, including both new tax arrears and interest on old tax arrears, of about 2% of GDP. Separate estimates for 1993 alone suggest a flow of tax arrears of about 2% of GDP in both countries, with new tax arrears and the real component of interest on old tax arrears being of comparable size.[5] Another complication concerns write-offs of tax arrears. I have no information on how much of this has taken place in these countries. Including the flow of write-offs of tax arrears would raise still further our estimate of the annual flow of tax arrears.

In both the Czech and Slovak Republics, the stock of tax arrears at the end of 1993 was about 4–5% of GDP (Table 5.8). The Czech figure is an estimate and in principle includes some but possibly not all interest and late penalties;[6] I have no information on how the Slovak figure was calculated. The Czech figures suggest a flow of tax arrears in 1993 of about 2% of GDP, again inclusive of interest and penalties. Thus, while the stocks of tax arrears in the Czech and Slovak Republics are substantial but smaller than those in Hungary and Poland, the recent flow of tax arrears in the Czech Republic appears to be comparable in scale to those in Hungary and Poland.

Finally, aggregate data from Hungary suggest that only a small portion of tax arrears are likely to be recovered. The Hungarian Tax Office (APEH) estimated that only about 15–20% of the end-1993 stock of tax arrears was recoverable (Table 5.9). The annual collection rate in Hungary in 1993–94 for overdue social security debts was about 7–8% (Table 5.9). These aggregate data support the view that tax arrears can be considered a form of government subsidy (we consider the firm-level evidence in favour of this in the next section).

The flow of tax arrears in the Visegrád countries is therefore substantial but not enormous: at roughly 2% of GDP per annum, it is about the same size or smaller than the flow of budgetary subsidies to enterprises. Total tax revenue in these countries is on the order of 40–50% of GDP. If we remove the interest component from the annual flow of tax arrears in these countries (say half),[7] we find that something like 98% of taxes accrued (excluding, of course, taxes evaded) are actually paid.

Table 5.9   Tax and social security arrears in Hungary and the composition of
government tax revenue (stocks are end-period)

	1991	1992	1993	1994 June 30
Tax and social security arrears: Interest included, rescheduled arrears not included. (*Sources:* National Bank of Hungary, press reports, author's estimates)				
In billion forints:				
Total tax and social security arrears	n.a.	160–165	243	n.a.
Taxes	n.a.	65–70	95	n.a.
Social security	~55	94	148	182
o.w. interest on social security arrears				~35
Memo items:				
Recoverable tax arrears (Tax Office estimate)		10–15	15–18	
Overdue social security debts collected			12.8	6.7
In % of GDP:				
Total tax and social security arrears	n.a.	~5.8	6.9	n.a.
Taxes	n.a.	~2.4	2.7	n.a.
Social security	2.3	3.4	4.2	~4.9
Composition of total tax revenue in % of GDP (*Source:* IMF (1994))				
Total tax revenue	45.5	42.7	43.6	
of which:				
Profit tax	5.7	2.6	2.2	
Personal income tax	7.5	7.9	8.4	
VAT and excises	13.9	13.6	14.3	
Customs duties	2.7	3.4	2.5	
Social security	14.1	14.1	14.3	
Other	1.6	1.1	1.9	

I now turn to the composition of tax arrears in Poland and Hungary. Tables 5.9
and 5.10 present a breakdown by type of tax of the stock of tax arrears in Poland
and Hungary, along with a corresponding breakdown of government tax revenue.
The main difference in the structure of tax arrears in the two countries derives
from the overrepresentation of the 'popiwek', the excess wage tax, in the stock
of tax arrears in Poland. Wages paid by Polish firms (after 1990, state-owned
firms only) above a certain norm were taxed at penal rates, and this tax was
highly unpopular. Firms could test the credibility of the government by paying
high wages anyway and not paying the tax. The most notorious such case is the
Polish state railways; this firm alone accounted for about half of all popiwek
arrears in 1991. Furthermore, popiwek arrears are relatively old compared to
other tax arrears, and much was accrued in 1990–91. An upward adjustment for
accrued interest would increase still further the proportion of the popiwek in
total tax arrears. These points apply as well to the 'dividend' tax (a lump-sum
assets-based tax), another SOE (state-owned enterprise) tax which is

Table 5.10   Tax and social security arrears in Poland and the composition of government tax revenue (stocks are end-period)

	1991	1992	1993
Tax and social security arrears: Interest not included, rescheduled arrears included. (*Sources:* Central Statistical Office, Social Security Fund, press reports, author's estimates)			
In trillion zloty:			
Total tax and social security arrears	30.3	43.2	71.6
Taxes	26.1	28.5	41.3
(of which, rescheduled)	(12.2)	(14.2)	(19.3)
of which:			
Turnover tax, VAT, excises	2.8	6.3	8.7
Profit taxes	3.8	4.2	7.1
Excess wage tax ('popiwek')	12.0	10.2	17.9
'Dividend' tax on state-owned firms	5.6	6.5	6.5
Other taxes	1.9	1.3	1.1
Social security	4.2	14.7	30.3
In % of GDP:			
Total tax and social security arrears	3.7	3.8	4.6
Taxes	3.2	2.5	2.6
Turnover tax, VAT, excises	0.3	0.6	0.6
Profit taxes	0.5	0.4	0.5
Tax on excess wage increases ('popiwek')	1.5	0.9	1.1
'Dividend' tax on state-owned firms	0.7	0.6	0.4
Other taxes	0.2	0.1	0.1
Social security	0.5	1.3	1.9
Composition of total tax revenue in % of GDP (*Sources:* IMF (1994) and author's estimates)			
Total non-tax revenue	37.6	40.2	42.0
of which:			
Turnover tax/VAT and excises	7.4	9.0	10.6
Profit tax	6.1	4.6	5.3
Tax on excess wage increases ('popiwek')	3.3	1.5	0.6
'Dividend' tax on state-owned firms	1.5	0.7	0.5
Wage tax/personal income tax	2.4	6.3	9.1
Customs duties	2.1	2.3	2.1
Social security	9.9	10.7	9.9
Other	4.9	5.7	4.5

disproportionately represented in the stock of tax arrears. While important in stock terms, in recent years arrears on these two taxes are now less important in flow terms. The principal due on these taxes increased relatively little in real terms in 1992–93 (Table 5.10), meaning the bulk of the flow of 'popiwek' and 'dividend' arrears in these years would be interest on past arrears. This is largely because these taxes declined in importance both in terms of budget revenue and in terms of economic policy.

If we exclude the popiwek and the dividend from the stock of tax arrears in Poland, we find that the structure of the remainder is similar to the structure of tax arrears in Hungary, where social security arrears make up over half of the total. Social security arrears also appear to be the main source of the current flow of tax arrears in these countries. I estimate the real flow of social security arrears alone in Poland and Hungary to be about 1% or so of GDP, again with the flow of new arrears and interest on existing arrears being of comparable size.[8] Social security tax rates in all the Visegrád countries are high by international standards, at about 40–50%. This tax is the single largest tax paid by enterprises; social security receipts in the Visegrád countries amount to about 10–15% of GDP, compared to about 10% for VAT and about 5% for corporate income tax. Unlike corporate income tax, it is accrued by all firms, not just profitable ones (this point will become relevant below).

The natural questions to ask are how is the stock of tax arrears distributed, and how is the flow allocated, in these countries. In the next section we investigate these questions using evidence from enterprise surveys in Hungary and Poland.

5.5 The Distribution and Allocation of Tax Arrears

The enterprise survey data we will use were collected as part of the World Bank Research Project on Enterprise Behaviour and Economic Reform. Surveys of approximately 200 manufacturing firms were conducted in late 1993 (Poland) and early 1994 (Hungary). The information collected included both detailed economic data (balance sheet, income statement, etc.) and responses of top management to a questionnaire. The firms surveyed included state-owned, privatized, and *de novo* private firms. A more detailed description of the survey, and an initial analysis of the Polish data, can be found in Belka *et al.* (1994). The data collected in the surveys include information on tax payables (including social security liabilities), broken down according to not in arrears, overdue less than 3 months, overdue 3 months to 1 year, and overdue more than one year.[9] These figures include both principal and interest on overdue taxes (but not, in principle, overdue taxes subsequently rescheduled). We will use these data to draw some conclusions about the distribution of tax arrears.

Total tax and social security arrears in the surveyed firms amount to about 4–5% of total 1993 annual sales in both samples. Applying this ratio to figures for aggregate manufacturing in the two countries yields a rough estimate of about 4% of GDP in (unrescheduled) tax arrears (including interest) in the manufacturing sector in late 1993/early 1994 in the two countries. As noted above, the aggregate Hungarian and Polish data on tax arrears in the total economy (not just manufacturing) yield a figure of about 8–10% of GDP, and manufacturing makes up about one-half of total enterprise sector activity. The surveys seem, therefore, to be at least moderately consistent with aggregate data on the volume of tax arrears.

Table 5.11   Firms with tax arrears in Polish and Hungarian enterprise surveys

	Poland (205 firms)	Hungary (174 firms)
Firms with no overdue taxes		
Number	134	104
Percentage of total firms	65.4	59.8
Firms with any overdue taxes		
Number	71	70
Percentage of total firms	34.6	40.2
of which:		
Firms with any taxes overdue 3 months or more		
Number	58	37
Percentage of total firms	28.3	21.3
of which:		
Firms with any taxes overdue 1 year or more		
Number	43	18
Percentage of total firms	20.1	10.3

Note: Figures may not sum due to rounding.

Table 5.11 shows the distribution of firms holding overdue tax liabilities according to how overdue the taxes are. In both Hungary and Poland, over one-third of all the firms surveyed had some overdue taxes, and about one-quarter were seriously in arrears with the tax authorities (some taxes overdue more than three months).

Table 5.12 shows the distribution of firms holding any overdue tax liabilities according to profitability in 1993, where profitability is defined as after-tax profit as a percentage of sales. The link between profitability and tax arrears is very clear: few highly profitable firms in either country had any overdue taxes, whereas most of the most unprofitable firms did. The picture is the same if we consider only taxes seriously in arrears (overdue more than three months).[10]

Although holding some tax arrears is fairly common in the surveyed firms, the bulk of tax arrears are concentrated in the most unprofitable firms. This is clear from Table 5.13, which presents the distribution of the volume of tax arrears according to firm profitability. In both the Hungarian and Polish surveys, highly unprofitable firms (after-tax profit/sales ratios less than –25%) with tax arrears make up about 10–15% of the total samples in both countries measuring either by number of firms or by their employment, but these very unprofitable firms account for about half of all tax arrears in the samples. It follows from this that the scale of overdue taxes is also closely related to profitability. In Table 5.14 we find the ratio of overdue taxes to annual sales (as a percentage), again grouping firms according to profitability. Highly profitable firms (after-tax profit margins greater than 10%) have very few tax arrears on average, whereas the most unprofitable firms hold on average tax arrears amounting to about one-half of annual sales. As these highly unprofitable firms are also on average very highly indebted, the bulk of these tax arrears are unlikely to be repaid, and so we may

Table 5.12 Profitability and overdue taxes

Profitability (after-tax profit/sales)	Poland (200 firms)			Hungary (167 firms)		
	Firms with no overdue taxes	Firms with any overdue taxes	All firms	Firms with no overdue taxes	Firms with any overdue taxes	All firms
Profit/sales < -25%						
Number	4	21	25	7	12	19
Percentage of firms in profitability class	16.0	84.0		36.8	63.2	
-25% < Profit/sales < -10%						
Number	7	18	25	7	6	13
Percentage of firms in profitability class	28.0	72.0		53.9	46.2	
-10% < Profit/sales < 0%						
Number	20	18	38	13	14	27
Percentage of firms in profitability class	52.6	47.4		48.2	51.9	
0% < Profit/sales < 10%						
Number	81	12	93	75	16	91
Percentage of firms in profitability class	87.1	12.9		84.2	17.6	
10% < Profit/sales						
Number	19	0	19	14	3	17
Percentage of firms in profitability class	100	0.0		82.4	17.7	
Total sample						
Number	131	69	200	116	51	167
Percentage of firms	65.5	34.5		69.5	30.5	

Note: Figures may not sum due to rounding.

Table 5.13   Concentration of tax arrears and firm profitability

Firms with	Poland (198 firms)	Hungary (138 firms)
Profit/sales < -25%		
Percentage of firms	12.6	11.6
Percentage of employment	13.4	10.7
Hold percent of total tax arrears	50.1	50.5
-25% < Profit/sales < -10%		
Percentage of firms	12.6	8.0
Percentage of employment	16.1	5.5
Hold percent of total tax arrears	32.5	16.5
-10% < Profit/sales < 0%		
Percentage of firms	19.2	14.5
Percentage of employment	16.8	12.1
Hold percent of total tax arrears	11.2	7.8
0% < Profit/sales < 10%		
Percentage of firms	46.0	57.3
Percentage of employment	44.2	64.2
Hold percent of total tax arrears	6.2	15.7
10% < Profit/sales		
Percentage of firms	9.6	8.7
Percentage of employment	9.5	7.6
Hold percent of total tax arrears	0.0	9.5

Note: Figures may not sum due to rounding.

Table 5.14   Tax arrears as a percentage of annual 1993 sales, and firm profitability

Profitability (after-tax profit/sales)	Tax arrears/sales in % Polish survey (200 firms)	Tax arrears/sales in % Hungarian survey (137 firms)
Profit/sales < -25%	52	46
-25% < Profit/sales < -10%	12	27
-10% < Profit/sales < 0%	4	6
0% < Profit/sales < 10%	0.7	1
10% < Profit/sales	0.0	2.4
Total sample	5	4

Weighted averages; unweighted averages are similar.

reasonably conclude that the flow of tax arrears to these firms constitutes in effect a subsidy from the government.

Neither size, nor ownership classification, nor industrial sector is as well correlated with tax arrears. Table 5.15 presents a breakdown of firms with tax arrears according to their number of employees. In Poland large firms are more likely to have tax arrears than small firms, but the difference is not as dramatic as with profitability. In Hungary there is no clear connection with size. In both countries the highly unprofitable firms which hold the bulk of tax arrears have employment levels close to the sample average (600–700 employees per firm in both samples). Table 5.16 shows that Polish state-owned firms are more likely

Table 5.15 Size and overdue taxes

Employment	Poland (199 firms)			Hungary (143 firms)		
	Firms with no overdue taxes	Firms with any overdue taxes	All firms	Firms with no overdue taxes	Firms with any overdue taxes	All firms
Employment <51						
Number	11	4	15	18	7	25
Percentage of firms in size class	73.3	26.7		72.0	28.0	
Employment 51–250						
Number	48	18	66	25	12	37
Percentage of firms in size class	72.7	27.3		67.6	32.4	
Employment 251–1000						
Number	49	26	75	44	16	60
Percentage of firms in size class	65.3	34.7		73.3	26.7	
Employment > 1000						
Number	22	21	43	14	7	21
Percentage of firms in size class	51.2	48.8		66.7	33.3	
Total sample						
Number	130	69	199	101	42	143
Percentage of firms	65.3	34.7		70.6	29.4	

Note: Figures may not sum due to rounding.

Table 5.16 Ownership and overdue taxes

Ownership (private or state)	Poland (205 firms)			Hungary (141 firms)		
	Firms with no overdue taxes	Firms with any overdue taxes	All firms	Firms with no overdue taxes	Firms with any overdue taxes	All firms
Private sector firms						
Number	72	13	85	60	18	78
Percentage of firms in ownership class	84.7	15.3		76.9	23.1	
State sector firms						
Number	62	58	120	40	23	63
Percentage of firms in ownership class	51.7	48.3		63.5	36.5	
Total sample						
Number	134	71	205	100	41	141
Percentage of firms	65.4	34.6		70.9	29.1	

Note: Figures may not sum due to rounding.

Table 5.17 Tax-based incomes policy and overdue taxes: Polish survey (state-owned firms only)

Tax-based incomes policy ('popiwek') binding in 1991–93?	Firms with no overdue taxes	Firms with any overdue taxes	Total
No			
Number	15	29	44
Percentage of firms in 'no' group	34.1	65.9	
Yes			
Number	47	29	76
Percentage of firms in 'yes' group	61.8	38.2	
All state-owned firms			
Number	62	58	120
Percentage of firms	51.7	48.3	

Note: Figures may not sum due to rounding.

to have tax arrears than private firms, but this is not the case with Hungarian state-owned firms. This pattern may result more from profitability patterns rather than ownership *per se*; nearly all the highly unprofitable firms (23 out of 26) in the Polish sample were state-owned, compared to about half (the average for the total sample) of the highly unprofitable Hungarian firms.

Finally, we consider wages and the special case of the Polish excess wage tax, the popiwek. One might expect *a priori* that the incidence of the popiwek would be positively correlated with tax arrears, given the remarks in the preceding section about well-known cases of firms defying the excess wage tax policy by paying wages but not the tax. In fact, the opposite is the case, as Table 5.17 shows. State-owned firms are grouped according to whether the popiwek was binding in the period 1991–93. Firms in which the popiwek was not binding in this period are significantly *more* likely to have tax arrears than firms which had to pay this tax. The reason is likely that state-owned firms which can afford to pay high wages and thereby incur popiwek liabilities also have enough money to pay their taxes, whereas SOEs in financial trouble tend to pay low wages. High-wage firms in the Polish survey thus tend to have lower tax arrears on average. No such simple correlation appears in the Hungarian data, however (Table 5.18).

We now consider more formally the correlates of tax arrears. We use two different tax arrears measures: the first is a binary 1/0 variable indicating the presence of tax arrears of any size; the second, tax arrears as a percentage of the firm's sales. As just noted, some correlations between tax arrears and another variable may be driven in part by underlying patterns in firm characteristics. We therefore calculate not only simple pairwise correlations, but also partial correlations between the tax arrears variable and some other variable of interest where we hold constant firm size (measured by log employment), industrial sector (using a set of two digit industrial dummy variables) and ownership (state owned, or not).

Table 5.18 Wages and overdue taxes

Wage level	Poland (196 firms)			Hungary (125 firms)		
	Firms with no overdue taxes	Firms with any overdue taxes	All firms	Firms with no overdue taxes	Firms with any overdue taxes	All firms
Low wage firms						
Number	24	41	65	30	11	41
Percentage of low-wage firms	36.9	63.1		73.2	26.8	
Medium wage firms						
Number	45	19	64	32	16	48
Percentage of medium-wage firms	70.3	29.7		66.7	33.3	
High wage firms						
Number	59	8	67	29	7	36
Percentage of high-wage firms	88.1	11.9		80.6	19.4	
Total sample						
Number	128	68	196	91	34	125
Percentage of firms	65.3	34.7		72.8	27.2	

Note: Figures may not sum due to rounding.

The correlations are summarized in Table 5.19. Profitability is highly negatively correlated with tax arrears in Poland, whether or nor we control for other firm characteristics in the partial correlations. The correlation between profitability and tax arrears in somewhat less striking in Hungary when we look at the presence of tax arrears and it disappears altogether when we look at tax arrears as a percentage of sales. If, however, we use as our profitability measure a 1/0 variable indicating whether or not the firm is very unprofitable (profit/ sales < -25%), we find highly significant correlations in both countries; severe financial distress is strongly associated with having tax arrears and with having large tax arrears, even controlling for other firm characteristics. In the Polish sample, state ownership is strongly correlated with tax arrears. This finding, however, is to a large extent driven by low profitability in state firms; when we control for profitability as well in the partial correlation between state ownership and tax arrears (the results are not reported in the table), the significance of the state ownership variable falls considerably or disappears altogether, while the significance of the profitability variable remains high. State ownership is rather less correlated with tax arrears in Hungary. For the most part, neither wages, nor size (employment), nor industrial sector are closely associated either with the presence of any tax arrears or with the presence of large tax arrears.

We now move on to the allocation of the flow of tax arrears. We do not have time series data on overdue tax liabilities for the surveyed firms, but we do have, for the Polish firms only, balance sheet data on total tax liabilities outstanding. These data have the advantage of including any tax arrears which have been rescheduled.

The flow of tax liabilities in the surveyed Polish firms was considered explicitly in a paper by myself and three colleagues (Belka *et al.*, 1994), and I will report (and expand on) our results here. We divide the sample of firms into two groups: 'severely financially distressed' firms, defined as firms with 1993 after-tax profit margins of less than -25% of annual sales, and the remaining firms. About 13% of the sample (26 firms, 23 of which are state-owned) is 'severely financially distressed' according to this definition. We then ask how these losses were financed in the course of 1993 on the liability side of the balance sheet: by (nominal) increases in trade credit received (suppliers shipping goods and not being paid), by (nominal) increases in bank credit, or by (nominal) increases in total tax liabilities.

The results are reproduced in Table 5.20. All nominal flows are measured as a percentage of annual sales. The severely financially distressed firms are receiving somewhat larger nominal flows of trade credit than the remaining firms, but the differences are not great and the flow is small relative to total losses. The picture is almost identical with respect to the nominal flow of bank credit: the financially distressed group receives a somewhat larger, but still small, nominal flow of bank credit than the non-distressed group. The key difference between the two groups is in the change in the nominal stock of tax liabilities in the course of 1993. The financially distressed group accumulates additional nominal

Table 5.19 Correlates of tax arrears

	Poland survey (195–205 firms)		Hungary survey (88–167 firms)	
	Tax arrears yes/no (1/0)	Tax arrears as % of sales	Tax arrears yes/no (1/0)	Tax arrears as % of sales
Profitability				
Pairwise correlation	- - -	- - -	- - -	0
Partial correlation	- - -	- - -	-	0
Financial distress				
Pairwise correlation	+++	+++	+++	+
Partial correlation	+++	+++	+++	+++
Wage				
Pairwise correlation	-	0	0	0
Partial correlation	0	0	0	0
Employment				
Pairwise correlation	+	+	0	0
Partial correlation	0	0	0	0
State ownership (1/0)				
Pairwise correlation	+++	+++	0	0
Partial correlation	+++	+++	+	+
Industrial dummy variables (partial correlation only)				
Food processing	0	0	- - -	0
Light	0	0	0	0
Chemicals etc.	0	0	-	0
Metallurgy	0	0	[n.a.]	[n.a.]
Metals	0	0	0	0
Machinery	0	0	0	0
Electronics etc.	0	0	0	0
Building materials	0	0	0	0
Other	[dropped]	[dropped]	[dropped]	[dropped]

+++ (- - -) Positively (negatively) correlated, significant at 0.1% level.
++ (- -)   Positively (negatively) correlated, significant at 1% level.
+ (-)   Positively (negatively) correlated, significant at 5% level.
0   Not correlated at 5% level.
n.a.   Not applicable.

Notes:
Tax arrears yes/no: = 1 if firm has any tax arrears , = 0 if not.
Profitability = ln(sales/costs).
Financial distress: = 1 if profit/sales < -25%, = 0 if not.
Wage = ln(wage).
Employment = ln(employment).
State ownership: = 1 if majority state owned, = 0 if not.
Pairwise correlations:
   If both continuous variables, significance of correlation coefficient.
   If one continuous variable and one 1/0 variable, significance for a *t*-test on continuous variable differing in two sub-samples as defined by the 1/0 variable.
   If both 1/0 variables, significance of coefficient of one variable in logit regression on the other variable.
Partial correlations:
   For presence of tax arrears (1/0), significance of coefficient of the variable of interest in a logit regression also including industry dummies, size (log employment) and a state-ownership dummy variable.
   For tax arrears as a percentage of sales, significance of partial correlation coefficient of the variable of interest, also holding constant industry, size (log employment) and state ownership.

tax liabilities amounting to the equivalent of a remarkable 46% of annual sales, compared to only 2% for the remaining firms.

A rough estimate based on the figures in Table 5.20 is that perhaps two-thirds of the increase in liabilities to the state could be due to penalty interest on tax arrears, meaning that a substantial portion of the flow of liabilities is new tax arrears (on the order of the equivalent of 15% of annual sales). This suggests the flow of new tax arrears is probably central to keeping these firms afloat. Another piece of evidence consistent with this can be seen from the figures in the table for operating profit, defined here as revenues minus accrued costs (included accrued taxes) before depreciation, interest charges and exceptional charges.[11] The severely financially distressed group are on average making significant losses (-16%) even by this definition, and the individual variation within the group is not great (three-quarters of these firms are failing to cover their core costs by this definition). Total taxes accrued by this group amounts to about 30% of annual sales, meaning that if on average they did not pay half their taxes they would be able to stay afloat.

Table 5.20 Polish survey: severely financially distressed firms and the financing of losses

All quantities measured as a percentage of 1993 sales	26 Financially distressed firms (1993 profitability < -25%)	177 Other firms
'Operating profit', 1993	-16.0	14.0
Net profit after tax, 1993	-76.1	0.5
Change in payables to suppliers 1.1.93–31.12.93	8.8	3.0
Change in bank debt 1.1.93–31.12.93	9.1	2.5
Change in tax and social security liabilities 1.1.93–31.12.93	46.3	2.0
Memo items: Tax and social security liabilities in % of 1993 sales		
1.1.93	34.0	4.7
31.12.93	80.3	6.7
Taxes and social security contributions during 1993, in % of 1993 sales (accruals basis)	31.2	17.0
Equity/debt ratio, end-1993	-0.1	1.2
Distribution of debt in % (end-1993)		
Total	100	100
Firms (trade creditors)	41	48
Banks	16	24
Government	41	22
Other	2	7

Source: Belka et al. (1994).

Note: Weighted averages (aggregates); unweighted means are similar.
Operating profit = revenues minus accrued costs (included accrued taxes) before depreciation, interest charges and exceptional charges.

Finally, Belka *et al.* show that these firms are indeed staying afloat. The financially distressed group is shedding substantial amounts of labour – over half of them shed 10% or more of their labour force in 1993, compared to about a quarter of the rest of the sample. What is striking is that these firms shared in the general economic expansion in Poland in 1993 – three-quarters of these firms actually increased their sales in real terms in 1993, almost as large a proportion as in the rest of the sample.

We can use the survey results to estimate in a very rough fashion the flow of tax arrears to Polish and Hungarian manufacturing firms in two ways. First, as calculated above, applying the aggregate tax arrears/sales ratio in the two country samples to total manufacturing sales yields a figure for tax arrears of manufacturing firms of about 4% of GDP, or on average about 1% p.a. in the transition period. This figure is an underestimate to the extent that rescheduled tax arrears are not reported by the firms in the sample as 'overdue taxes'.

Second, for the Polish survey only, we can make an estimate based on the increase in tax liabilities of the severely financially distressed firms. We first need to adjust the flow downwards to account for simple inflation effects, i.e. to remove the inflation component from the nominal interest charged on tax arrears. A very rough guess would be that perhaps half of the total nominal increase would result from the inflation component of penalty interest. We then make the extreme assumption that the rest (the equivalent of about 20–25% of annual sales) is composed entirely of new tax arrears plus real interest on existing tax arrears. Taking this figure as an upper-limit estimate of the flow of tax arrears to severely financially distressed manufacturing firms, and assuming financially distressed firms account for the same proportion of total manufacturing as they do in the sample (10% or so), we arrive at an annual flow of tax arrears to severely financially distressed manufacturing firms amounting to perhaps 2% of GDP or less. This estimate captures both rescheduled and unrescheduled tax arrears, but also legitimate (non-overdue) increases in tax liabilities; on the other hand, it misses the tax arrears of non-financially-distressed firms. The difference between the two estimates is not small, but the results are nevertheless striking: comparing these figures to those in the previous section on budgetary subsidies, we see that the flow of tax arrears to manufacturing firms is far larger than the flow of budgetary subsidies to manufacturing firms.

Belka *et al.* suggest the following interpretation of the observed flow of tax liabilities in the Polish survey. Most firms, including state-owned firms, try to stay current with their tax payments. When state-owned firms are in severe financial distress, however, they cannot stay current with all their creditors and must re-prioritize their payments. Such firms apparently respond by running tax arrears so as to be able to continue to pay suppliers and workers and thus continue to survive. So long as the government (or other creditors) do not put the firm into bankruptcy, the strategy is successful and firms are able to avoid immediate closure. In effect, severely financially distressed firms are able in this way to extract subsidies from the government. (We saw earlier the importance of social security arrears in the total stock of tax arrears; non-payment of social security means that these firms in effect start to receive a 40–50% wage subsidy.)

To summarize: over one-third of the firms in the Polish and Hungarian surveys have some overdue taxes. A relatively small number of highly unprofitable firms hold the bulk of these overdue taxes, and the scale of overdue taxes held by these firms is very large relative to their turnover. In the Polish survey, these unprofitable firms with lots of tax arrears are nearly all state-owned firms; in the Hungarian survey, about half are state-owned. In neither country sample are tax arrears well correlated with size (employment). With respect to the flow of tax arrears, the analysis by Belka *et al.* of the Polish survey data indicates that the firms in severe financial distress, nearly all of which are state-owned, are in effect being financed largely by a flow of tax liabilities; and thus financed, they are managing to survive.

Why is it that government tax collectors do not respond by vigorously pursuing these firms into bankruptcy? I offer here a few possible reasons.

The priority of government in satisfying claims of bankrupt firms is probably *not* central to the explanation. In Poland, the state treasury and social security authorities have top priority in bankruptcy proceedings, and yet the tax authorities do not move in and shut down financially distressed firms running tax arrears. The likely low rate of return to such an action is probably important, however. Financially distressed firms are highly indebted (the 26 such firms in the Polish survey were on average negative equity firms), and the market value of their assets is probably very low. I note here in passing that in the Czech Republic tax claims also get top priority in the settlement of claims, but that in Hungary these claims come after secured creditors. This would suggest that in Hungary the tax authorities will be still more reluctant to take firms into bankruptcy.

Another important factor is probably the social and political consequences of shutting down a firm. We might reasonably expect the local tax authorities to face political pressures to tolerate tax arrears instead of bankrupting a firm and making its workforce redundant. It is surprising, though, that the survey results showed that tax arrears are not significantly correlated with employment. A related point is that one can make an economic argument for tolerating tax arrears: these firms, to the extent they are able to survive by selling their products and paying their suppliers, are generating positive value added, and the reallocation of the productive resources they use would be slow given the economic environment.

Finally, local tax authorities might see a potential pay-off to waiting, e.g. for the firm to be rescued by central government, or for a bad debt workout scheme to be applied to the firm, or for the firm to share in general economic recovery.

5.6   Conclusions

The purpose of this chapter has been to document magnitudes and look for empirical patterns. What I shall do by way of conclusion is summarize the main findings and consider some policy implications.

Budgetary subsidies in the Visegrád countries, at 3–5% of GDP, are close to the Western European norm; they are, moreover, mostly sector specific and relate primarily to remaining price regulations, e.g. public transport. Manufacturing, and hence the tradables sector, is mostly budgetary-subsidy-free. Some of the more potentially contentious policy issues regarding budgetary subsidies – notably that of state aids to industry – are therefore not likely to become very pressing in practice.

Tax arrears are a much different story. Aggregate data suggest that the flow of tax arrears in the Visegrád countries is significant but not enormous. Although nearly all taxes accrued are actually collected, the flow of tax arrears, on the order of 2% of GDP per annum, is not much less than the flow of budgetary subsidies. Firm-level data from Hungary and Poland suggest the flow of tax arrears to the manufacturing sector is on the order of 1% or so of GDP per annum, considerably more than the flow of budgetary subsidies to manufacturing. Both aggregate and firm-level data suggest most of these tax arrears are uncollectable and hence we can regard the flow of tax arrears as essentially a subsidy. Finally, tax arrears are being accumulated primarily by financially distressed firms, which are able to use this subsidy to help keep themselves in business. In a limited but still important sense, we are seeing the re-emergence of the 'soft budget constraint' in these transition countries.

An obvious lesson from the above is that a full analysis of state aids to industry should include tax arrears as a possible form of state aid; the finding that the flow of tax arrears to the manufacturing sector is much larger than the flow of budgetary subsidies is striking. But what to recommend that these countries should do about their tax arrears problems is less obvious. I will offer here only a few observations. First, governments should engage in formal tax forgiveness programmes only with extreme caution or avoid them altogether, primarily because of moral-hazard problems. Any formal tax forgiveness programme runs the serious risk of decreasing subsequent tax discipline. Tying tax forgiveness to one-off events is a help but may not be enough. The Polish government, for example, recently introduced a partial tax forgiveness programme for taxes which were being discontinued or phased out;[12] but this may have deleterious effects on the government's ability now and in the future to collect taxes which are perceived to be temporary (e.g. a re-introduced incomes policy tax), let alone on its ability to collect taxes which are permanent.

A second point is that, so long as the integrity of the overall tax system is not in danger, a continuation of the status quo is tolerable. Nearly all taxes accrued are being collected and tax discipline is fairly high; the main culprits running tax arrears are severely financially distressed firms which for the most part do not have the money to pay. Heavy-handed attempts to collect taxes from these firms (e.g. shutting them down and trying to liquidate the assets of the firm) would not yield much revenue, and redeployment of their assets and labour forces would be difficult in practice. In the meantime, since they appear to be covering their costs to suppliers, they are, with the aid of the tax arrears subsidy, generating positive value added.

If the status quo is tolerable in the short run, we may conclude as follows. First, CEEC governments should maintain existing tax collection efforts and possibly introduce new measures to keep the tax arrears flow problem under control but should try to avoid tax forgiveness programmes. Second, introduction of effective debt workout schemes and reorganization and liquidation procedures would help solve the tax arrears problem. Both the tax arrears stock problem and the tax arrears flow problem are located primarily in financially distressed and highly indebted firms, and so these problems should gradually decline in scale as debt workout schemes are introduced, as bankruptcy and liquidation procedures become more frequently used, as market demand for assets of liquidated firms increases, etc. The design of workout schemes should moreover take account of the fact that there is apparently a continuing tax arrears flow problem to distressed and highly indebted firms.[13]

Notes

1. The Polish category is actually for 'subsidies and other income', but the upward bias introduced is on average very small.
2. Because the Czech data derive from several different databases, the employment coverage excludes a number of (mostly small) firms.
3. In Hungary in 1993 the penalty interest rate was about 40% (defined as twice the National Bank of Hungary refinancing rate, which in 1993 was about 20% p.a.). By comparison, the average commercial bank lending rate was about 25%, and the maximum commercial bank lending rate was close to 40% (NBH *Monthly Review* 8.94). December–December CPI inflation in 1993 was 21.1%.
4. The amount of interest on social security arrears in mid-1994 was about 35 billion forints. Six months' of interest on the end-1993 stock of arrears amounts to nearly this much (leaving no room for all the interest accrued prior to end-1991). This discrepancy could have been caused by reschedulings, since rescheduling arrears has the effect of removing interest on the arrears from the stock. Another possibility is that the social security authorities have not been charging full interest on arrears.
5. If inflation is substantial it is important not to take the entire nominal increase in tax arrears as an estimate of the real flow; to obtain the real flow, one must subtract the inflation component of the nominal increase. Why this is so can be seen most simply from a hypothetical case in which all firms pay their taxes in full (including interest) one year late, and hence the real flow of tax arrears is zero. In a steady state with inflation, the tax arrears/GDP ratio will be constant, but the nominal stock of tax arrears grows at the rate of inflation.

   The nominal increase in unrescheduled tax arrears in Hungary in 1993, including interest, was about Ft 80 billion (Table 5.9). CPI inflation in Hungary in 1993 was 21.1% (December–December). The pure inflation component of the nominal increase was about Ft 40 billion, making for a real flow of about Ft 40 billion, or about 1% or so of GDP. This is underestimated, possibly significantly, because decreases due to reschedulings are not accounted for (see note 4). The nominal increase in tax arrears in Poland in 1993, excluding interest, was zloty 28 billion (Table 5.10). CPI inflation in Poland in 1993 was 37.6% (December–December). The pure inflation component of the nominal increase was about zloty 16 trillion, making for a real increase in principal only of about zloty 12 trillion. The real interest rate component of the flow of tax arrears in 1993 would have been (assuming the stock figures in Table 5.10 need to be doubled to allow for accrued interest) perhaps zloty 15–25 trillion, making for a total real flow of tax arrears in 1993 of about 2% of GDP.

6. There are two reasons why not all late penalties may be included. First, the end-1993 figure is the sum of the end-1992 stock of tax arrears and tax arrears deriving from the 1993 tax year; it is not clear if penalties on end-1992 tax arrears accrued in the course of 1993 would be included. Second, 1993 was the first year of the new tax system in the Czech Republic, and it has been reported that the tax authorities may understandably have been lenient in assessing penalties on late tax payments resulting from mistakes made by tax-payers, etc.

7. Annual real interest on a stock of 5% of GDP in tax arrears (the average for the transition period) would amount to about 1% of GDP in Poland or Hungary. See also note 5.

8. In Hungary, the stock of unrescheduled social security arrears (including interest) amounted to 3.4% of GDP at end-1992. Nominal arrears (including interest) increased in 1993 by about 50–60%. CPI inflation in 1993 was 21.1%, which would make for a real increase in 1993 of about 1% of GDP, with interest on old arrears and the flow of new arrears of comparable size. However, the reported figure for interest due on these arrears in mid-1994 is quite low, suggesting that these are underestimates because of outflows of unscheduled arrears and the associated interest following reschedulings (see note 4).

In Poland, the increase in the stock of social security arrears in 1993 (excluding interest) was zloty 16 trillion; minus the pure inflation component gives an increase in principal of about zloty 10 trillion. Real interest on the stock adds perhaps another zloty 15 trillion or so, for a total increase of about 2% of GDP.

9. Tax liabilities are not the same thing as tax arrears; a firm may have a tax liability which is not yet due to be paid.

10. The link between profitability and overdue taxes in the Hungarian data becomes nearly as marked as in the Polish data if we consider only taxes overdue 3 months or more (results not reported here).

11. Penalty interest on tax arrears is apparently included in exceptional charges rather than in financial costs.

12. 50% of interest due and 10% of the principal due was to be forgiven if firms paid the remainder.

13. For a detailed analysis of the framework for and experience with workouts, reorganizations and liquidations in both Hungary and Poland, see Baer and Gray (1995).

References

Baer, H. L. and Gray, C. W. (1995), 'Debt as a control device in transitional economies: the experiences of Hungary and Poland', World Bank, mimeo, 6 January.

Barbone, L. and Marchetti, D. jr. (1994), 'Economic transformation and the fiscal crisis', World Bank Policy Research Working Paper 1286, April.

Belka, M., Estrin, S., Schaffer, M. E. and Singh, I. J. (1994), 'Enterprise adjustment in Poland: evidence from a survey of 200 private, privatized and state-owned firms', paper presented at the World Bank Workshop on Enterprise Adjustment in Eastern Europe, Washington, DC, September.

IMF (1994), *World Economic Outlook*, October.

6

Unemployment Insurance and Incentives in Hungary: Preliminary Evidence*

John Micklewright and Gyula Nagy

6.1   Introduction

Throughout Eastern Europe, an economic system that guaranteed jobs is being replaced by one that guarantees unemployment benefit – subject to certain conditions – in the event of job loss. Payment of unemployment benefit therefore helps underpin economic reform and the introduction of an unemployment benefit system is an important step in the transition to a market economy.

Notwithstanding their important enabling role in the transition process underway in Eastern European economies, the fear is often voiced that the benefit systems that were introduced in the region are too generous and create serious disincentives for the unemployed to find new jobs. There is a shortage of firm evidence on the issue, however. Too often a belief in widespread disincentives is based on inadequate analysis, such as cross-country comparison of illustrative benefit calculations for hypothetical individuals. This chapter provides a more rigorous analysis of the issue with very large samples of data on actual unemployed people in Hungary. The evidence uncovered casts light on whether the design of unemployment insurance should be largely influenced by its impact on incentives for re-employment, or whether such considerations as equity and sustaining support for the transition to a market economy, tempered by fiscal realism, are the more important factors.

*   We thank other participants in the EC PHARE project on 'Taxation and Tax Reform in Central and Eastern Europe' for comments on an earlier version of this chapter. We are grateful for financial support for the research to the EC ACE programme under the project 'Tax and Budget Reform in Hungary', and to the EUI Research Council. We thank the National Labour Centre for providing us with anonymized micro-data from the unemployment insurance records (we alone bear responsibility for the way they have been used and interpreted). We also thank György Lázár for his support and advice, and Ms Zsuzsa Kovács for assistance in data processing.

A notable feature of the labour market in Hungary is the low outflow rate from unemployment, a characteristic in common with labour markets in several other Eastern European countries. The rise in registered unemployment to about 14% of the labour force in early 1993 resulted more from a very low outflow rate than from a high inflow rate. Inflows each month in 1992 were about 1.0% of the labour force – a level similar to that in several Western European countries (Boeri, 1994) – whereas only 5% of the unemployed stock left the register each month, a very low figure by Western European standards.

This situation poses two problems for those concerned with design of income support for the unemployed. On the one hand, the low outflow rate implies that a person's need for income support will on average last a long time, and well beyond the sort of period usually covered by unemployment insurance (UI) benefit. The data we use in this chapter show that exhaustion of entitlement to benefit is the single most likely way for a spell of UI in Hungary to finish. Data from the labour force survey show that people unemployed over a year made up more than 40% of the unemployed stock by the spring of 1994, up from little more than 10% at the start of 1992. Large numbers of unemployed then lack income support from the state altogether or they must rely on support from a social assistance scheme which until recently had received little attention from the Hungarian government (and which is much less generous than UI). By June 1994 the numbers of registered unemployed receiving social assistance equalled the number receiving UI, who made up little more than a third of the unemployed stock.

On the other hand, the question arises of whether the low outflow rate is in part caused by disincentives present in the unemployment benefit system. The principal cause of unemployment in Hungary to date has surely been a sharp fall in output caused by demand and supply side shocks, with GDP falling by over 20% during 1990–93. However, a number of commentators have argued that the UI system in Hungary is generous both in absolute terms and relative to systems in other countries inside and outside Eastern Europe, with the implication that this has been a contributory factor to the emergence and the continuation of high levels of unemployment. The existence of a large informal economy in pre-reform Hungary – which has undoubtedly continued – fuels fears that the benefit system provides a substantial subsidy to this form of activity.

We have argued elsewhere that the Hungarian benefit system is more complicated than is often appreciated, making difficult both assessment of its generosity and comparison with other countries (Micklewright and Nagy, 1994a). And allegations of large disincentives ignore the point that unemployment benefit in Eastern Europe was introduced *in order to permit* unemployment to emerge in economies where it had not previously occurred in open form. Nevertheless, the question remains whether at the margin the benefit system in Hungary induces a low level of search behaviour. Data from the Labour Force Survey are suggestive – a third of unemployment benefit recipients interviewed in the third quarter of

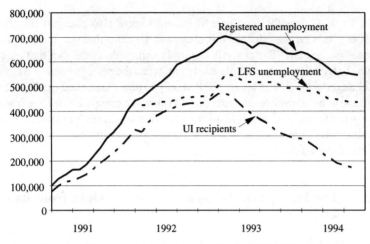

Notes: LFS: 'Labour Force Survey unemployment' is the ILO/OECD definition of
unemployment.

Figure 6.1 Numbers of unemployed in Hungary and numbers receiving
unemployment insurance (UI), 1991–94

1993 were not classified as unemployed in the ILO/OECD sense of both searching
and available for work, although many of these were classified as discouraged
workers.

Our aim in this chapter is to produce more concrete evidence than has hitherto
been available on disincentives within the Hungarian unemployment benefit
system. In particular, we look at the extent to which differences in the speed at
which people leave registered unemployment in Hungary are caused by
differences in their UI benefit entitlements. Preoccupation with incentives might
seem an issue of second-order magnitude in the face of sharp drops in output
during transition and the restructuring of the economic system. But at the very
least the issue is worthy of attention so as to allow the income support role of the
benefit system to be discussed more dispassionately. Moreover, there has been a
steady fall in unemployment since its peak in the first quarter of 1993 (something
true of both registered unemployment and unemployment defined on ILO/OECD
criteria of search and availability – see Figure 6.1) and the weak recovery in
1994 may imply that attention to the supply side of the labour market should
take on more relevance.

If the benefit system in Hungary has had a significant impact on behaviour,
then we can expect policy changes in the last few years to have had a substantial
effect. There have been repeated changes to the system since unemployment
benefit was first introduced in 1989. The last major reform occurred in January
1993 when entitlement periods to UI were cut by a third (the maximum falling

from 18 to 12 months) and benefit amounts were also changed (in general reduced). It is on the effect of this change in UI rules that our analysis in this chapter is focused.[1] The analysis is simple and exploits the fact that existing claims to UI in Hungary are 'grandfathered' when the rules governing UI receipt are changed – the new rules are applied only to new claims and existing claims continue to be administered under the old rules. We compare exit rates from the UI register for claims starting in the month before and the month after the change in rules, this comparison providing a 'quasi-experiment' (Meyer, 1988) of the effects of the UI changes.

6.2   The Hungarian UI System and the Data from its Registers

This section has two purposes. First, we need to provide the reader with sufficient information about the Hungarian UI system to understand the analysis of its effects that follows. Second, we have to explain the micro-data from the administrative registers of the UI system that we use, and ask whether inflow samples drawn from immediately before and after the new rules were introduced on 1 January 1993 can be reasonably viewed as providing a 'controlled experiment' of the effects of UI change. We refer to the rules applying before and after that date as the '92 scheme' and the '93 scheme', respectively.

6.2.1   Unemployment Insurance in Hungary

The Hungarian UI system is quite complex, with substantial variation in entitlement periods and benefit formula (Micklewright and Nagy, 1994a). Eligibility depends in the first instance on employment history in the four years prior to a claim. At least 12 months' of work is required in this period in order to qualify for any benefit. The period of entitlement then depends on the length of the work record; 12 months work results in the minimum period and 4 years of work brings the maximum. Length of entitlement is a step function of the work record and there are ten different entitlement periods in all (including the maximum and minimum). The January 1993 changes cut all ten entitlement periods by one third. The minimum fell from $4\frac{1}{2}$ months to 3 months and the maximum from 18 months to 12 months. Long entitlement periods are common – in the sample we analyse, nearly two-thirds of claimants have entitlement periods at or near the maximum.

The level of benefit is a function of (unindexed) gross earnings in the four complete calendar quarters prior to the claim and depends on the duration of unemployment. There is a more generous formula in the early part of the spell – 'period 1' – than in the latter part – 'period 2'. Period 1 lasted for the first two-thirds of the total entitlement

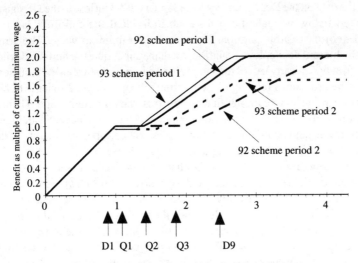

Previous earnings (unindexed) as multiple of current minimum wage

Notes: The arrows below the horizontal axis refer to quantiles of the ratio of unindexed previous earnings to the February 1993 minimum wage, calculated using the December 1992 and January 1993 inflow samples. D1 is the bottom decile, Q1 the lower quartile, Q2 the median, Q3 the upper quartile and D9 the upper decile.

Figure 6.2   Benefit–earnings formulae in the 1992 and 1993 Hungarian UI schemes

period in the 92 scheme but since 1 January 1993 it lasts only for the first quarter.

The schedules relating benefit to earnings have the piece-wise linear formulae shown in Figure 6.2. Benefit in period 1 in the 92 scheme was set at 70% of past earnings, shown by the thick solid line in the figure. If the application of this formula produced a monthly benefit figure less than the current minimum wage then benefit was set equal to the latter. But if the past earnings fell below the current minimum wage then benefit was set equal to past earnings. Maximum benefit was twice the minimum wage. The thick dashed line shows how the schedule was modified in period 2 when the formal benefit-earnings ratio was 50%. The January 1993 changes actually increased the formal benefit-earnings ratios in both period 1 and period 2 to 75 and 60%, respectively, but the maximum benefit in period 2 was reduced to about 1.7 times the minimum wage and a figure about 5% lower than the minimum wage was taken as the criterion for modifying the formula at the lower end of the distribution.

The higher incidence of unemployment among the lower paid and the lack of any indexing provisions for past earnings result in the bottom two pieces of the formula in each period determining the benefit of the majority of claimants. This may be seen from the arrows pointing to the horizontal axis in Figure 6.2.

Using the data on the December 1992 and January 1993 inflow to the UI registers described below we calculated for each individual the ratio of his or her (unindexed) past earnings to the February 1993 minimum wage. The arrows show the bottom decile, lower quartile, median, upper quartile and top decile of this distribution. Nearly half of the sample have earnings that would be sufficiently low for the provisions relating to the minimum wage in the 92 scheme to bind. About one in five have earnings that are less than the minimum wage. There are substantial differences in the position for men and women since the latter are on average lower paid and the domination of the low-earnings provisions in their case is really striking (Micklewright and Nagy, 1994a).

It can be seen from the above that the changes introduced in January 1993 were substantial ones and in general reduced the generosity of the UI system. The cut in the period of total entitlement by one-third is the most obvious feature. If the actual spell of unemployment is short then the total benefit received in the spell can be higher in the 93 scheme on account of the increase in the formal benefit–earnings ratios in both periods. This would be true if someone with maximum entitlement period were to have a spell shorter than about 20 weeks. But beyond this point the increase in importance of period 2 in the 93 scheme would result in total benefit falling and the low outflow rate from the register means that the great majority of claimants have lower total benefit over a spell under the 1993 rules. A person exhausting UI under the 93 scheme after a maximum entitlement period of 12 months would have received total benefit by this time of about 10% less than under the 92 scheme rules, under which there would also be a further 6 months of entitlement to run. Moreover, these calculations presume that the formal benefit–earnings ratios apply throughout. Figure 6.2 shows that those affected by the maximum benefit rule and by the formulae applying to low earnings would be unlikely to ever receive higher benefit under the 93 scheme.

What happens after UI exhaustion? This question is clearly critical to an analysis of the impact of changes in rules relating to the duration of UI entitlement. On exhausting UI an individual may apply for social benefit, eligibility for which depends on household income. The scheme is administered and paid for by local governments, although recipients are obliged to remain registered as unemployed with the local employment office. Per capita household income must not exceed 80% of the minimum pension, a level equal to about two-thirds of the minimum wage. However, the amount of social benefit paid is not means tested and is paid at a flat rate equal to the value of this cut-off line (although local governments can pay more at their discretion.) The simple per capita adjustment used in calculating eligibility would appear to favour families with children, although it should be noted that family allowance (which is generous in Hungary) is taken into account in the calculation. A married claimant with a spouse earning two-thirds of the average wage and with two dependent children would not qualify for social benefit and receipt seems likely to be restricted to those with large families where no other household member works. Given the large numbers of unemployed now receiving social benefit (which may also be claimed by those entering unemployment who have exhausted their UI entitlement in earlier spells) surprizingly little is known about its receipt. Less than 50% of UI exhausters are thought to qualify and we show below that termination of UI will typically lead to a big drop in benefit income for those that do manage to qualify, which is not surprizing given the level of social benefit in relation to the minimum wage.

6.2.2   Data from the UI Registers

To study the effects of the introduction of the 93 scheme we use data on persons entering the UI registers in December 1992 and January 1993. We start with the complete inflow in those months, which is 100 392 individuals – about 2¼% of all economically active persons aged 20–59. From this population we discard two types of persons. The first are those who quit their last job voluntarily. Quitting led to a three month delay in UI receipt under the 92 scheme and to one of six months under the 93 scheme. Our January sample should therefore contain no spell of benefit starting under the 93 scheme as the result of a quit. The data for both December and January contain UI spells administered under the 92 scheme relating to claims for benefit made in the Autumn of 1992 but we discard these to achieve a sample for December 1992 which matches that for January 1993 as closely as possible. For the same reason we discard those receiving statutory severance pay prior to UI. This also delays the start of UI payments (from one to six months depending on the work record) and again means that no spell of UI following a period of severance pay and administered under the 1993 rules should be found in our January data. As a result of these two decisions we discard more than 25% of spells administered under the 1992 rules (in about three-fifths of cases due to severance pay).[2] We are left with a sample of 80 711 spells, all relating to people who lost their job and who did not receive statutory severance pay. Of these, 50 441 are administered under the 92 scheme and 30 270 under the new rules operating from 1 January 1993.

The 92 scheme sample is the substantially larger one. Is it possible that people who would otherwise have entered the register in January 1993 made their claim to UI in December 1992 in order to benefit from the more generous set of rules in operation at that time? If so *and* if the people concerned had a lower desire to leave the register we would then be unable to tell whether differences in the speed of return to work between 92 and 93 scheme people were due to the lower taste for work of the former or the reduced benefit entitlement of the latter.

In considering this issue we need to remember that the individuals under investigation are all officially job losers rather than quitters, although of course some may have volunteered for redundancy. This must limit the extent to which they can control their date of registering a claim to benefit. In the first instance

Table 6.1   Characteristics of 92 scheme and 93 scheme claimants among new spells of UI starting in December 1992 and January 1993

	All work history groups		Continuous employment group	
	1992 scheme	1993 scheme	1992 scheme	1993 scheme
Days between date of last employment and start of UI payment				
Median	2	7	2	5
Upper quartile	9	33	4	7
Top decile	94	212	8	15
Proportion:				
Male	0.686	0.680	0.649	0.656
Age (average years)	36.5	35.2	39.0	37.8
Education				
Primary and below	0.428	0.426	0.424	0.441
Vocational	0.491	0.491	0.482	0.472
General secondary and above	0.081	0.083	0.094	0.087
Manual	0.854	0.873	0.806	0.846
Area				
Budapest city	0.063	0.112	0.043	0.075
Szabolcs	0.114	0.069	0.103	0.066
High outflow county	0.382	0.391	0.372	0.406
Previous spell of UI	0.300	0.270	0.013	0.012
Entry to UI from employment	0.936	0.896	0.994	0.990
Base period earnings indexed January 1993 (gross Forints per month)	17 222	16 980	17 621	17 510
Work history in previous four years				
12–27 months	0.139	0.158		
28–43 months	0.206	0.260		
44–47 months	0.195	0.211		
Continuous employment	0.460	0.371	1.000	1.000

Notes:
1. Figures based on 50 002 individuals receiving benefits under the 1992 scheme and 30 110 receiving under the 1993 scheme.
2. Vocational schooling includes vocational secondary schooling.
3. High outflow counties are Békés, Fejér, Gyor, Hajdu, Somogy, Tolna, Vas, Veszprém and Zala. They are the counties with the highest three-month outflow rates for spells of UI starting during the period 20 March 1992–19 April 1992 (see Micklewright and Nagy, 1994b).

this obviously depends on the date of job loss which may be entirely out of their control. Following job loss the date of claim to UI is, however, an individual decision and the 92 scheme people are in fact somewhat quicker at registering their claims – see columns 1 and 2 of Table 6.1. The median lag from the date of job loss is only 2 days for them and the upper quartile 9 days, compared to 7 and 33 days for the 93 scheme claimants.[3]

Awareness of the introduction of the change in the rules of the UI system at the end of 1992 is difficult to judge. The amendment to the relevant employment law was made as late as 23 December but the main measures, including the changes in entitlement periods, had been discussed within the Ministry of Labour since at least September (although there had been substantial uncertainty surrounding the date the new measures would be introduced). At least one mass circulation daily newspaper announced the substance of the forthcoming changes (but not of course the date they would be effective) in October. It is possible that some enterprises shedding staff in December may have warned their employees of imminent changes and advised them to claim quickly.[4]

As far as the size of the two inflows are concerned, it is – surprisingly – impossible to establish from published figures whether or not the December 1992 inflow was abnormally large. Monthly inflow figures published by the National Labour Centre are from the 20th of one month to the 19th of the following month and they do not record entrants reported late by local employment offices, which appears to result in a substantial underestimate of the inflow (Micklewright and Nagy, 1994b). Enterprises may only make large layoffs with prior notification to the Ministry of Labour of one or three months (depending on the numbers of involved). Given the uncertainty surrounding the date of introduction of the new benefit rules it seems unlikely that layoffs in December 1992 were substantially affected by the introduction of the new scheme. The tax year coincides with the calendar year in Hungary and this may be one reason for enterprises shedding more staff in December than in January.[5] It should be noted that the majority of those on the 93 scheme actually lost their jobs in December, rather than January – 61% have a last date of employment in December and among these nearly half lost their jobs on the last day of the year.

Table 6.1 compares a number of observed personal characteristics of the 92 and 93 scheme samples, a comparison that is in any case important when interpreting any non-parametric analysis of the spell data that does not control for observables. Columns 1 and 2 relate to the full sample (obtained after the selection rules given above). The gender composition is virtually identical, men making up over two-thirds of the inflow, and there are only slight differences in educational level, manual/non-manual status, average age and average base period earnings. There are rather larger differences in the geographical breakdown of the two groups. The biggest differences are for the two areas with the lowest and highest unemployment rates, the capital Budapest city and the county of Szabolcs in the north-east of the country. The former is much more strongly represented in the 93 scheme sample and the latter in the 92 sample. Looking at several other months of inflow data it seems that the representation of these two counties in the 93 scheme inflow is the more typical. When, however, we divide the 20 Hungarian counties into two groups on the basis of the outflow rate from the register in the summer of 1992, the composition of the 92 and 93 scheme samples in terms of high and low outflow counties is very similar. The incidence of an earlier spell of UI in the register records (this can be at any time since 1989) is somewhat higher in the 92 scheme sample. (The quite high incidence in both samples – around 30% – is of some interest and shows that as in Western labour markets there is a significant degree of recurrent unemployment in Hungary.)

The last characteristic considered in Table 6.1 is employment history, where we have grouped the first 8 of the 10 possible work history periods into two (12–27 months and 28–43 months). Those with a history of continuous work in the four years prior to claiming benefit obtain the maximum entitlement, and this is easily the modal period for claimants under both schemes. But the maximum is notably more common among 92 scheme claimants, applying to 43% of men and 52% of women compared to 36% and 40% respectively under the 93 scheme. (The contrast between the schemes is rather less marked if we also include the group with the next best work history.) It is difficult to know how to interpret these differences. It might be argued that those with the best work history had the biggest incentive to register a claim under the 92 scheme and what we are seeing in Table 6.1 is consistent with income-maximizing claim behaviour. On the other hand, all entitlement periods were longer by the same proportion under the 92 scheme. Columns 3 and 4 in Table 6.1 compare the characteristics of claimants in this modal work history group. Differences in the speed of claim are somewhat smaller than in the full sample, while differences in occupation, education and county are slightly bigger.

Are these differences in characteristics of 92 and 93 scheme claimants greater than those we would expect from looking at the inflow in a pair of consecutive months when there was no change in the UI rules? We also have data from the inflow in April and May 1994 (from which we again exclude those with severance pay and voluntary quitters).[6] The differences between the characteristics of claimants in these two months are small. Notably, differences are also small between geographical distribution and work histories in the April–May 1994 samples in contrast to the December 1992 and January 1993 samples. For example, the proportions with a maximum entitlement period differ by only 2 percentage points compared to 9 points with the earlier pair of months. Of course, the comparisons may be affected by the seasonal difference. A better comparison would be between December 1991 and January 1992, which would also have the advantage of spanning a change in tax year.

It is clear that the December 1992 and January 1993 inflow samples differ in several respects, although they are very similar in others. On balance we think it unlikely that the former contains a disproportionate number of persons with a high propensity to stay on benefit, who made sure that they claimed under the more generous 92 scheme.

To complete our description of the data, Table 6.2 provides some information on the levels of UI benefit in payment. The first part of the table shows benefit in period 1 and period 2 as a percentage of previous earnings, where the latter are the earnings during the relevant base period used to calculate benefit but indexed to January 1993. Period 1 lasts for the first two-thirds of the benefit period in the 92 scheme but only the first quarter in the 93 scheme. Both benefit

Table 6.2   Benefit levels on the two schemes

(a) Ratio of gross UI benefit to indexed base period gross earnings (%)

	92 scheme period 1		93 scheme period 1	
	Men	Women	Men	Women
Bottom decile	56.1	57.9	54.3	56.3
Median	59.3	68.4	67.2	67.2
Top decile	84.7	84.7	84.7	87.8
	92 scheme period 2		93 scheme period 2	
	Men	Women	Men	Women
Bottom decile	42.4	42.4	46.4	48.3
Median	54.1	68.4	53.7	66.1
Top decile	84.7	84.7	84.7	87.8

(b) Ratio of period 2 net UI benefit to social benefit in January 1994

	92 scheme		93 scheme	
	Men	Women	Men	Women
Bottom decile	1.46	1.20	1.42	1.21
Median	1.56	1.56	1.49	1.49
Top decile	2.01	1.58	2.47	1.89

and earnings are gross. (The effect of personal income taxation on the comparison is not obvious and is discussed in Micklewright and Nagy, 1994a.) The adjustment of the basic benefit–earnings formula for low and high earnings together with wage inflation during the base period (and in any lag before entry to unemployment) means that the 'standard' period 1 rates of 70% in the 92 scheme and 75% in the 93 scheme are a poor guide to replacement rates faced in practice. Median period 1 replacement rates on the 92 scheme are 59% for men and 68% for women – more women being affected by the rules governing low earnings. The median is notably higher for men on the 93 scheme but not for women.

Viewed relative to previous earnings, UI benefit may appear to be quite generous for the majority of claimants. In absolute terms the benefits are much less generous. The minimum wage, which played a big part in the determination of benefit for many unemployed people in the 92 scheme, was about equal in December 1992 to the per capita minimum subsistence income level calculated by the Hungarian Central Statistical Office for a two-adult/two-child household. Of course, this also illustrates the low living standards provided by jobs at the bottom of the earnings distribution.

The bottom part of Table 6.2 gives information on the ratio of UI benefit in period 2 (net of the 6% social insurance contribution levied on the unemployed) to the level of social benefit paid in January 1994 (the time when the modal work history group on the 93 scheme would exhaust UI). The calculation is made for all claimants in the sample and not just those who actually exhaust UI entitlement. The table shows the distribution of the drop in benefit income that would be experienced were all the sample to qualify for social benefit. In reality less than a half of those who do exhaust UI would probably get this form of benefit. UI in period 2 exceeds the social benefit level by over 40% for more than 90% of the sample and by over 50% for more than half. Broadly speaking, we can say that about half of people exhausting UI will not qualify for social benefit and among those that do about half will lose at least a third of their benefit income. The exhaustion of UI therefore has considerable consequences for benefit income in the majority of cases.

6.3   Spell Durations and Exit Rates – Non-Parametric Analysis

If the 92 and 93 scheme samples are sufficiently similar in observable and unobservable characteristics, then differences in spell durations between claimants on the two schemes should be the result of different entitlements to benefit. The shorter entitlement periods of the 93 scheme should exert a downward pressure on reservation wages and in addition have a positive effect on search intensity. (The same is true of the – in general – lower levels of benefit on the 93 scheme.) It is worth noting that the individual is fully informed of his or her benefit entitlement after a claim has been decided upon by the local employment office; national guidelines require local offices to inform the claimant in writing of the level of benefit in both period 1 and period 2 and of the day that entitlement will expire.

Each spell in the data is traced through the administrative registers of the UI system until it finishes through an exit to a job, a government labour market programme, exhaustion of entitlement to UI, or some other reason. Investigation of local office practices indicates that the exit state coded on each spell is very reliable and in only a few cases is the state unknown (those labelled as censored in

Table 6.3   Exit states from the UI register

Exit state	92 scheme		93 scheme		All
	Men (%)	Women (%)	Men (%)	Women (%)	(%)
Employment	49.0	34.4	47.0	31.6	43.5
Subsidized employment	1.3	1.1	0.6	0.5	1.0
Subsidized self-employment	1.9	1.2	1.5	0.8	1.5
Public works	1.7	0.8	1.4	0.8	1.3
Training scheme	1.2	2.7	1.4	3.5	1.8
Early retirement	3.5	6.8	1.8	4.5	3.8
Normal retirement	1.5	2.4	0.4	1.7	1.5
Disqualified	2.0	2.6	2.6	2.6	2.3
Other	1.4	2.8	1.5	1.7	1.9
UI exhausted	32.8	40.3	38.5	47.8	37.5
Spell censored	3.7	4.9	3.3	4.5	3.9
Total	100.0	100.0	100.0	100.0	100.0

Table 6.3). The distribution of exit states is shown in Table 6.3. Exit to a job is the most common outcome overall but there is a big difference in its importance for men and women – nearly half of men on both the 92 and 93 schemes leave to a job but only one-third of women, for whom exhaustion of UI entitlement is the single most common way of leaving the register. (Taking 93 scheme claimants of both sexes together, exhaustion is the most common form of exit overall and this is the basis for our comment on the frequency of exhaustion in section 6.1.) Some form of labour market programme (including early retirement) accounts for nearly 1 in 10 exits. The fact that the job exits are almost as common for 93 scheme claimants as for 92 scheme claimants, despite their shorter entitlement periods, is of some note although exhaustion is certainly more common on the 93 scheme.

In comparing the speed of exit of claimants in the two schemes we divide the sample into the four groups of work history identified in Table 6.1.

6.3.1 Continuous Employment History

We start with the modal group of continuous employment in the last four years, which brings a maximum entitlement period to benefit. Everyone in this subsample had continuous employment in the four years prior to the claim. Survivor functions (i.e. the fraction remaining on the register after a given spell length) are shown in Figure 6.3. The functions finish at the end of the entitlement periods to benefit, 360 days for the 93 scheme and 540 days for the 92 scheme.[7]

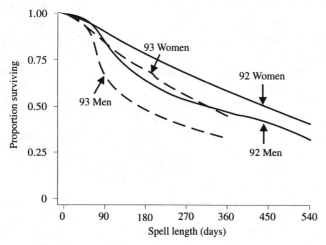

Notes: Sample sizes are 14 908 men on 92 scheme, 7 334 men on 93 scheme, 8 071 women on 92 scheme, 3 845 women on 93 scheme.

Figure 6.3 Survivor functions for claimants with continuous employment in last four years

We see immediately that the survivor functions for both men and women on the 93 scheme lie well below those for 92 scheme claimants – people receiving under the 1993 rules move off the register more quickly than those receiving under the 1992 rules. At the one year point, when entitlement ceases under the 1993 rules, only 32% of men in the 93 scheme were still receiving UI while 47% of their counterparts under the 92 scheme were still in the register – nearly half as many again. Among women, 45% of 93 scheme claimants survived to one year whereas 57% of those on the 92 scheme were still receiving UI at this point. The comparison of the survivor functions for men and women reflects what we saw in Table 6.3 – women leave the register more slowly and are much more likely to exhaust UI.

At first sight, the sharply contrasting rates of survival in the register for 92 and 93 scheme claimants seems strong evidence in support of the hypothesis that the shorter benefit period (and somewhat lower benefit level) faced by the latter increased their intensity of search and/or reduced their reservation wages. However, closer inspection of the survival functions casts some doubt on such a simple explanation for the observed differences. In particular, the male survivor functions diverge sharply at an early point – at around 70–90 days – and thereafter run roughly parallel to each other. It is difficult to think why benefit-induced differences in the behaviour of claimants on the two schemes should be concentrated so early in the spell when even under the 93 scheme there was still some nine months of benefit entitlement to run.

Figure 6.4 sheds more light on the issue by looking at the empirical hazards. The diagrams give the probability of leaving the register to go to a job (Figures 6.4(a) and 6.4(b)) and any other register exit (Figures 6.4(c) and 6.4(d)) in a given interval of time conditional on surviving all risks of exit up until the start of the interval. The intervals are defined as two weeks long. Figure 6.4(a) shows an enormous surge in the job hazard for men on the 93 scheme just before the three month point, the hazard increasing some four- or five-fold from its average level in the first few weeks (or that around the six month point). (This increase is highly significant, the 95% confidence interval around the peak, of 0.0086, is from 0.008 to 0.0093.) There is also a rise for men on the 92 scheme at the same point in calendar time (on average the 92 scheme men entered the register about 30 days earlier) although it is notably lower, about half that of the 93 scheme hazard. From this point onwards the hazards are very similar, although the 93 scheme hazard remains a little higher.

The second point to note from Figure 6.4(a) is that there is little apparent rise in the 93 scheme hazard as the point of exhaustion of entitlement at one year draws near. This is true both in relation to the hazard for claimants under the 93 rules in earlier periods (which could be explained by seasonal factors in late 1993) but also in relation to the hazard for 92 scheme claimants over the same period. In the final two week period there is a slight upturn in the 93 scheme hazard that we do not see for the 92 scheme. The difference is significant but it

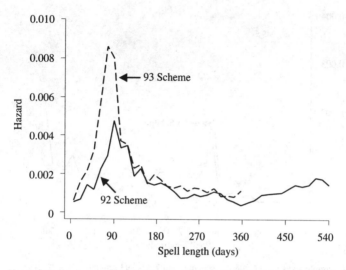

Notes: Sample sizes are 14 908 (92 scheme) and 7 334 (93 scheme).

Figure 6.4a   Hazard functions for male claimants with continuous employment in last four years: exit to a job

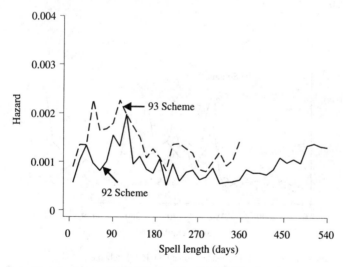

Notes: Sample sizes are 8 071 (92 scheme) and 3 045 (93 scheme).

Figure 6.4b   Hazard functions for female claimants with continuous employment in last four years: exit to a job

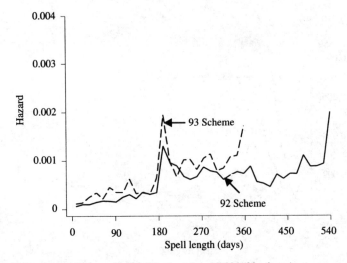

Notes: Sample sizes are 14 908 (92 scheme) and 7 334 (93 scheme).

Figure 6.4c   Hazard functions for male claimants with continuous employment in last four years: non-job exits

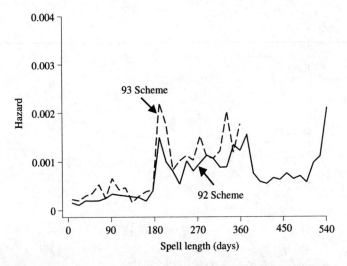

Notes: Sample sizes are 8 071 (92 scheme) and 3 045 (93 scheme).

Figure 6.4d   Hazard functions for female claimants with continuous employment in last four years: non-job exits

is very small. Similarly, there is no surge in the hazard for 92 scheme claimants just before their entitlement expires 6 months later at the 18 month point. We cannot tell whether the steady gradual rise in the hazard during the first half of 1994 for these claimants is benefit-induced due to the approaching end of entitlement or whether it is due to an upturn in the labour market.

It seems likely that seasonal factors combined with an exceptional increase in hiring by employers is the principal cause of the surge in the male job hazard at around the 90 day mark. (The rise seems exceptional since there is no similar sized increase a year later for the 92 scheme claimants who are still on the register, although this may represent a sorting affect.) The stock of registered vacancies hit a three year high in spring 1993 and reached the highest level yet recorded in the 1990s, before falling back substantially in the rest of the year. (The change, as opposed to the level, does seem seasonal however; vacancies rose 50% between January and May 1993 and 125% and 25% between the same two months in 1991 and 1993, respectively.) Figure 6.5 shows the outflow rate to jobs from the *stock* of UI recipients during the period March 1992–December 1993. The outflow rate increased almost three-fold between December 1992 and April 1993, the latter date seeing the highest monthly outflow rate during the 19 months in the diagram. In other words, the outflow rose sharply for *all* UI recipients at this time and not just for the December and January inflow cohorts that we investigate in this chapter. Looking back at Figure 6.1 we see that this is the period when unemployment began to fall in Hungary.

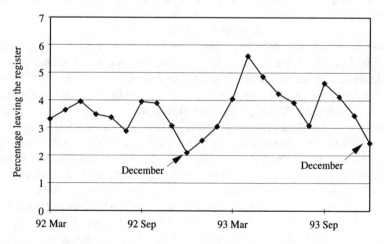

Source: National Labour Centre.
Notes: Figures include Career Beginner's Benefit Recipients.

Figure 6.5 Proportion of the stock of UI recipients leaving the register to a job, March 1992 – December 1993

There remains the issue of why the 93 scheme hazard increases more sharply in spring 1993 than that for 92 scheme claimants and it seems unlikely that it is associated with their shorter period of entitlement to benefit.[8] The three month point is the time at which the more generous period 1 finishes for those with maximum entitlement but it is difficult to think of an argument explaining what we see that involves this. The formal benefit–earnings ratio at this time is higher on the 93 scheme than on the 92 scheme and it falls at the three month point rather less than that at the (later) switch from period 1 to period 2 under the 92 scheme. This leaves the possibility that the 93 scheme claimants have characteristics that on average allowed them to benefit more from the upsurge in demand at this time, although we have seen in Table 6.1 that in terms of observable characteristics the two groups are quite similar. One characteristic we cannot control for is being on temporary layoff. It is possible that a greater proportion of men with a continuous employment history who enter the registers in January were on temporary layoff than those entering the register in December and that the upswing in the labour market in spring 1993 led to higher numbers of 93 scheme claimants being recalled.

Figure 6.4(b) shows the job hazards for women and we draw attention to the difference in vertical scale from Figure 6.4(a). The hazard for 93 scheme women lies everywhere above that for the 92 scheme, in general being between 10 and 50% higher. Note that there is a much smaller rise around the three month point, of about 50% for the 93 scheme claimants compared to other periods. Whatever happened in the Hungarian labour market in spring 1993 seems to have favoured the job prospects of unemployed men with good work histories much more than unemployed women.

Figures 6.4(c) and 6.4(d) show the hazards of exit to the other labour market states described in Table 6.3 for men and women respectively (in this case the graphs have the same scale). These include various active labour market programmes of subsidized work and training together with normal and early retirement. For both men and women the other exits hazard jumps at 180 days since it is at this point that eligibility for various labour market programmes begins and those within three years of normal retirement age become eligible for early retirement (the decision to allow early retirement is at the discretion of the local employment office). The 93 scheme hazards are in general somewhat above those for the 92 scheme. Hazards for both schemes and both sexes rise sharply and significantly just before the exhaustion point (less so for women on the 93 scheme). This suggests that both claimants and/or local employment offices look harder for available labour market programmes when benefit entitlement is close to expiry, although it should be noted that the rises in the hazards at this point are not enormous and the great majority of those leaving the register at some time to go to labour market programmes are not leaving just before UI exhaustion.

6.3.2 Employment History of 44–47 Months

Figure 6.6 and Figures 6.7 give survivor and hazard functions for claimants with 44–47 months work in the previous four years – a group that makes up a fifth of the sample (the most numerous group after those with a continuous employment history). There are some marked differences from the graphs for the continuous employment history group. Looking first at the survivor functions, which in this case end at the slightly shorter entitlement periods of 330 days and 495 days, we again see a big difference between men and women that emerges early on. This is of course what we saw in Figure 6.3 but in Figure 6.6 the values of the survivor functions for both sexes at the point when benefit expires in the 93 scheme are almost identical for 92 and 93 scheme claimants. Comparison with Figure 6.3 shows that it is the survivor functions *of the 92 scheme claimants* that are different in this case. Whereas 93 scheme claimants in the two work history groups – 48 months and 44–47 months employment – leave the register at more or less the same speed as each other (something true of both sexes) the 92 scheme claimants with continuous work history leave the register much more slowly than those with a small interruption in their work record (or those too young to have worked four complete years).

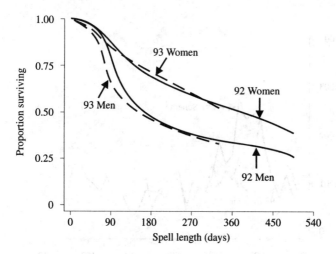

Notes: Sample sizes are 7 612 men on 92 scheme, 4 694 men on 93 scheme, 2 170 women on 92 scheme, 1 662 women on 93 scheme.

Figure 6.6 Survivor functions for claimants with 44–47 months employment in last four years

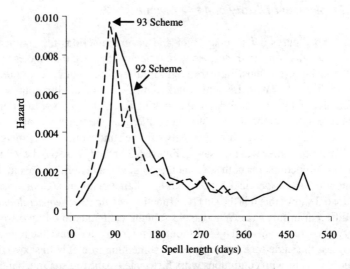

Notes: Sample sizes are 7 612 (92 scheme) and 4 694 (93 scheme)

Figure 6.7a   Hazard functions for male claimants with 44–47 months employment in last four years: exit to a job

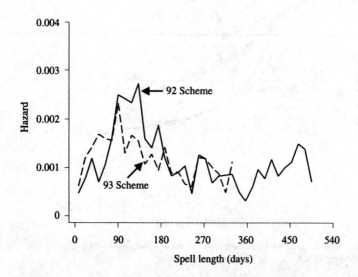

Notes: Sample sizes are 2 170 (92 scheme) and 1 662 (93 scheme)

Figure 6.7b   Hazard functions for female claimants with 44–47 months employment in last four years: exit to a job

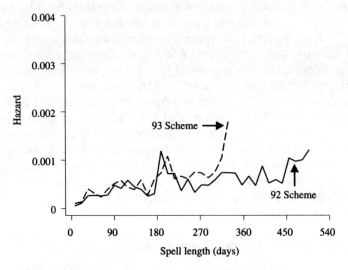

Notes: Sample sizes are 7 612 (92 scheme) and 4 694 (93 scheme).

Figure 6.7c   Hazard functions for male claimants with 44–47 months employment in last 4 years: non-job exits

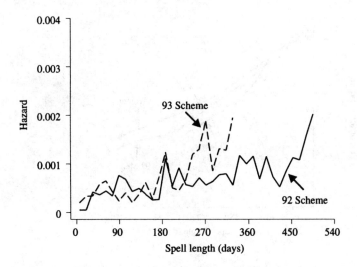

Notes: Sample sizes are 2 170 (92 scheme) and 1 662 (93 scheme).

Figure 6.7d   Hazard functions for female claimants with 44–47 months employment in last four years: non-job exits

The hazards in Figures 6.7 again shed more light. The job exit hazards for men (Figure 6.7(a)) on the two schemes are virtually identical when one bears in mind that the 92 scheme men enter the register a month earlier (so they are 'hit' by the spring surge in outflows a month later). And they are also very similar to that for 93 scheme claimants with continuous work history shown earlier in Figure 6.4(a), underlining the fact that it is the hazard of the 92 scheme continuous work history group that is exceptional. The peak of the job exit hazard for women is higher on the 92 scheme than on the 93 scheme. And, as for the continuous employment history group, for neither sex is there a jump in the job exit hazard shortly before expiry of UI entitlement, although we again see increases in the other exits hazard on both schemes at this point. The conclusion for this employment history group seems to be that the introduction of the 93 scheme had no effect at all on the job exit hazards but that it somewhat hastened the other exits.

6.3.3   Employment History of up to 43 Months

Figures 6.8 and 6.9 show the survivor functions for the remainder of the sample who all have shorter employment histories.[9] We have grouped the eight work history periods concerned into two, 28–43 months and 12–27 months. In both cases the survivor functions for the 93 scheme lie somewhat below those of the

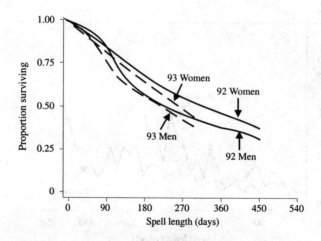

Notes: Sample sizes are 7 275 men on 92 scheme, 5 412 men on 93 scheme, 3 005 women on 92 scheme, 2 442 women on 93 scheme.

Figure 6.8 Survivor functions for claimants with 28–43 months employment in last four years

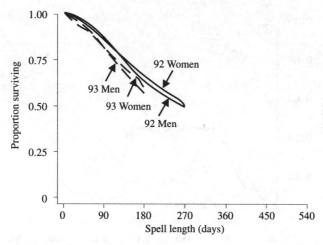

Notes: Sample sizes are 4 598 men on 92 scheme, 3 089 men on 93 scheme, 2 363 women on 92 scheme, 1 642 women on 93 scheme.

Figure 6.9   Survivor functions for claimants with 12–27 months employment in last four years

92 scheme and in the case of the 28–43 months group we again see evidence that the upturn in the labour market in spring 1993 benefited men more than women. The job exit hazards are shown in Figure 6.10. Figure 6.10(a) shows quite clearly that once we have taken into account the one month earlier entry of those receiving under the 1992 rules, the job exit hazards of 92 and 93 scheme claimants with 28–43 months employment are very similar – the 92 scheme group being affected by the 'spring surge' one month later, this accounting for the relative positions of the survivor functions in Figure 6.8. The same appears to apply (although with somewhat less clarity) for women in Figure 6.10(b) and for men with 12–27 months employment history in Figure 6.10(c).[10] Again, the conclusion for these employment history groups appears to be that the introduction of the 93 scheme had little effect on job exit hazards.

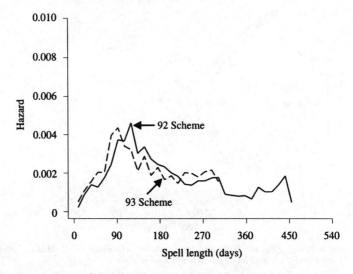

Notes: Sample sizes are 7 275 (92 scheme) and 5 392 (93 scheme).

Figure 6.10a Hazard functions for male claimants with 28–43 months employment in last four years: exit to a job

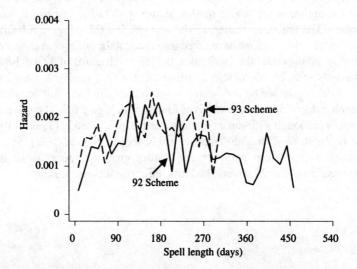

Notes: Sample sizes are 3 005 (92 scheme) and 2 442 (93 scheme).

Figure 6.10b Hazard functions for female claimants with 28–43 months employment in last four years: exit to a job

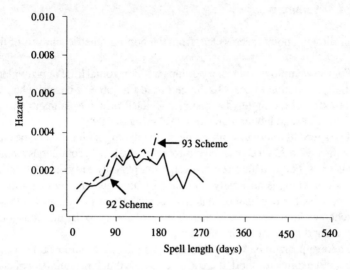

Notes: Sample sizes are 4 598 (92 scheme) and 3 099 (93 scheme).

Figure 6.10c Hazard functions for male claimants with 12–27 months employment in last four years: exit to a job

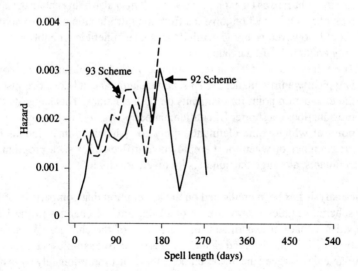

Notes: Sample sizes are 2 363 (92 scheme) and 1 642 (93 scheme).

Figure 6.10d Hazard functions for female claimants with 12–27 months employment in last four years: exit to a job

6.3.4   Summary

The following points seems clear from the non-parametric analysis of the data.

- For most employment history groups we have found little or no evidence that the introduction of the 93 scheme raised the job exit hazard when we take into account the slightly later point at which 92 scheme claimants encountered the increase in labour demand in the spring of 1993.
- The speed of return to work is only markedly higher for 93 scheme claimants compared to 92 scheme claimants for individuals with continuous employment histories. For men the hazards diverge sharply only early on in the entitlement period, which is not easily explained by an argument involving incentives. One possible explanation that may contribute to this pattern is that the 93 scheme claimants had a higher recall probability to the previous job, but at present this must remain speculation.
- There appears to be very little rise in the job exit hazard near the time when benefit expires. In short, there is no evidence that large numbers of claimants are putting off taking a job until just before their UI entitlement runs out. Of course, it is an open question as to what happens after UI expiry. The possibility of social benefit following exhaustion of UI entitlement, albeit paid at a substantially lower rate than UI, may be one reason for the lack of any sharp rise in the hazard as UI expiry draws near. It may also help explain the apparent lack of much impact on job exits from the introduction of the 93 scheme. It should, however, be borne in mind that social benefit is probably received by only about half of UI exhausters.
- The exit rate to other labour market states (including subsidized employment) is typically a little higher for 93 scheme claimants and does rise just before the exhaustion point for claimants on both schemes. This suggests that the introduction of a shorter UI entitlement period in 1993 did bring forward the point at which some claimants apply for participation in labour market programmes or when local employment offices offer such programmes to claimants, although the numbers involved are small.

Our analysis has been predicated on the assumption that comparison of 92 and 93 scheme samples drawn from around the time of changes in the UI rules provides a 'natural experiment' of the effects of the changes. We showed in section 6.2 that the observed characteristics of the two samples were reasonably similar and we argued that it was unlikely that a disproportionately large number of those with a higher propensity to stay on benefit managed to claim under the more generous 1992 rules. If we are wrong, then we should see higher hazards for the 93 scheme claimants. The fact that we do not in general find large differences between the hazards of claimants on the two schemes is therefore some evidence against the hypothesis that there was widespread income-maximizing claim behaviour at the time of the changes in UI rules.

6.4   Conclusions

In this chapter we have looked at whether differences in the speed at which people leave registered unemployment in Hungary are caused by differences in their UI benefit entitlements, focusing on the effect of major changes in the UI system in January 1993 which substantially reduced entitlements. Broadly speaking, we find that the introduction of the new rules was not associated with large increases in exit rates from the UI register that are easily explained by a story of increased incentives to find work or to move off the register to other destinations. The conclusion is that the unemployed in Hungary are rather unresponsive to changes in UI benefits.

The work presented has been simple non-parametric analysis of administrative data from UI registers. These data have their advantages (large sample sizes and precise measurement of benefit entitlements) but any more definite conclusions about unemployment benefits and incentives to work in Hungary need further information. We need to observe claimants after the point of UI expiry when we know whether they have qualified or not for social benefit, a form of income support for the unemployed in Hungary about which far too little is currently known, to assess its incentive and welfare impacts. We need data that provide information on the household characteristics of claimants and on other sources of income. One aspect, which will be hard to discover, is the involvement of the unemployed in the informal economy. Anecdotal evidence suggests this is quite common and the existence of significant income from this source may be one reason for changes in UI rules having little effect. This said, the main finding that changes in benefit rules have little impact on the behaviour of the unemployed may be unsurprizing given the principal reason for the emergence of large-scale unemployment during the transition.

Notes

1. In one sense the impact of the reduction of entitlement periods on the level of registered unemployment is obvious. It appears that less than half of those who exhaust UI qualify for means-tested social benefit and there is little incentive for the others to remain registered. So one would expect a reduction in entitlement periods to reduce the registered unemployed stock (albeit with a lag since changes affect only new claims) even if there were no change in behaviour. What we are concerned with shedding light on in this chapter, however, are the behavioural changes that may result from cuts in the generosity of benefit.
2. For reasons that are not clear there are a few spells under the 93 scheme of benefit following severance pay or voluntary quit. We discard these spells as well.

172 J Micklewright and Gy Nagy

3. If a shorter lag signifies a greater willingness to live on benefit, then these differences would still be a concern even if there had been complete ignorance of the imminent change in the benefit rules among those becoming unemployed in December 1992. Those with less desire to live on benefit would have got caught by the change in the rules, and the December and January inflows would still differ in their mix of people with higher and lower propensities to remain on benefit.
4. Large enterprises do appear to keep abreast of changing legislation affecting unemployment benefit. A local employment office manager told us in October 1994 that he had heard of new draft changes to the unemployment benefit system from an employer and not from head office!
5. Checking a sample of the stock of UI recipients in March 1992 we find that entry in December 1991 was substantially more common than in January 1992.
6. The April data record spells of benefit starting only after the 9th of the month.
7. The survivor functions are estimated using the usual Kaplan–Meier method, which ensures that the small amount of spell censoring in the data does not affect the estimates.
8. It might be argued that the 93 scheme claimants perceive the spring of that year as being their only chance of benefiting from a favourable seasonal upswing in demand while those on the 92 scheme perceive that they have a further chance the following year before their benefit expires, but this seems far-fetched.
9. The survivor functions in both Figures 6.8 and 6.9 (and the hazards in Figure 6.10) are estimated using groups with various entitlement periods and we treat UI exhaustion as censoring when obtaining the estimates.
10. It should be noted that standard errors of the estimated hazards are quite large in some instances in Figure 6.10. For example, the hazard of 0.0039 in the last fortnight of entitlement for men with 12–27 months employment on the 93 scheme has a 95% confidence interval of 0.0026–0.0053 and that for women of 0.0037 has an interval of 0.0019–0.0055.

References

Boeri, T. (1994), ' 'Transitional' unemployment', *Economics of Transition*, 2, No. 1, 1–25.
Meyer, B. (1988), 'A quasi-experimental approach to the effects of unemployment insurance', NBER Working Paper 3159, Cambridge. MA.
Micklewright, J. and Nagy, Gy. (1994a), 'How does the Hungarian unemployment insurance system really work?', *Economics of Transition*, 2, No. 2, 209–32.
Micklewright, J. and Nagy, Gy. (1994b), 'Flows to and from insured unemployment in Hungary', EUI Working Paper in Economics No. 94/41, Florence.

7

The Impact of Active Labour Market Policies
A Closer Look at the Czech and Slovak Republics*
Michael C Burda and Martina Lubyova

7.1   Introduction

The economic transformation in Central and Eastern European countries (CEECs) has been associated with a dramatic increase in unemployment, with jobless rates typically rising to 15% or higher. An notable exception to this development has been the Czech Republic, where unemployment persistently remains in the 3–4% range. With output growth now returning and unemployment stabilizing in the Visegrád countries, it is clear that either the Czechs did something right, or had an enormous amount of good luck, or both. Even more puzzling is the fact that the Slovak Republic, which shared institutions and policies with the Czech Republic for decades, experienced the same increase in unemployment as did Poland, Hungary, Bulgaria and Romania.

Explanations for the Czechoslovak puzzle abound. Observers usually appeal to differential output declines, industrial structure, demographics, wage and productivity developments, as well as relative proximity to richer industrial economies. One prominent hypothesis is a decidedly different degree of active labour market policy between the two countries before, and especially after the 'velvet divorce'. Active labour market policies are generally understood as those policies which increase the exit rate from unemployment, and include job

*   This research is sponsored by the PHARE Programme of the European Commission, with support of the Sonderforschungsbereich 373, Deutsche Forschungsgemeinschaft (Burda) and the 1994 PHARE-ACE Programme of the European Union (Lubyova). We thank Vit Subert and Borivoj Vyjídák of the Czech Labour Ministry and Lubica Gajdosova of the Slovak Labour Ministry for providing and explaining the data used in the analyses. We are grateful to Tito Boeri, Michael Funke, and Stephen Smith for extensive comments on an earlier draft of this chapter. Stefan Profit provided expert research assistance, gave helpful comments, and discovered an error in the preliminary version of this chapter; Matthias Almus assisted with keying in data.

counselling and information, training, direct job creation as well as marginal job subsidies.

This chapter exploits the devolution of the Czech and Slovak Federation into two separate autonomous states on 1 January 1993 to learn about the effects of active labour market policy over the period 1991–4. As with all economic 'experiments', not all factors can be controlled for precisely, and several differences can be identified which might have led to differential rates of unemployment incidence in the two countries. Yet on the whole, these can only account for half of the Czech–Slovak unemployment gap; the rest is due to different exit rates from unemployment, and thus might have been influenced by differential intensities of active labour market policies (ALMPs) in the Czech and Slovak Republics.

After surveying the economic rationale behind ALMPs, we summarize the level and extent of their implementation in the Czech and Slovak Republics. Events leading up to and including the 'velvet divorce' may have affected the administration of these programmes. In fact, we find that Slovak ALMP spending per unemployed person was already lower in 1991, the result of a rigid system of federal funding which paid little attention to the distribution of unemployment across the two regions. While this inequity was corrected to some extent by a large rerouting of spending to the Slovak Republic in 1992, political forces were already in motion which would ultimately lead to the split-up of the country. After 1993, Slovak ALMP spending – both total and per unemployed – declined precipitously. The question then arises: how much difference did this make?

On the basis of a panel of monthly observations of labour market districts in the two countries, we are able to estimate econometrically the effects of active labour market policies.

Concretely, we find that an additional 100 000 crowns spent per quarter in an average district in our sample is associated with an additional 0.75 outflows into employment per month in the Czech Republic, and 2.5 outflows per month in the Slovak Republic. Our results suggest that, while the Slovak Republic suffered some inherent disadvantages with respect to industry structure and demographics, the sharp cut in ALMP spending which ensued after the dissolution can also be blamed for some of the rise in unemployment after 1992. Had Slovak ALMP spending been restored in 1993 to 1992 levels, outflows to jobs would have been more than 30% higher and steady state unemployment roughly 2 percentage points lower in 1993, all other things equal.

7.2 Success or Failure? The Labour Market Performance of the Czech and Slovak Republics

Unlike any other transforming economy in Central and Eastern Europe, the Czech Republic succeeded in maintaining a low rate of unemployment. Table 7.1 displays the evolution of unemployment rates over the first five years after the

Table 7.1 Labour market indicators in the Czech and Slovak Republics

	1990	1991	1992	1993	1994*
Unemployment rate (% of labour force)					
Czech Republic	0.8	4.1	2.6	3.5	3.2
Slovak Republic	1.5	11.8	10.4	14.4	14.3
Labour force participation rate (% of working age population)					
Czech Republic	86.4	84.2	81.9	79.6	n.a.
Slovak Republic	79.8	79.5	77.7	77.1	n.a.
Labour force activity rate (% of working age population)					
Czech Republic	90.2	87.8	85.3	82.3	n.a.
Slovak Republic	83.3	82.5	80.3	79.7	n.a.

Sources: Unemployment: EBRD (1994) Tables 3 and 8.
Labour force participation and activity rates: computed from CEC (1994) p. 29 'civilian labour force' respectively 'active population' divided by 'working age population'.

Note: *All numbers refer to year end, except 1994, which refer to September 1994 as reported by *Business Central Europe,* November/December 1994.

'velvet revolution' in 1989 for the two regions now corresponding to the Czech Republic (CR) and the Slovak Republic (SR). The CR has one of the lowest joblessness rates in Europe, earning it the status of an 'economic miracle' (e.g. Raiser, 1994). Despite its previous union with the Czech Republic, the Slovak Republic experienced a dramatic rise in unemployment to levels comparable with those in Poland, Hungary and Bulgaria.

A stable unemployment rate could disguise large declines in both employment and labour force participation (Boeri 1994, Scarpetta and Reutersward 1994); it could be claimed that low Czech unemployment simply reflects higher rates of exit from the labour force. The second half of Table 7.1 shows, however, that the Slovak Republic has experienced a similar, if not as severe, reduction of labour force participation which has accelerated over time, so this cannot alone explain the Czech labour market 'miracle.' Furthermore, Czech labour force participation was higher at the outset of the transformation.

Some analysts attribute divergent Czechoslovak labour market outcomes to differing degrees of economic contraction in the two countries. According to popular belief, the Slovak Republic was more heavily scarred by socialist planning, which located heavy industry and armaments production far from cold-war front lines. Yet, as Ham *et al.* (1994) have pointed out, the decline of output and production was virtually identical in both countries until 1993, and Table 7.2 confirms this for both GDP as well as industrial production.

Nor is it likely that the relative evolution of real wages or unit labour costs is to blame. On the whole, unions are weak in both countries and unit labour costs have fallen dramatically since 1990. The liberalization of prices was accompanied by a sharp nominal depreciation of the crown of roughly 50%, and Table 7.2 confirms a large drop in real product wages in both countries. While it is true

Table 7.2   Macroeconomic indicators (percentage change per annum)

	1990	1991	1992	1993	*Memo*: 1990–3 cumulative
Czech Republic					
Real GDP	-1.2	-14.2	-6.6	-0.3	-21.1
Industrial production	-3.5	-22.3	-10.6	-5.3	-36.5
Total employment	-0.1	-5.5	-2.6	-1.5	-10.2
Labour productivity	-0.2	-9.4	-4.1	1.2	-12.1
Real product wages	-0.8	-31.5	12.0	6.1	-19.2
Slovak Republic					
Real GDP	-2.5	-11.2	-7.0	-4.1	-22.8
Industrial production	-2.7	-21.6	-13.7	-13.5	-43.1
Total employment	-0.8	-7.9	-5.2	-1.6	-14.8
Labour productivity	-1.7	-3.5	-2.0	-2.5	-9.4
Real product wages	-0.7	-31.0	14.5	6.3	-16.5

Sources: Real product wages: computed from Ham *et al.* (1994) Table 1, using formula above. All other data: CEC (1994), p.38–39 and authors' calculations.

Note: Labour productivity growth is calculated as $(1+ g_Y)/(1+g_E) -1$, where g_Y and g_E are annualized real GDP and employment growth rates, respectively. Real product wage growth is computed in an analogous way.

that minimum wages have evolved differently since the divorce (Franz, 1994), they are currently unindexed and not strictly enforced in either country, but define the 'social minimum' (a yardstick for minimum welfare payments in the two countries). It seems equally implausible that provision of social welfare programmes, which might vitiate incentives to engage in the restructuring process, can account for differences between the CR and the SR. Table 7.3 shows that, in contrast to Poland and Hungary, average benefits have been maintained well below minimum wage levels in both countries.[1]

While it is clear that the CR has been a success story in dealing with unemployment, it is less clear why the Slovak Republic has been such a failure. Arguments attributing the entire rise in unemployment to industrial decline, real wages and unemployment benefit generosity have little basis. Indeed, the evidence seems to indicate a higher rate of unemployment incidence in the SR from the very beginning of the transformation. Table 7.4 compares inflow rates into unemployment (measured as a fraction of the employed), with outflow rates out of unemployment (measured as a fraction of the unemployed). Neglecting movements in and out of the labour force for the moment, the steady-state rate of unemployment is the ratio of an inflow rate into unemployment (as a fraction of employment) to a gross turnover rate (the sum of the inflow and outflow rates).[2] The table reveals that the Slovak Republic has experienced a stable but persistently higher rate of inflow over the sample, more comparable to inflow rates in the United States than Western Europe (see Layard *et al.*, 1991).

Table 7.3 Minimum wage and average unemployment benefit (as percentage of average wage)

	1991	1992	1993	1994:1
Czech Republic				
Minimum wage	51.1	45.9	36.5	36.7
Average benefit	46.3	24.8	n.a.	n.a.
Slovak Republic				
Minimum wage	52.0	47.5	42.1	44.4
Average benefit	43.8	31.6	29.2	31.1
Memo: Hungary				
Minimum wage	39.0	36.0	33.0	35.0
Average benefit	41.0	39.3	36.6	36.7
Poland				
Minimum wage	34.7	37.0	40.1	39.3
Average benefit	n.a.	36.0	36.0	36.0

Source: CEC (1994), p.38.

Table 7.4 Gross unemployment flows in the Czech and Slovak Republics (annual average of monthly rates)

	1991	1992	1993
Inflow rate into unemployment			
(as % of employment stock)			
Czech Republic	0.71	0.62	0.70
Slovak Republic	1.76	1.44	1.96
Outflow rate from unemployment			
(as % of unemployment stock)			
Czech Republic	18.02	23.94	20.78
Slovak Republic	5.66	10.06	8.06
Outflow rate from unemployment			
to employment (as % of			
unemployment stock)			
Czech Republic	11.50	16.61	15.39
Slovak Republic	3.76	5.21	3.39

Implied steady-state unemployment rates, average monthly data, 1993 (%)

	Outflow Rate	
Inflow rate	CR	SR
CR	3.3	8.0
SR	8.6	19.6

Source: Czech and Slovak Ministry of Labour and Social Affairs.

Note: Stocks are measured at beginning of month.

This important fact provides support for the argument that the *composition* of employment may have played a greater role in the differential unemployment performance than aggregate data imply. If Slovak employment was concentrated in 'loser industries' or in demographic groups with high rates of unemployment incidence, then this, rather than a collapse of production itself, could explain the unemployment differential.[3] Judging from Figure 7.1, which displays the structure of employment in 1991, this compositional effect must be subtle indeed. With the exception of agriculture, only minimal differences are evident. One important difference not evident in Figure 7.1 is employment in armaments manufacture, which in the Slovak Republic accounted for about 60% of pre-divorce military output and about 6% of Slovak industrial production, versus 1.5% in the Czech Republic (OECD, 1994). In 1990 President Havel ordered a large reduction in weapons production, which had peaked in 1987 at Kcs 29 billion (Czechoslovakian crowns), to Kcs 4 billion in 1992; of this, roughly 80% fell on Slovak enterprises and many of these cuts began to take effect in 1991.[4] Employment in Slovak armaments production declined over the period from 1990 to 1992 by more than 30 000, or roughly 10% of the increase of unemployment over the period (Huber and Ochotnicky, 1994).[5]

Finally, the overall high (and possibly higher) rate of exit from the labour force in the CR may have a different interpretation than in the SR. The underground or informal economy has emerged in virtually all CEECs as a systematic byproduct of the transformation. These activities are a natural response to profit opportunities and represent a key source of 'primary capital' which frees entrepreneurs from credit restrictions associated with the still-inefficient banking system. The informal economy may be crucial in accounting for the 'missing people' in the CR; from January 1991 to April 1992, roughly 450 000 Czechs voluntarily left state enterprises, without appearing elsewhere in the unemployment, employment or official migration statistics (Benácek, 1994; Raiser, 1994). The Institute of Labour and Social Affairs in Prague estimated that roughly 250 000 individuals received income from underground activity in 1992, up from 40 000 in 1990 (Bastyr, 1993). Strict administration of unemployment benefits have forced jobless workers into non-activity or into make-work jobs, or as 'private contractors' with lower social security burdens for their employers. Early retirement programmes, which were designed to ease older people out of the labour force, encouraged underground economic activity by forbidding supplemental income; high tax rates, described in detail in Appendix 7.1, also make it attractive to engage in the underground economy.

Indirect evidence can be found in sharply different patterns of self-employment in the two countries. At 9% in 1993, the rate of self-employment in the CR labour force is conspicuously higher than in the SR, which was 4.4% in the same year (CEC, 1994). Two factors have influenced the development of entrepreneurship in the two countries. The first is the extent of small business grants in the CR and the SR; Czech spending on entrepreneurial startups was 15

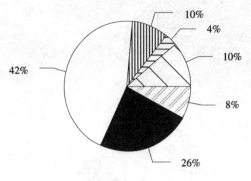

Czech Republic

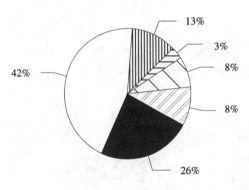

Slovak Republic

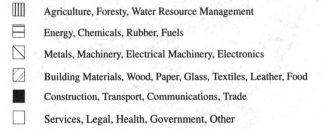

Agriculture, Foresty, Water Resource Management

Energy, Chemicals, Rubber, Fuels

Metals, Machinery, Electrical Machinery, Electronics

Building Materials, Wood, Paper, Glass, Textiles, Leather, Food

Construction, Transport, Communications, Trade

Services, Legal, Health, Government, Other

Source: Statistical Yearbook of the CSFR, 1992, Tables 7.2, 12 and 13.

Figure 7.1 The composition of employment in the Czech and Slovak Republics in 1991

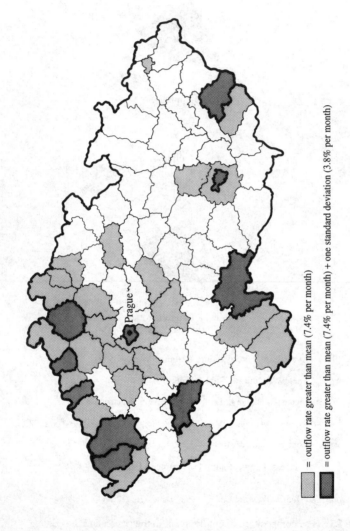

= outflow rate greater than mean (7.4% per month)

= outflow rate greater than mean (7.4% per month) + one standard deviation (3.8% per month)

Figure 7.2a Geographic distribution of exits from unemployment into non-participation in the Czech Republic, October 1990 – July 1994

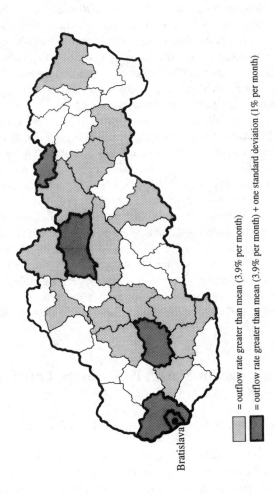

Figure 7.2b Geographic distribution of exits from unemployment into non-participation in the Slovak Republic, October 1990 – December 1993

times greater in the Slovak Republic in 1992, 80 times greater in 1993! The second factor is location. Proximity to the border, especially with developed industrial economies, is positively correlated with exits from unemployment into non-participation. Figure 7.2 present maps of the two countries with district patterns of labour force exit from unemployment expressed as deviation from the respective national means. Not only is variation across districts higher in the CR than in the SR, but high rates of exit from the labour force in the CR are concentrated along the border with the former GDR and central Bavaria, Austria and near large cities such as Prague, Pilsen and Brno. In contrast, the distribution of labour force exits in the Slovak Republic is random. Furthermore, regions which have high outflow rates also have high outflow rates into employment, which would militate against the discouraged worker interpretation. This evidence supports the hypothesis that a large part of the CR miracle may simply be underground or unregistered cross-border activity.[6]

In any case, a key difference evident from Table 7.4 that could reflect the effect of policy interventions is the rate of outflow out of unemployment to jobs, which is two to three times higher in the Czech Republic. The extent to which inflows and outflows can account for differences in unemployment rates is presented in the second part of Table 7.4, where we compute the steady-state unemployment rates that would obtain were the Czechs to have Slovakian outflow rates and were the Slovaks to have Czech inflow rates. Differences in outflow rates can account for almost half of the divergent experience in the two countries. The level of active labour market policies (ALMPs), which began to diverge already before but especially after the divorce, could have played a role in maintaining high unemployment turnover in the Czech Republic.

In the next section we discuss the theoretical rationale for government action in the realm of active labour market policy and describe the evolution of ALMP in both countries.

7.3 Active Labour Market Policy in the Czech and Slovak Republics

7.3.1 The Rationale for Active Labour Market Programmes

Active labour market policies (ALMPs) are generally understood as those measures which increase the exit rate from unemployment and include the provision of job counselling and information exchange, training, direct job creation as well as marginal job subsidies in general or to problem groups in particular (women, young people, the less-skilled). As a matter of principle, they should always be justified by the existence of market failures or distortions in the labour market relative to some ideal outcome. Yet the source of distortions which justify ALMPs are rarely if ever explicitly discussed. In developed industrial economies, these distortions might arise through unions, monopsonies, or efficiency wages; governments themselves may distort incentives via taxation, unemployment benefits and minimum wages. Labour supply may be affected by income taxation and the social safety net, early retirement policies and the minimum working age. Many interventions can be justified on efficiency as well as redistributive and political economic grounds; for example, unemployment benefits protect certain types of human capital investments from overly hasty depreciation or abandonment. In the context of a systemic transformation, distortions may arise from incomplete information, a lack of well-defined or conventionally defined property rights, as well as search externalities in labour markets.

Calmfors (1994) classifies ALMPs into three groups. *Job broking* addresses information, congestion or network externalities. Information is to some extent a public good, so the government might be able to improve matters by collecting and disseminating it, especially in emerging, transforming economies. *Labour market training* is designed to improve skills of workers, but is called for on efficiency grounds only when workers lack access to capital markets to finance human capital investments themselves. Since capital markets do not lend excessively in this area, it is safe to conclude that capital market imperfections can rationalize training programmes, as long as the training is for those skills in excess demand.

Direct job creation, which is most often a large component of ALMPs, is aimed at supporting the demand for labour, which is lower than normal for business cycle or structural reasons. During such periods, long-term unemployment can emerge, which may have deleterious effects on worker re-employability. There is ample evidence that unemployment durations are time dependent; the longer the duration, the lower the exit probability, controlling for observable worker characteristics. If pure sorting effects are the cause, there is little for the government to do to improve matters. Even if unemployment depreciates skills, rational workers should respond by choosing lower initial reservation wages and, subject to caveats about capital markets, the market should provide the correct incentives unless already distorted, e.g. by suboptimal provision of unemployment pay.

On the other hand, labour market intervention could be justified if workers are 'scarred' or 'ranked' by the duration of unemployment spells. Suppose there are two types of workers which can only be identified after some period of employment. 'Good workers' possess higher skills, more motivation and energy, or greater loyalty. 'Bad workers' have lower levels of these characteristics and are more likely to be unemployed than good ones, but workers of both types can become unemployed for economic reasons. Under these conditions, employers would always prefer to hire from the pool of employed workers; employment is a (noisy) signal that the worker comes from a better distribution of abilities and qualities. For a model in which employers 'rank' unemployed job candidates by duration of the current spell, see Blanchard and Diamond (1994). As is usually the case in such signalling problems, inefficiencies may arise. Job creation may give the unemployed the ability to break the bad signal of unemployment to the extent it really is a false positive.

Not only can job creation for problem groups increase outflows out of unemployment, but well-targeted wage subsidies can reduce the power of insiders that block downward adjustment of real wages. See Lindbeck and Snower (1985) and Blanchard and Summers (1986) for elaboration of these ideas. At the same time, these programmes may also have negative effects on the functioning of labour markets. Calmfors (1994) adduces evidence, especially from the Swedish experience, that these effects may outweigh benefits.[7] Most importantly, dead-weight loss and substitution effects can be quite large and under such conditions, it is questionable whether they are an efficient use of public resources. At the same time, the evidence supports programmatic targeting of problem groups as a means of getting around this problem (OECD, 1993).

Another often neglected aspect of ALMPs is advisory and information services for the jobless. A consensus has emerged that intensified counselling and search assistance positively affect re-employment probabilities via a 'prodding effect', especially for long-term unemployed (see the reviews in OECD (1993) and Calmfors (1994); for evidence on the United Kingdom, see Lehmann (1993)). Training also seems to have a small but negative aggregate effect on wages, which would support the view that they increase the supply of those workers; their greatest effects are on groups with the least experience or who have systematic difficulties re-entering the labour force, such as women (Dolton, 1993).

In summary, evidence on the effectiveness of ALMPs at the individual level is mixed. This may have as much to do with econometric problems due to endogenous reactions of policy-makers as well as the displacement, dead-weight, substitution and incentive effects described above. Ironically, much new criticism of ALMPs originates in Sweden (Calmfors and Nymoen, 1990), where programmes in place seem ill-equipped to respond to mass unemployment. Yet cross-country evidence on ALMP spending consistently shows a small but statistically significant negative association with average unemployment rates (Burda, 1988; Jackman et al., 1990; Layard et al., 1991; OECD, 1993), indicating a role for these programmes in explaining divergent labour market outcomes of the CR and the SR. In the next section, specifics of Czech and Slovak ALMPs are discussed in more detail.

7.3.2   Active Labour Market Programmes: Description and History[8]

In the Czech and Slovak Republics, a rich mixture of ALMP programmes has been implemented since the passing of enabling legislation in June 1991. Inspired by the Swedish experience, Federal Labour Minister Petr Miller and his Czech counterpart Milan Horalek proposed a proactive, local-based employment policy which could react flexibly to diverging regional fortunes. Because these reforms were enacted at federal level, they were simultaneously adopted by both republics.

The first element of this approach, which was implemented in late 1990, was the establishment of a computerized information system at the employment office district level and the adequate staffing of these offices. Second, the maximal duration of unemployment was fixed at one year and later reduced in 1992 to six months; benefit eligibility was linked to a regime of frequent contacts with the employment office, training offers and alternative employment. Third, the labour ministry initiated several job creation programmes, often tailored to specific groups and designed as an alternative to unemployment benefits. The following paragraphs discuss the primary components of these programmes in greater detail.

Publicly useful jobs (PUJ) are locally administered, communal make-work designed primarily for the unemployed who have exhausted entitlement to normal benefits. Jobs created under this programme are temporary, usually lasting up to six months, and they usually involve public works projects arranged with local

Table 7.5 Job creation ALMPs in the Czech and Slovak Republics (000's and percentage of labour force)

	1992		1993		1994	
Czech Republic						
Publicly Useful Jobs (PUJ)	20.8	(0.4)	10.4	(0.2)	10.6	(0.2)
Socially Purposeful Jobs (SPJ)	121.1	(2.4)	102.0	(2.1)	61.2	(1.2)
of which:						
For self-employed	23.5	(0.5)	25.7	(0.5)	12.0	(0.2)
By employers	72.6	(1.4)	74.7	(1.5)	49.0	(1.0)
Trainees	19.0	(0.4)	1.2	(0.0)	0.1	(0.0)
Assistants	4.5	(0.1)	0.2	(0.0)	0.0	(0.0)
Youngsters	1.6	(0.0)	0.2	(0.0)	0.0	(0.0)
Training Posts (TP)	-	10.2	(0.2)	5.7	(0.1)	
of which:						
Secondary	-	7.6	(0.2)	4.4	(0.9)	
Graduated	-	1.6	(0.0)	0.9	(0.0)	
Youngsters	-	1.0	(0.0)	0.3	(0.0)	
Total	**141.9**	**(2.8)**	**122.6**	**(2.5)**	**77.5**	**(1.6)**
Slovak Republic						
Publicly useful Jobs (PUJ)	24.0	(1.0)	8.2	(0.3)	7.5	(0.3)
Socially Purposeful Jobs (SPJ)	52.3	(2.2)	119.3	(5.0)	121.8	(5.1)
of which:						
Created by legal entities	24.5	(1.0)	59.1	(2.5)	90.6	(3.8)
By private individuals	31.7	(1.3)	61.2	(2.5)	30.5	(1.3)
Retraining (RET)	1.9	(0.1)	3.4	(0.1)	2.6	(0.1)
of which:						
Unemployed	1.6	(0.1)	1.8	(0.1)	1.7	(0.1)
Memo: completed training						
within current year	13.8	(0.6)	16.5	(0.7)	n.a.	
Total	**78.2**	**(3.2)**	**130.9**	**(5.4)**	**131.9**	**(5.5)**

Sources: Czech and Slovak Ministry of Labour and Social Affairs, CEC (1994).

Note: Data are positions created with employers (not necessarily filled), at mid-year (July) except SR retraining in 1992 (June). Numbers may not add to totals due to rounding. The 1994 ALMP data of both the CR and SR are normalized by the labour force at year end 1993. Labour force are from CEC (1994), p. 30.

authorities. The street sweepers one frequently sees in Prague are an example of this programme. According to Ham *et al.* (1994), local authorities have not been particularly successful in creating these jobs, although the data above show that PUJs constitute about 10% of all publicly supported job creation. Two important functions of PUJ are to provide a 'workfare' option for those whose benefits durations expire, and to test the willingness to work of the currently unemployed. In 1993, the average wage in PUJs was roughly equal to the legal minimum, whereby the monthly contribution by local offices was roughly Kc 1 800 in the Czech Republic and Sk 1 450 in the Slovak Republic.[9]

The much more important Socially Purposeful Jobs (SPJ) programme, in contrast, is designed either to create new positions with existing employers or to encourage self-employment among the unemployed. In principle, it is not designed to subsidize existing jobs. District labour offices have considerable discretion over the types of job creation that are to be subsidized as well as over the individuals to whom the vacant positions are offered.[10] Most of the support takes the form of targeted marginal wage subsidies. In addition, traineeships, assistantships and positions for teenagers without skills are subsidized by local employment authorities. In 1993, a programme was launched which targets secondary school leavers and university graduates (TPSY); another minor programme is targeted towards the disabled. Tables 7.5 and 7.6 display some summary statistics on Czech and Slovak ALMPs since 1992.

Table 7.6 Overall spending on ALMPs in the Czech and Slovak Republics (in millions of Kcs for 1991, 1992 and Kc/Sk for 1993; per unemployed in parentheses[1])

	1991		1992		1993	
Czech Republic						
Publicly Useful Jobs (PUJ)	78	(526)	223	(1 397)	160	(1 015)
Socially Purposeful Jobs (SPJ)	497	(3 334)	968	(6 068)	331	(2 099)
of which:						
Startup Grants	167	(1 119)	232	(1 454)	160	(1 015)
Retraining	40	(268)	94	(589)	73	(466)
Training Posts (TP)	48	(320)	326	(2 039)	245	(1 559)
Other[2]	110	(736)	107	(607)	53	(339)
Total	**773**	**(5 185)**	**1 718**	**(10 763)**	**749**	**(4 764)**
Slovak Republic						
Publicly Useful Jobs (PUJ)	108	(601)	403	(1 420)	164	(500)
Socially Purposeful Jobs (SPJ)	352	(1 958)	2 871	(10 119)	750	(2 290)
of which:						
Startup Grants	0	(0)	14	(50)	2	(7)
Retraining	55	(304)	292	(1 029)	118	(361)
Training Posts (TP)	-		98	(345)	54	(165)
Other[2]	-		149	(523)	20	(62)
Total	**515**	**(2 863)**	**3 813**	**(13 436)**	**1 107**	**(3 379)**

[1] Average unemployment over the year. Numbers may not add to totals due to rounding.

[2] Including retirements, maternity leaves, military service and the imprisoned.

The most salient fact that emerges is that these programmes are relatively small in both spending per person and relative to the size of the labour force. *In this direct sense, they cannot explain the difference between the Czech and other CEEC unemployment rates.* Job creation ALMPs, especially of the SPJ type, are more likely to stimulate the supply of private vacancies. Indeed, in aggregate data, vacancies and ALMP measures are positively correlated. Figure 7.3 displays a weak positive correlation over time between aggregate private vacancies and both aggregate overall ALMP expenditures and job slots created in both countries. This positive correlation has two plausible interpretations.[11] The first is that ALMP either improve the attractiveness of job creation for firms, or simply increase local aggregate demand. A second interpretation is that a common third factor, business conditions, is responsible for both: when times are good, more vacancies are created, tax revenues are higher and more ALMP programmes can be financed; alternatively, when the unemployment budget is fixed, lower unemployment means lower benefits paid, and more resources for active policy. That SPJ is more strongly correlated with vacancies than PUJ (neither are necessarily included in official vacancy listings) supports the hypothesis that the SPJ programme acts as direct spur to job creation.

At the same time, information on the geographic distribution of ALMP programmes in the Czech and Slovak Republics indicates that labour offices respond to local conditions. The scatterplots in Figure 7.4 illustrate the extent to which ALMP programme allocation to the local districts or micro-regions is correlated with local labour market outcomes. Presumably, the provision of ALMPs should be moderate in those districts in which vacancies are already relatively abundant and unemployment rates are low.[12] The responsiveness to local labour market conditions is more evident in the CR than in the SR, which is also the finding of Slovak researchers looking at the same question (Ochotnicky and Kohutova, 1994).

A second salient fact emerging from Tables 7.5 and 7.6 is the different level of active labour market policies in the Czech and Slovak Republics, even before the 'velvet revolution'.[13] Table 7.6 documents the evolution of expenditures over the period 1991–3. Low spending per unemployed in the SR despite rising unemployment may be due to a rigid per capita formula used in 1991 to distribute federal funds for employment policies. A sharper increase in unemployment in the Slovak Republic resulted in fewer resources per head for ALMPs, first due to a dilution effect and, second, to a diversion of money to unemployment benefits expenditures. In 1992, massive efforts were made to rectify the asymmetry; ALMP spending increased by more than 600% over 1991. The money was not spent particularly efficiently: using the data from the tables, an average Slovak SPJ (PUJ) position cost 24 100 (49 100) crowns in 1992, compared with 9 500 (21 400) crowns in the Czech Republic.

The 'velvet divorce' ended implicit federal transfers via the employment policy budget. The fiscal situation of the new Slovak Republic was deteriorating; the

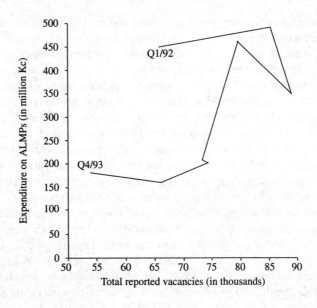

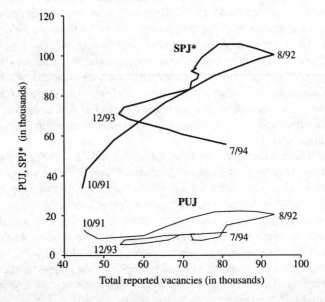

SPJ*: Socially Purposeful Jobs net of participants in self-employment schemes, but including Training Posts for School-Leavers and Youngsters (TPSY).

Figure 7.3a Aggregate ALMPs, vacancies and unemployment: Czech Republic

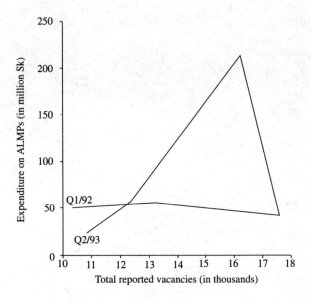

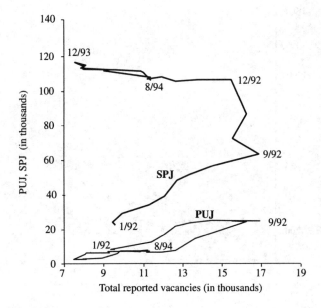

Figure 7.3b   Aggregate ALMPs, vacancies and unemployment: Slovak Republic

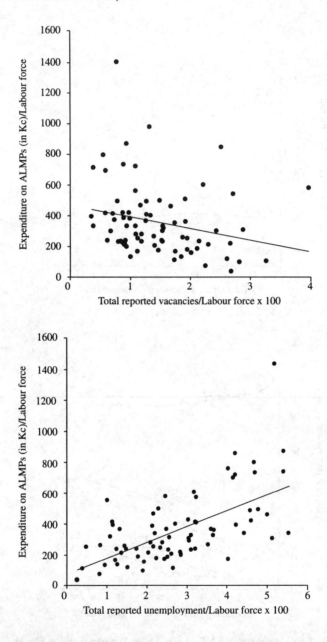

Figure 7.4a ALMP spending, vacancies and unemployment in cross section, yearend 1992: Czech Republic (76 district labour offices)

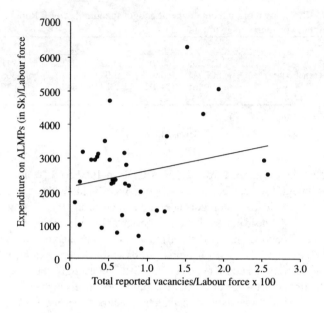

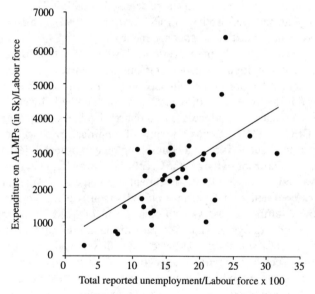

Figure 7.4b   ALMP spending, vacancies and unemployment in cross section, yearend 1992: Slovak Republic (38 district labour offices)

Table 7.7   Breakdown of total employment budget spending, Slovak Republic millions of crowns (percentage of total)

	1991		1992		1993*	
Total	3 206	(100.0)	5 521	(100.0)	1 941	(100.0)
Passive (benefits)	2 745	(85.6)	1 711	(31.0)	1 305	(67.2)
Active	461	(14.4)	3811	(69.0)	636	(32.8)

*Until September only

Source: Slovak Ministry of Labour and Social Affairs.

state budget deficit jumped from 2.8% of GDP in 1992 to 6.7% in 1993, and mounting unemployment benefits payments were paid for by cuts in active employment policies. The consequences are evident from Table 7.6: in 1993, a year of a sharp decline in industrial production and rising unemployment, spending in the Slovak Republic on ALMPs was reduced by more than two-thirds (71%), versus 56% in the CR; on a per unemployed basis the decline was even steeper: 75% in the SR versus a constant 56% in the CR. Interestingly, the data in Tables 7.5 and 7.6 imply that while programme participation levels in the SR were high, overall spending and spending per person has declined sharply. The curtailment of ALMP spending in the Slovak Republic depicted in Table 7.7 is an example of the crowding out observed in other CEECs. See Burda (1993) for a description of this process in the context of an economic model.

As discussed above, an often overlooked aspect of active labour market programmes is employment office staffing. Evidence exists that OECD unemployment rates are highest in those countries in which staffing per unemployed is the lowest, but the causality might well be in reverse, as static staffs are overwhelmed by increased numbers of jobless. The *Employment Outlook* (OECD, 1993) contains a review of empirical evidence pointing to positive effects of supervision and counselling on exit probabilities. Table 7.8 displays the evolution of staffing in the Czech and Slovak Republics since 1991. Uldrichova and Karpisek (1994) document a divergence in the number of supervisory (counselling) staff per unemployed person, with the Slovaks showing sharply lower staffing levels. As with other forms of ALMP spending, sharp increases in unemployment are likely to dilute the employment office's effectiveness in advising the unemployed and in disseminating information.

In contrast, spending on retraining programmes appears to be a minor source of difference between the two countries. A legal right to retraining exists, and local districts are involved in arranging training programmes. Although spending has increased, it remains a minor fraction of total spending in both countries; both the CR and SR spend little on retraining compared with Hungary and Poland (CEC, 1993, p.29). In general, retraining is seen as an introduction to a new job, and may have aspects similar to SPJ programmes. Firms seem much more willing to hire qualified individuals from the unemployment pool than to retrain; in addition,

The Impact of Active Labour Market Policies 193

Table 7.8 Labour Office staffing in the Czech and Slovak Republics, numbers

	1991	1992	1993[1]
Czech Republic			
Total Staff	4 434	n.a.	4 392
of which:			
Consulting staff	377	n.a.	353
Unemployed/Total staff	50	n.a.	32
Unemployed/Consulting staff	588	n.a.	393
Slovak Republic			
Total Staff	2 026	2 686	2 882
of which:			
Staff on the district level	851	994	1 125
Staff on the local level	1 117	1 692	1 757
Unemployed/Total staff	149	97	128
Unemployed/Consulting staff	1 118	n.a.	n.a.

[1] For the CR: Staffing as of 30 June 1993.

Source: CR: Uldrichova and Karpisek (1994), OECD, authors' calculations; Slovak Ministry of Labour and Social Affairs

public retraining programmes only pay 70% of the previous wage, marginally better than the unemployment benefit (reduced in November 1993 to 60%). As a result, most enter training programmes after having become unemployed.

7.4 Econometric Evidence on the Effectiveness of ALMPs in the Czech and Slovak Republics

In this section, we employ econometric methods to explore the effectiveness of ALMPs in the Czech and Slovak Republics. Specifically, we would like to answer the following question: have active labour market programmes, measured in various ways, affected the rate at which the unemployed exit unemployment into employment? All other things given, this can yield insights into the effect of such programmes on the rate of unemployment. The basis for our investigation is the so-called 'matching function', an empirical relationship linking the flow number of exits from unemployment to the lagged stocks of unemployed and vacancies, as well as other factors:

$$\ln x_{it} = \alpha_0 + \alpha_1 \ln u_{it-1} + \alpha_2 \ln v_{it-1} + Z_{it}'\beta + \varepsilon_{it} \tag{7.1}$$

where x_{it} = the outflow during period t of unemployed individuals in district i into employment, u_{it} = the stock of unemployed individuals registered at the employment agency at the end of period t, v_{it} = the stock of unfilled vacancies reported by firms to the employment agency at the end of period t, Z_{it} = a vector of other time- and/or district-dependent attributes, α_0, α_1, α_2 are coefficients, β is a vector of coefficients, and ε_{it} = a random error term.

There is a substantial literature on the matching function, which we do not review here.[14] The underlying idea is that, under given conditions, the number of exits from unemployment into jobs is a stable positive function of the number of unemployed and the stock of vacancies in the previous period. We estimate a logarithmic form of a 'Cobb–Douglas' specification which exhibits constant elasticities of matches with respect to its argument. Under constant returns to scale, $\alpha_1 + \alpha_2 = 1$. In augmented form, the equation is

$$\ln x_{it} = \alpha_0 + \alpha_1 \ln u_{it-1} + \alpha_2 \ln v_{it-1} + Z_{it}'\beta + \gamma \ln(\text{ALMP}_{it}) + \varepsilon_{it} \qquad (7.2)$$

or, alternatively,

$$(1-\gamma(L))\ln x_{it} = \alpha_0 + \alpha_1 \ln u_{it-1} + \alpha_2 \ln v_{it-1} + Z_{it}'\beta +$$
$$\gamma \ln(\text{ALMP}_{it}) + \varepsilon_{it} \qquad (7.3)$$

where ALMP_{it} is some measure of the local activity in active labour market programmes at time t, and may include lagged values. A potential lag structure $\gamma(L)$ on the endogenous variable captures partial adjustment in the matching process.[15]

7.4.1   Data

The data were obtained from the Czech and Slovak Ministries of Labour and Social Affairs. The unit of observation is a district labour office, of which there are 76 in the Czech Republic and 38 in the Slovak Republic. Observation intervals span the period November 1990 – July 1994 for the Czech Republic and November 1990 – December 1993 for the Slovak Republic. We report descriptive statistics for the two data sets in Table 7.9. The initial observations for both the CR and SR were collected when the district labour offices were being established and appear somewhat unreliable. Following previous work, most econometric estimates involve shorter time intervals. Since most observations on ALMP began in January 1992, the sample used in estimation begins in 1992.

The key hypothesis to be tested is that the effectiveness of matching at the district level is positively affected by various ALMP measures. We include as additional regressors several variables available in the CR and SR, which unfortunately are not always comparable for both countries. From the CR, we have monthly data on the stocks of socially purposeful jobs (SPJ) and publicly useful jobs (PUJ) created at the district level in the form of 'agreements' concluded with municipalities or private employers. These created positions represent the total potential stock of subsidized jobs. The SPJ measure used in estimation includes newer job creation programmes for school leavers and youngsters (the Training Posts for School Leavers and Youngsters (TPSY) reported in Table 7.5) but excludes business grants (participants in self-employment schemes).

Table 7.9 Data employed in regression analysis: descriptive statistics

	Period	Frequency	Mean	Standard deviation	Minimum	Maximum
Czech Republic						
Outflows into						
employment	1/92–7/94	m	337.44	245.00	16	2 500
Unemployed	1/92–7/94	m	2 164.43	1 639.33	123	11 330
Vacancies	1/92–7/94	m	935.75	1 903.33	55	20 965
Spending on ALMPs						
(000s Kcs/Kc)	1/92–4/93	q	4 116.14	4 161.13	114.46	39 594.30
SPJ*	1/92–7/94	m	1 076.93	981.55	8	6 082
PUJ	1/92–7/94	m	147.76	140.68	0	854
Slovak Republic						
Outflows into						
employment	1/92–12/93	m	333.82	232.13	2	1 588
Unemployed	1/92–12/93	m	7 973.30	3 097.82	1 671	21 123
Vacancies	1/92–12/93	m	318.98	502.62	13	4 306
Spending on ALMPs						
(000s Kcs/Sk)	1/92–2/93	q	1 688.55	1 725.12	72.97	1 3815.38
Staff	2/92–12/93	m	68.24	22.56	21	142
of which:						
District Staff	2/92–12/93	m	26.34	7.14	10	50
Local Staff	2/92–12/93	m	41.90	17.02	9	104

Source: CR, SR Labour Ministries of Labour and Social Affairs.

Note: Spending on ALMPs in CR and SR are not directly comparable. SPJ* denotes Socially Purposeful Jobs net of participants in self-employment schemes, but including Training Posts for School-Leavers and Youngsters (TPSY). See Table 7.6 and text for discussion.

In the Slovak Republic, monthly staffing data are available at the district labour office level (DISTSTAFF) as well as local labour office level (LOCSTAFF).[16] According to arguments made in section 7.3, staffing enhances matching efficiency. If local labour market consultants contribute to the matching process, an equiproportional increase in unemployment and vacancies without an increase in staffing – the usual thought experiment made under 'constant returns to scale' – may lead to a *reduction* of matching efficiency. Put differently, the external effect of the unemployed on the contact and job finding probabilities of others is greater, since there is competition for a given amount of assistance at the employment agencies.

Finally, quarterly data are available on spending on ALMPs at the district level for both Czech and Slovak Republics (EXP). The Czech data are for total district spending, including equipment and staffing, as well as PUJ, SPJ and other programmes. The Slovak ALMP data include only three categories of spending: (1) training (2) benefits for those in retraining and (3) counselling. This is clearly a poor proxy for total spending, but if the proportions remain constant, the log of this variable will be an acceptable proxy for the total.[17]

7.4.2   Results

The estimation results for the matching function of the forms (7.1), (7.2) and (7.3) are reported in Table 7.10.[18] The first column for both countries is the 'bare bones' matching function often found in the literature. Fixed time and individual district effects control for time-invariant district attributes as well as country-wide, time-dependent factors, for example, a trend in matching efficiency. Results are consistent with those reported by Burda (1993), Boeri (1994) and Boeri and Scarpetta (1994). The coefficients on both unemployment and vacancies are less precisely estimated in the Slovak Republic. The sum of the estimated coefficients $\alpha_1 + \alpha_2$ is always less than unity, and constant returns can

Table 7.10   OLS matching function estimates, dependent variable: flows into jobs, $\ln F_t$

(a)   Czech Republic

Coefficient on:	(1)	(2)	(3)	(4)	(5)	(6)
$\ln u_{t-1}$	0.7740	0.5959	0.7430	0.5857	0.7220	0.5958
	(0.0318)	(0.0322)	(0.0334)	(0.0336)	(0.0387)	(0.0390)
$\ln v_{t-1}$	0.1339	0.0912	0.1406	0.1062	0.0971	0.0668
	(0.0183)	(0.0176)	(0.0188)	(0.0180)	(0.0218)	(0.0212)
$\ln PUJ_{t-1}$	—	—	0.0337	0.0086	—	—
			(0.0078)	(0.0077)		
$\ln SPJ^*_{t-1}$	—	—	0.0492	0.022	—	—
			(0.0157)	(0.0152)		
$\ln EXP_t$	—	—	—	—	0.1041	0.0666
					(0.0150)	(0.0150)
$\ln F_{t-1}$	—	0.2375	—	0.2363	—	0.2091
		(0.0197)		(0.0203)		(0.0224)
$\ln F_{t-2}$	—	0.0655	—	0.0703	—	0.0486
		(0.0199)		(0.0203)		(0.0224)
$\ln F_{t-3}$	—	0.0332	—	0.0411	—	0.0177
		(0.0195)		(0.0198)		(0.0218)
$\ln F_{t-4}$	—	0.0115	—	-0.0013	—	0.0028
		(0.0179)		(0.0181)		(0.0199)
R^2	0.9071	0.9165	0.9133	0.9213	0.9051	0.9117
$F: H_0 = CRTS$	5.6418*	0.8276	0.6446	2.8510	15.1203**	1.5844
N	2356	2356	2238	2238	1824	1824
Sample	1/92–7/94	1/92–7/94	2/92–7/94	2/92–7/94	1/92–12/93	1/92–12/93

Data: Ministry of Labour and Social Affairs of the Czech Republic.

Note: All regressions include individual district and fixed time effects.
Regressions (2), (4) and (6) include lagged dependent variables.
Regressions (3) and (4) include the number of participants in Active Labour Market Programs (ALMPs): Publicly Useful Jobs (PUJ), Socially Purposeful Jobs (SPJ*) net of participants in self-employment schemes, but including Training Posts for School-Leavers and Youngsters (TPSY).
F-test in (2), (4) and (6): null hypothesis is long-run constant returns scale restriction; in (3) and (4), the *F*-test includes the coefficients on the ALMPs.
An asterisk denotes significance level of 1% (**) and 5% (*). Critical Values are 6.63 and 3.84, respectively.

(b) Slovak Republic

Coefficient on:	(1)	(2)	(3)	(4)	(5)	(6)
ln u_{t-1}	0.8290	0.6258	0.6996	0.5156	0.9407	0.7094
	(0.2027)	(0.1713)	(0.2126)	(0.1745)	(0.2349)	(0.2104)
ln u_{t-1}	0.0566	0.0334	0.0418	0.0123	0.1278	0.0854
	(0.0405)	(0.0342)	(0.0410)	(0.0336)	(0.0449)	(0.0403)
ln DISTSTAFF$_t$	—	—	-0.0896	-0.1534	—	—
			(0.1899)	(0.1559)		
ln LOCSTAFF$_t$	—	—	0.4239	0.1465	—	—
			(0.1531)	(0.1262)		
ln EXP$_t$	—	—	—	—	0.1201	0.0681
					(0.0426)	(0.0383)
ln F_{t-1}	—	0.4784	—	0.4755	—	0.4200
		(0.0350)		(0.0334)		(0.0409)
ln F_{t-2}	—	0.0576	—	0.0555	—	0.0675
		(0.0382)		(0.0372)		(0.0434)
ln F_{t-3}	—	0.0807	—	0.1185	—	0.0205
		(0.0357)		(0.0365)		(0.0414)
ln F_{t-4}	—	-0.0147	—	-0.0152	—	-0.0535
		(0.0329)		(0.0319)		(0.0388)
$\bar{R}^2$	0.6012	0.7170	0.6134	0.7407	0.6351	0.7102
$F: H_0 = $ CRTS	0.2996	2.1290	1.3963	0.7945	0.0786	1.2825
N	912	912	872	872	636	636
Sample	1/92–12/93	1/92–12/93	2/92–12/93	2/92–12/93	1/92–6/93	1/92–6/93

Data: Ministry of Labour and Social Affairs of the Slovak Republic.

Note: All regressions include individual district and fixed time effects.
Regressions (2), (4) and (6) include lagged dependent variables.
Regressions (3) and (4) include staffing data for on a local and district level.
F-Test in (2), (4) and (6): null hypothesis is long-run constant returns scale restriction.
An asterisk denotes significance level of 1% (**) and 5% (*). Critical values are 6.63 and 3.84, respectively.

be rejected at conventional significance levels for the Czech data. The results support the lagged adjustment specification, although roughly two-thirds of the adjustment occurs in the first month in both countries. Constant returns under this specification are no longer rejected.[19]

Columns (3)–(6) report estimates of the same function when the above-mentioned measures of active labour market policy are included, as in equation (7.2). All interventions have the expected sign, and are uniformly statistically significant in specifications without lags. There is, however, strong evidence of serial correlation in the district residuals, so henceforth we focus on the dynamic specifications. One robust conclusion is that *expenditures* at the district level are statistically significant in both countries, even in the lagged adjustment specification. Estimated coefficients are similar in both countries, and yield a short-run impact elasticity of spending on outflows into employment of 0.067 in the Czech Republic and 0.068 in the Slovak Republic; the corresponding long-run elasticities are 0.092 and 0.125, respectively. The higher long-run elasticity in the SR reflects a higher degree of estimated persistence in outflows compared to the CR, which is true of all the estimates reported in Table 7.10. This higher persistence may be related to administration of benefits and active labour market programmes (see Ham *et al.*, 1994).

We compare the results in two ways. First, we compute the comparative effectiveness of active labour market policy spending in the two countries or, equivalently, the 'cost' of an additional exit from unemployment to employment, all other things being equal. Evaluating the elasticities at respective sample means in the two countries, an additional 100 000 crowns spent per quarter in an average Czech district in our sample is associated with 0.76 additional outflows per month in the long run, as compared with roughly 2.5 outflows per month in the Slovak Republic. Inversely, an additional outflow into employment would cost 132,000 Kc per quarter in the Czech Republic, compared with 40,500 Sk per quarter in the Slovak Republic.[20]

A second approach is to estimate the impact of the drastic reduction in Slovak ALMP spending in 1993. How high would outflows have been had the Slovaks maintained spending at average levels in 1992? From Table 7.6, raising ALMP spending in 1993 to 1992 levels represents an increase of 244.4%. The estimates imply an increase in the monthly outflow rate of (2.444)(0.125)=30.6%. Assuming all other things equal at inflow and outflow rates reported in Table 7.4, this implies a 1.9% reduction in the 1993 steady-state unemployment rate. (The *actual* unemployment rate in the Slovak Republic at yearend 1993 was 14.4%).[21] While the Slovak Republic suffers a disadvantage with respect to industry structure and demographics, the sharp cut in ALMP spending which ensued after the dissolution can explain more than half of the increase in unemployment in 1993. The cut in spending in the Czech Republic can also explain part of the decline in outflow rates observed in 1993 (see Table 7.4). Spending fell by 56%, on both a total and per unemployed basis; all other things given, our estimates above imply that restoring Czech spending to 1992 levels would be associated with a 12.4% increase in outflows, or a reduction in the steady-state unemployment rate from 3.3% to 3%.

Naturally, several caveats should be made with respect to these estimates. The first and most important is the general equilibrium impact of a large increase in expenditures. It is likely that such an increase could give rise to wage pressure, making some marginal vacancies less profitable. A second caveat is that the supply of ALMP is potentially endogenous, as Figure 7.4 seems to suggest. It is plausible that ALMP programmes respond to anticipated future unemployment inflows, stocks or general labour market conditions. Under these conditions, the effect of spending we estimate will be biased downwards and our results can be interpreted as lower bounds for the true impact.

A final caveat involves the Lucas critique: a massive intervention of the order discussed may well represent a regime change and alter the aggregate matching function on which the experiment is based. Not only might search behaviour of agents change in response to policy variation, but the behaviour of the labour offices may react as well. The data seem to suggest that ALMP implementation in the SR and CR follow different rules. Slovak spending at the local level is less likely to flow to problem regions where job creation is low and unemployment is high. In addition, much variation in the ALMP observed over the period 1991–93 occurred during the run-up to divorce, when a number of conflicting incentives may have been operative.

7.5 Conclusions

Subject to the caveats and usual caution which should be exercised when interpreting econometric results, we offer the following conclusions.

- Job creation and subsidized ALMPs in the CR represent a modest fraction of the labour force. At best, their use can be seen as a 'catalyst' for increasing exit rates from unemployment. In the Slovak Republic, programme volume is higher, but on a spending per capita basis the data suggest the same conclusion.
- Spending on ALMPs at the district level is associated with outflows from unemployment into jobs in both countries. In contrast, our results show no direct impact of 'socially purposeful jobs' or 'publicly useful jobs' on the matching process, but do not rule out an indirect effect working through the supply of vacancies. Evidence on staffing also suggests at best a weak impact on job matching.
- In the aggregate, job subsidy (SPJ) programmes are correlated with aggregate private vacancies, suggesting that (1) they cause job creation directly by creating profitable opportunities for firms to create vacancies, either via supply (subsidies) or aggregate demand; or (2) a common third factor drives both the stocks of private vacancies as well as the public resources available for active policies. Evidence on PUJ and SPJ supports rather the former interpretation in the CR, but less so in the SR.
- Reported estimates should be considered as lower bounds when active labour market policy is endogenous. A strong negative correlation can be observed between slack in local job markets and ALMP activity across local labour offices in the CR, whereby this relationship is less evident in the SR, even when spending was high, as in 1992.

While it is premature to translate our econometric results into concrete policy proposals, our results do provide a complementary explanation of the striking difference in labour market performance between the Czech and Slovak Republics. Of the usual explanations, industry structure (rather than a collapse of activity relative to the CR) and demographics (although the evidence is poor) can explain persistently higher rates of unemployment incidence in the Slovak

Republic. Higher rate of outflow from unemployment in the Czech Republic is in part attributable to the underground economy. At the same time, higher outflow rates are also related to well-implemented active labour market policies. The econometric evidence supports a small but consistent impact of active labour market policy spending at the local level in both countries.

It follows that the split-up, which was associated with a 71% reduction in ALMP spending in the Slovak Republic, bears some of the blame for the further deterioration of Slovak labour market conditions. At the same time, the estimated size of the effects are modest, and on the order of 2% in 1993. In this respect, ALMPs should not be regarded as a general panacea for the woes of Central and Eastern European labour markets. This chapter does, however, provide evidence that they can be an important flanking manoeuvre, which in times of high unemployment can often be crowded out by passive expenditures.

Appendix 7.1:   Labour Taxation and Tax Reform in the Czech and Slovak Labour Markets

Taxes are likely to play an important role in labour markets in transforming economies, just as they do in established ones. The abandonment of central planning means that the old system of profit confiscation by the state must be replaced by other types of taxation. Due to the extreme extent of cross subsidization, the net tax burden over time may not change very much as a result of the abolition of subsidies and profit taxes (Barbone and Marchetti, 1994). In the Czech and Slovak Republics, tax reform started by gradually amending the former tax laws while preparing a new tax law package which was passed by the Federal Assembly in the course of 1992 and came into effect on 1 January 1993. The new system consists of income taxes (corporate and personal income tax), a value-added tax, excise duties, property (real estate) taxes, inheritance and gift taxes, taxes on transfers of movable or immovable property, and a road tax. In addition to these, environmental taxes and number of local taxes and specific payments have been introduced. The novel feature of tax administration is a switch from direct to indirect taxation, which began with the replacement of turnover tax with a value-added tax. In both Czech and Slovak Republics the two VAT tax rates were originally 5% (for goods) and 23% (for services). These rates were later increased in the Slovak Republic to 7 and 25%, respectively. The introduction of VAT resulted in sharp price increases in January 1993. This was partially brought about by the insufficient information about the new tax practices: some firms included into their prices VAT together with the former turnover tax, so the price increase was higher than was anticipated.

Labour markets in the two republics were influenced mostly by changes in the wage-related taxes: income tax and payroll tax. Personal income tax ('tax on income of physical persons') has been reformed in two important ways.

(1) The tax rates were unified for all categories of persons and incomes. Before, taxes were applied according to personal characteristics (e.g. marital status, sex, age). Under the new system, these distortions were removed. The new tax rate is progressive, based on the system of five income brackets ranging from 15% on the first 60 000 crowns to 45% on incomes above 1 080 000 crowns.

(2) The payroll tax (tax on volume of wages) paid by employers was abolished. This tax was effectively replaced by contributions to three newly established social insurance funds. In both republics, the social insurance system was radically reformed. The new system was implemented in January 1993. A new National Insurance Company was created to administer three insurance funds: the old age pensions fund, the health insurance fund and the hospital insurance fund.

Labour taxes are rather high in the two republics in comparison to OECD countries. Contributions of dependent-status employees are divided between employees and their employers in the following way: the employee pays 11% of his gross monthly wage, out of which 5.9% goes to the pension fund, 3.7% to the health insurance fund and 1.4% to the hospital insurance fund. Employers pay a contribution for each employee amounting to 35% from employee's gross monthly wage, out of which 20.6% is for the pension fund, 10% for the health insurance fund and 4.4% for the hospital insurance fund. The contributions paid by employers constitute a replacement of the former payroll tax. They add to roughly a 46% tax rate on labour, which is comparable to the higher end of Western European rates. These rules hold for both the Czech and Slovak Republics. The self-employed also pay monthly contributions of 46% from monthly gross income; 26.5% goes to the pension fund, 13.7% to the health insurance fund and 5.8% to the hospital insurance fund.

In addition to the three insurance funds, an employment fund was created to support active labour market policies. Contributions towards the employment fund are generated by a 4% payroll tax on of gross wages; employees contribute 1%, employers 3%. The funds thereby generated are used to finance retraining programmes and other ALMP measures. Self-employed must also contribute 4% of their reported income to the fund.

Another type of labour tax exists in addition to income taxes and insurance contributions. In both countries, a punitive wage bill tax, primarily a stop-gap measure to prevent decapitalization of state enterprises while corporate control was being established, is still employed as a incomes policy mechanism. This tax, which is set in tripartite negotiations each year, applies officially to state firms with more than 25 employees. The excess wage tax works as follows. Each year 'target rates' for wage bill growth are established in negotiations surrounding the tripartite agreement. Settlements which lead to wage bills exceeding the growth parameters are subject to tax. In 1992, for example, firms with profit/cost ratios of up to 12% were allowed 12% wage bill growth; those greater than 12% were allowed wage growth of up to 16%. Banks and insurance companies were allowed zero wage growth (a subtle means of recapitalization of these institutions, perhaps) and other firms were limited to 6%. The punitive tax rates on excess beyond allowed growth are quite high. For those firms with wage bill growth of 3–5% above target, a tax of 200% is levied; above 5% growth, the tax rate rises to 750%!

The total labour tax burden described above in the CR and SR is similar in both countries. To some extent this is a legacy of the communist system, but also one of Western European tradition (see Barbone and Marchetti, 1994). While TIP (tax-based incomes policy) may have had positive short-run macroeconomic effects on inflationary expectations, it certainly added to the tax burden in enterprises experiencing success and may have vitiated the allocative function of wages. There is a suspicion that in periods of systemic transformation when rates of return on entrepreneurial activity are high so are incentives to engage in the underground economic activity.

Notes

1. The minimum wage was first introduced in February 1991 by the Directive of the Federal Govt. No. 99/1991. Coll., with a monthly minimum of 2000 Kcs (Czechoslovak crowns) and an hourly minimum of 10.80 Kcs/hour. It was increased in January 1992 to 2200 Kcs/month and 12.00 Kcs/hour. In the Slovak Republic, the wage was raised as of November 1993 to 2450 Sk (Slovak crowns)/month, and as the result of tripartite negotiations should be raised again to Sk 2600 in 1995. In the CR, the minimum has not been raised since the divorce.
2. Ignoring gross entry and exit from the labour force, the unemployment rate u is the solution to the differential equation $du/dt = s(1 - u) - fu = s(s + f)u$, where s and f are job separation and job finding rates, respectively. In the steady state, $u = s/(s+f)$. See Hall (1979). In the more general case with a third state 'out of the labour force', the corresponding steady-state unemployment rate will depend negatively on the rate of worker discouragement.
3. The low rate of CR inflow into unemployment has led many to claim that the Czechs have only successfully postponed unemployment to a later date. Raiser (1994) adduces convincing evidence, however, that restructuring has been extensive in the Czech Republic, especially with respect to privatization and banking sector recapitalization.
4. *Hospodarske Noviny*, CSFR, No. 105, 1991. These cuts were not fully implemented, however.
5. Higher unemployment rates among Gypsies and other demographic groups may also play a role. According to Munich et al., (1994), however, there little hard support for this hypothesis. Our own informal detective work revealed the following facts: the fraction of total unemployed in the Slovak Republic who are registered as Gypsies has been relatively stable at 13–15%, reflecting their population in the country (estimated as high as 11% in the Slovak Republic, compared with 3% in the Czech Republic (see Fidrmuc, 1994). Second, while cross-sectional correlation across 38 employment office districts between inflow rates and overall unemployment are high (0.74 and 0.79 in April 1992 and 1993, respectively), they are much lower between inflow rates and the fraction of unemployed Gypsies (0.42 and 0.45). It is more plausible the high correlation between Gypsy population and unemployment rates (Fidrmuc, 1994) is due to lower outflow rates, which in turn reflects low skill levels or discrimination.
6. Munich et al. (1994) find a strong positive association between outflows out of unemployment with proximity to the western German border.
7. The most important negative effects cited by Calmfors are (1) reduction in search intensity of programme participants; (2) a labelling or lock-in-effect which stigmatizes participants (see Burtless, 1985); (3) dead-weight loss effects (some of those who receive subsidies would have found a job anyway); (4) substitution effects of the favoured at the expense of others (naturally, what one would hope for!); (5) fiscal displacement effects (local governments undertake projects

that would have occurred anyway) and (6) 'crowding out' effects in local labour markets, in which wages rise due to labour market tightness, leading to unemployment elsewhere.

8. This follows in part the excellent discussion in Ham, *et al*. (1994) and Uldrichova and Karpisek (1994).

9. See Ham *et al*. (1994). At the end of 1992, the exchange rate was roughly Kcs 36/ECU.

10. According to Ham *et al*. (1994) these jobs are often offered to the best applicants, rather than those with problematic job profiles and re-employment prospects, suggesting dead-weight losses.

11. Note that Table 7.6 reports 'agreements' concluded by district labour offices with public and private employers, which may support a vacancy but continues to exist after the position has been filled. The possibility of a mere *report* (the ALMP positions are simply reported as normal vacancies) can therefore be discounted.

12. Alternately, one might interpret a negative correlation as evidence of 'crowding out' (see Calmfors, 1994), but this appears rather implausible.

13. See Uldrichova and Karpisek (1994). On benefit policy, the evidence is less convincing, although Ham *et al*. (1994) argue that, before January 1992, Slovak benefit administration was more generous than in the CR (for example, allowing workers to collect unemployment benefits and severance pay simultaneously). In addition, while school leavers qualify for both benefits in both countries, eligibility is conditioned on the non-availability of SPJ or PUJ jobs, which is less likely in the CR than in the SR.

14. See Pissarides (1986), Blanchard and Diamond (1989), and Burda and Wyplosz (1994) for estimates of the matching function. Some theory can be found in Pissarides (1991). Estimates of matching functions in Central and Eastern European countries can be found in Boeri (1994) and Burda (1993).

15. Suppose that matching between unemployed and vacancies sometimes takes longer than one month. This could be modelled by including further lags of ln *u* and ln *y* and ln *v*, or assuming partial adjustment to a steady state implied by contemporaneous values (an autoregressive adjustment process). The latter specification seems more plausible and is supported by unreported results.

16. Czech staffing data, in contrast, are currently available only sporadically.

17. The original data file consisted of accumulated expenditures since the beginning of each year on a quarterly basis from 1992:1 until 1993:2. Quarterly expenditure levels were calculated by differencing these series. The Slovak data contain several missing or implausible values which were set equal to the average of surrounding values: observations with unreasonable values were excluded. A detailed list of all corrections can be obtained on request.

18. All regressions were carried out using SAS 6.08.

19. The inclusion of fixed effects in dynamic specifications with short panels leads to biased estimates: see Nickell (1981); for this sample, the number of months is always roughly half the number of districts, so this issue is probably of second-order importance.

20. Denoting estimated long-run elasticities and sample means by η and μ, respectively, we have for the CR: (dF/dALMP) = h(mF/mALMP) = [0.0666/(1 - 0.2091 - 0.0486 - 0.0177 - 0.0028] x 337.44/4116 140 = 7.56421 x 10^{-6} outflows/Kc or 132 000 Kc per outflow. For the SR: (dF/dALMP)= h(mF/mALMP)= [0.0681/(1 - 0.4200- 0.0675- 0.0205 + 0.0535)] x 333.82/1688 550 = 2.468 x 10^{-5} outflows/Sk or 40 500 Sk per outflow.

21. From the steady-state formula given in footnote 2 and data in Table 7.4, the steady-state unemployment rate is 1.96/(1.96 + 8.06) = 1.96/(1.96 + 3.39 + 4.67) = 19.6% as reported in the table, whereby the second step simply decomposes the exit rate from unemployment into exits into jobs plus exits from the labour force. A 30.6% increase in the exit rate into jobs increases 3.39 to 4.43, and reduces the steady-state unemployment rate to 1.96/(1.96 + 4.43 + 4.67) = 17.7%.

References

Barbone, L. and Marchetti, D. (1994), 'Transition and the fiscal crisis in Central Europe'. mimeo, World Bank.

Bastyr, I. (1993), 'Prijmy a mzdy v Ceske Republice 1990–1992' (Incomes and wages in the Czech Republic 1990–2), Institute of Labour and Social Affairs, Prague, August.

Benácek, V. (1994), 'Small businesses and private entrepreneurship during transition. The case of the Czech Republic', mimeo, April.

Blanchard, O. and Diamond, P. (1989), 'The Beveridge curve', *Brookings Papers on Economic Activity*, **1**, 1–60.

Blanchard, O. and Diamond, P. (1994), 'Ranking, unemployment duration and wages', *Review of Economic Studies*, **61**, 417–34.

Blanchard, O. and Summers, L. (1986), 'Hysteresis and the European unemployment problem', *NBER Macroeconomics Annual*, **1**, 1–78.

Boeri, T. (1994), 'Transitional unemployment', *Economics of Transition*, **2**, 1–25.

Boeri, T. and Scarpetta, S. (1994), 'Convergence and divergence of regional labour market dynamics in Central and Eastern Europe', OECD Technical Workshop on Regional Unemployment in Central and Eastern Europe, IAS, Vienna, November.

Burda, M. (1988), 'Wait unemployment in Europe', *Economic Policy*, **7**, 391–426.

Burda, M. (1993), 'Unemployment, labour markets and structural change in Eastern Europe', *Economic Policy*, **16**, 101–37.

Burda, M. and Wyplosz, C. (1994), 'Gross worker and job flows in Europe', *European Economic Review*, **38**, 1287–315.

Burtless, G. (1985), 'Are targeted wages subsidies harmful? Evidence from a voucher experiment', *Industrial and Labor Relations Review*, **39**, 105–14.

Calmfors, L. (1994), 'Active labour market policy and unemployment: A framework for the analysis of crucial design features', Institute for International Economic Studies, Stockholm, Seminar Paper No. 563, January.

Calmfors, L. and Nymoen, R.(1990), 'Active labour market policies in the Nordic Countries', *Economic Policy*, **11**, 397–438.

CEC (Commission of the European Communities) (1993), *Employment Observatory: Central and Eastern Europe*, No. 4.

CEC (Commission of the European Communities) (1994), *Employment Observatory: Central and Eastern Europe*, No. 6.

Dolton, P. (1993), 'The economics of youth training in the UK', *Economic Journal*, **103**, 1261–78.

EBRD (1994), 'Statistical tables', *Economics of Transition*.

Fidrmuc, J. (1994), 'Ethnic minorities and regional unemployment', OECD Technical Workshop on Regional Unemployment in Central and Eastern Europe, Vienna, November.

Franz, W. (1994), 'Central and Eastern European labour markets in transition: Developments causes, and cures', mimeo, Konstanz.

Hall, R. (1979), 'A theory of the natural unemployment rate and the duration of unemployment', *Journal of Monetary Economics*, **5**, 153–69.

Ham, J., Svejnar, J. and Terrell, K. (1994), 'The Czech and Slovak labour markets during the transition', mimeo, CERGE, February.

Havemann, R. and Hollister, R. (1991), 'Direct job creation: economic evaluation and lessons for the US and Western Europe', in A. Björklund *et al.* (eds.) *Labour Market Policy and Unemployment Insurance* in FIEF Studies in Labour Markets and Economic Policy, Oxford University Press, Oxford.

Horelek, M., Kux, J., Bastyr, I. and Formanova, J. (1994), 'Main economic and social indicators of Czech Republic 1990-1994', mimeo, Research Institute of Labour and Social Affairs, Prague.

Huber, P. and Ochotnicky, P. (1994), 'Problems of the local labour market dominated by one large enterprise: An overview of Central and Eastern Europe and a case-study of a Slovakian Region', OECD Technical Workshop on Regional Unemployment in Central and Eastern Europe, IAS, Vienna, November.

Jackman, R., Pissarides, C. and Savouri, S. (1990), 'Labour market policies and unemployment in the OECD,' *Economic Policy*, **10**, 450–83.

Layard, R., Nickell, S. and Jackman, R. (1991), *Unemployment*, Oxford University Press, Oxford.

Lehmann, H. (1993), 'The effectiveness of the Restart Programme and the Enterprise Allowance Scheme', Centre for Economic Performance DP No. 139.

Lindbeck, A. and Snower, D. (1985), 'Wage setting, unemployment and insider–outsider relations,' *American Economic Review*, **76**, 235–39.

Munich, D., Svejnar, J. and Terrell, K.(1994), 'Regional unemployment dynamics and mismatch in the Czech and Slovak Republics', OECD Technical Workshop on Regional Unemployment in Central and Eastern Europe, IAS, Vienna, November.

Nickell, S. (1981), 'Biases in dynamic models with fixed effects', *Econometrica*, **49**, 1417–26.

Ochotnicky, P. and Kohutova, J. (1994), 'Regional unemployment and employment policy in Slovakia', mimeo, Centre for Strategic Studies of the Slovak Republic.

OECD (1991), *Evaluating Labour Market and Social Programmes*, OECD, Paris.

OECD (1993), *Employment Outlook*, OECD, Paris.

OECD (1994), *Industry in the Czech and Slovak Republics*, OECD, Paris.

Pissarides, C. (1986), 'Unemployment and vacancies in Britain', *Economic Policy*, **3**, 499–59.

Pissarides, C. (1991), *Equilibrium Unemployment*, Basil Blackwell, Oxford.

Raiser, M. (1994), 'Ein tschechisches Wunder? Zur Rolle politikinduzierter Anreizstrukturen im Transformationsprozeß', Kiel Diskussionspaper Nr. 233, June.

Scarpetta, S. and Reutersward, A. (1994), 'Unemployment benefit systems and active labour market policies in Central and Eastern Europe: An overview' in *Unemployment in Transition Economies: Transient or Persistent?* OECD. Paris.

Uldrichova, V. and Karpisek, Z. (1994), 'Labour market policy in the former Czech and Slovak Republic', in *Unemployment in Transition Economies: Transient or Persistent?* OECD, Paris.

Index